GENESIS

Genesis

A LIFE APPLICATION™ BIBLE STUDY

Study questions written and edited by
REV. NEIL S. WILSON
DR. JAMES C. GALVIN
REV. DAVID R. VEERMAN
DR. BRUCE B. BARTON

Tyndale House Publishers, Inc.
Wheaton, Illinois

Life Application Bible Studies: Genesis. Copyright © 1989 by Tyndale House Publishers, Inc. Wheaton, IL 60189

The *Life Application Bible* is a trademark of Tyndale House Publishers, Inc.

The text of Genesis is from *The Living Bible* copyright © 1971 owned by assignment by KNT Charitable Trust. All rights reserved.

Front cover photo by Comstock, Inc.

ISBN 0-8423-2714-2

Printed in the United States of America

2 3 4 5 6 7 8 9 10 95 94 93 92 91 90 89

Have you ever opened your Bible and asked the following:

- What does this passage really mean?
- How does it apply to my life?
- Why does some of the Bible seem irrelevant?
- What do these ancient cultures have to do with today?
- I love God; why can't I understand what he is saying to me through his Word?
- What's going on in the lives of these Bible people?

Many Christians do not read the Bible regularly. Why? Because in the pressures of daily living they cannot find a connection between the timeless principles of Scripture and the ever-present problems of day-by-day living.

God urges us to apply his Word (Isaiah 42:23; 1 Corinthians 10:11; 2 Thessalonians 3:4), but too often we stop at accumulating Bible knowledge. This is why the *Life Application Bible* was developed—to show how to put into practice what we have learned.

Applying God's Word is a vital part of one's relationship with God; it is the evidence that we are obeying him. The difficulty in applying the Bible is not with the Bible itself, but with the reader's inability to bridge the gap between the past and present, the conceptual and practical. When we don't or can't do this, spiritual dryness, shallowness, and indifference are the results.

The words of Scripture itself cry out to us, "Won't even one of you apply these lessons . . . ?" (Isaiah 42:23). The *Life Application Bible* does just that. Developed by an interdenominational team of pastors, scholars, family counselors, and a national organization dedicated to promoting God's Word and spreading the Gospel, the *Life Application Bible* took many years to complete, and all the work was reviewed by several renowned theologians under the directorship of Dr. Kenneth Kantzer.

The *Life Application Bible* does what a good resource Bible should—it helps you understand the context of a passage, gives important background and historical information, explains difficult words and phrases, and helps you see the interrelationship of Scripture. But it does much more. The *Life Application Bible* goes deeper into God's Word, helping you discover the timeless truth being communicated, see the relevance for your life, and make a personal application. While some study Bibles attempt application, over 75% of this Bible is application-oriented. The notes answer the questions, "So what?" and "What does this passage mean to me, my family, my friends, my job, my neighborhood, my church, my country?"

Imagine reading a familiar passage of Scripture and gaining fresh insight, as if it were the first time you had ever read it. How much richer you life would be if you left each Bible reading with a new perspective and a small change for the better. A small change every day adds up to a changed life—and that is the very purpose of Scripture.

The best way to define application is to first determine what it is *not*. Application is *not* just accumulating knowledge. This helps us discover and understand facts and concepts, but it stops there. History is filled with philosophers who knew what the Bible said but failed to apply it to their lives, keeping them from believing and changing. Many think that understanding is the end goal of Bible study, but it is really only the beginning.

Application is *not* just illustration. Illustration only tells us how someone else handled a similar situation. While we may empathize with that person, we still have little direction for our personal situation.

Application is *not* just making a passage "relevant." Making the Bible relevant only helps us to see that the same lessons that were true in Bible times are true today; it does not show us how to apply them to the problems and pressures of our individual lives.

What, then, is application? Application begins by knowing and understanding God's Word and its timeless truths. *But you cannot stop there.* If you do, God's Word may not change your life, and it may become dull, difficult, tedious, and tiring. A good application focuses the truth of God's Word, shows the reader what to do about what is being read, and motivates the reader to respond to what God is teaching. All three are essential to application.

Application is putting into practice what we already know (see Mark 4:24 and Hebrews 5:14) and answering the question, "So what?" by confronting us with the right questions and motivating us to take action (see 1 Timothy 4:8 and James 2:20). Application is deeply personal—unique for each individual. It is making a relevant truth a personal truth, and involves developing a strategy and action plan to live your life in harmony with the Bible. It is the biblical "how to" of life.

You may ask, "How can your application notes be relevant to *my* life?" Each application note has three parts: (1) an *explanation* that ties the note directly to the Scripture passage and sets up the truth that is being taught, (2) the *bridge* which explains the timeless truth and makes it relevant for today, (3) the *application* which shows you how to take the timeless truth and apply it to your personal situation. No note, by itself, can apply Scripture directly to your life. It can only teach, direct, lead, guide, inspire, recommend, and urge. It can give you the resources and direction you need to apply the Bible; but only you can take these resources and put them into practice.

A good note, therefore, should not only give you knowledge and understanding, but point you to application. Before you buy any kind of resource study Bible, you should evaluate the notes and ask the following questions: (1) Does the note contain enough information to help me understand the point of the Scripture passage? (2) Does the note assume I know too much? (3) Does the note avoid denominational bias? (4) Do the notes touch most of life's experiences? (5) Does the note help me *apply* God's Word?

NOTES

In addition to providing the reader with many application notes, the *Life Application Bible* offers several explanatory notes that help the reader understand culture, history, context, difficult-to-understand passages, background, places, theological concepts, and the relationship of various passages in Scripture to other passages.

BOOK INTRODUCTION

The Book Introduction is divided into several easy-to-find parts:

Timeline. A guide that puts the Bible book into its historical setting. It lists the key events and the dates when they occurred.

Vital Statistics. A list of straight facts about the book—those pieces of information you need to know at a glance.

Overview. A summary of the book with general lessons and applications that can be learned from the book as a whole.

Blueprint. The outline of the book. It is printed in easy-to-understand language and is designed for easy memorization. To the right of each main heading is a key lesson that is taught in that particular section.

Megathemes. A section that gives the main themes of the Bible book, explains their significance, and then tells why they are still important for us today.

Map. If included, this shows the key places found in that book and retells the story of the book from a geographical perspective.

OUTLINE

The *Life Application Bible* has a new, custom-made outline that was designed specifically from an application point of view. Several unique features should be noted:

1. To avoid confusion and to aid memory work, the book outline has only three levels for headings. Main outline heads are marked with a capital letter. Subheads are marked by a number. Minor explanatory heads have no letter or number.

2. Each main outline head marked by a letter also has a brief paragraph below it summarizing the Bible text and offering a general application.

3. Parallel passages are listed where they apply.

PERSONALITY PROFILES
Another unique feature of this Bible is the profiles of key Bible people, including their strengths and weaknesses, greatest accomplishments and mistakes, and key lessons from their lives.

MAPS
The *Life Application Bible* has a thorough and comprehensive Bible atlas built right into the book. There are two kinds of maps: A book introduction map, telling the story of the book, and thumbnail maps in the notes, plotting most geographic movements.

CHARTS AND DIAGRAMS
Many charts and diagrams are included to help the reader better visualize difficult concepts or relationships. Most charts not only present the needed information, but show the significance of the information as well.

CROSS-REFERENCES
An updated, exhaustive cross-reference system in the margins of the Bible text helps the reader find related passages quickly.

TEXTUAL NOTES
Directly related to *The Living Bible* text, the textual notes provide explanations on certain wording in the translation, alternate translations, and information about readings in the ancient manuscripts.

HIGHLIGHTED NOTES
In each Bible study lesson you will be asked to read specific notes as part of your preparation. These notes have been highlighted by a bullet (●) so that you can find them easily.

It's always exciting to get more than you expect. And that's what you'll find in this Bible study guide—much more than you expect. Our goal was to write thoughtful, practical, dependable, and application-oriented studies of God's Word.

This study guide contains the complete text of the selected Bible book. The commentary is accurate, complete, and loaded with unique charts, maps, and profiles of Bible people.

With the Bible text, extensive notes and helps, and questions to guide discussion, these Life Application Study Guides have everything you need in one place.

The lessons in this Bible study guide will work for large classes as well as small group studies. To get everyone involved in your discussions, encourage participants to answer the questions before each meeting.

Each lesson is divided into five easy-to-lead sections. The section called "Reflect" introduces you and the members of your group to a specific area of life touched by the lesson. "Read" shows which chapters to read and which notes and other features to use. Additional questions help you understand the passage. "Realize" brings into focus the biblical principle to be learned with questions, a special insight, or both. "Respond" helps you make connections with your own situation and personal needs. The questions are designed to help you find areas in your life where you can apply the biblical truths. "Resolve" helps you map out action plans for that day.

Begin and end each lesson with prayer, asking for the Holy Spirit's guidance, direction, and wisdom.

Recommended time allotments for each section of a lesson:

Segment	60 minutes	90 minutes
Reflect on your life	5 minutes	10 minutes
Read the passage	10 minutes	15 minutes
Realize the principle	15 minutes	20 minutes
Respond to the message	20 minutes	30 minutes
Resolve to take action	10 minutes	15 minutes

All five sections work together to help a person learn the lessons, live out the principles, and obey the commands taught in the Bible.

Also, at the end of each lesson, there is a section entitled, "More for studying other themes in this section." These questions will help you lead the group in studying other parts of each section not covered in depth by the main lesson.

And remember, it is a message to obey, not just to listen to. So don't fool yourselves. For if a person just listens and doesn't obey, he is like a man looking at his face in a mirror; as soon as he walks away, he can't see himself anymore or remember what he looks like. But if anyone keeps looking steadily into God's law for free men, he will not only remember it but he will do what it says, and God will greatly bless him in everything he does. (James 1:22-25, TLB)

GENESIS

VITAL STATISTICS

PURPOSE:
To record God's creation of the world and his desire to have a people set apart to worship him

AUTHOR:
Moses

TO WHOM WRITTEN:
The people of Israel

DATE WRITTEN:
1450–1410 B.C.

SETTING:
The region presently known as the Middle East

KEY VERSES:
"So God made man like his Maker. Like God did God make man; man and maid did he make them" (1:27). "God had told Abram, . . . I will cause you to become the father of a great nation; I will bless you and make your name famous, and you will be a blessing to many others" (12:2, 3).

KEY PEOPLE:
Adam, Eve, Noah, Abraham, Sarah, Isaac, Rebekah, Jacob, Joseph

BEGIN . . . start . . . commence . . . open. . . . There's something refreshing and optimistic about these words, whether they refer to the dawn of a new day, the birth of a child, the prelude of a symphony, or the first miles of a family vacation. Free of problems and full of promise, beginnings stir hope and imaginative visions of the future. Genesis means "beginnings" or "origin," and it unfolds the record of the beginning of the world, of human history, of family, of civilization, of salvation. It is the story of God's purpose and plan for his creation. As the book of beginnings, Genesis sets the stage for the entire Bible. It reveals the person and nature of God (Creator, Sustainer, Judge, Redeemer); the value and dignity of human beings (made in God's image, saved by grace, used by God in the world); the tragedy and consequences of sin (the fall, separation from God, judgment); and the promise and assurance of salvation (covenant, forgiveness, promised Messiah). Read Genesis and be encouraged. There is hope! No matter how dark the world situation seems, God has a plan. No matter how insignificant or useless you feel, God loves you and wants to use you in his plan. No matter how sinful and separated from God you are, his salvation is available. Read Genesis . . . and hope!

God. That's where Genesis begins. All at once we see him creating the world in a majestic display of power and purpose, culminating with a man and woman made like himself (1:26, 27). But before long sin entered the world and Satan was unmasked. Bathed in innocence, creation was shattered by the fall (the willful disobedience of Adam and Eve). Fellowship with God was broken, and evil began weaving its destructive web. In rapid succession, we read how Adam and Eve were expelled from the beautiful garden, their first son turned murderer, and evil bred evil until God finally destroyed everyone on earth except a small family led by Noah, the only godly person left.

As we come to Abraham on the plains of Canaan, we discover the beginning of God's covenant people and the broad strokes of his salvation plan: salvation comes by faith, Abraham's descendants will be God's people, and the Savior of the world will come through this chosen nation. The stories of Isaac, Jacob, and Joseph which follow are more than interesting biographies. They emphasize the promises of God and the proof that he is faithful. The people we meet in Genesis are simple ordinary people, yet through them, God did great things. These are vivid pictures of how God can and does use all kinds of people to accomplish his good purposes . . . even people like you and me.

THE BLUEPRINT

A. THE STORY OF CREATION (1:1—2:3)

Because God created people, we have dignity and worth.

B. THE STORY OF ADAM (2:4—5:32)
   1. Adam and Eve
   2. Cain and Abel
   3. Adam's descendants

Through Adam and Eve we learn about the destructive power of sin and its bitter consequences.

C. THE STORY OF NOAH (6:1—11:32)
   1. The great flood
   2. Repopulating the earth
   3. The tower of Babel

Just as God protected Noah and his family, he protects those who are faithful to him today.

Pride is making ourselves more important than God.

D. THE STORY OF ABRAHAM (12:1—25:18)
   1. God promises a nation to Abraham
   2. Abraham and Lot
   3. God promises a son to Abraham
   4. Sodom and Gomorrah
   5. Birth and near sacrifice of Isaac
   6. Isaac marries Rebekah
   7. Abraham dies

Through sharp testing, Abraham remained faithful to God. Abraham's example teaches us how to live a life of faith.

We are to trust God completely, even when it hurts.

E. THE STORY OF ISAAC (25:19—28:9)
   1. Jacob and Esau, Isaac's twin sons
   2. Isaac and King Abimelech
   3. Isaac blesses Jacob instead of Esau

Isaac did not resist when he was about to be sacrificed, and he gladly accepted a wife chosen for him by others. We must put God's will ahead of our own as Isaac did.

F. THE STORY OF JACOB (28:10—36:43)
   1. Jacob starts a family
   2. Jacob returns home

Although Jacob made many mistakes, his hard work teaches us about living a life of service for our Lord.

God is in the business of changing lives, despite our inadequacies.

G. THE STORY OF JOSEPH (37:1—50:26)
   1. Joseph is sold into slavery
   2. Judah and Tamar (a parenthesis)
   3. Joseph is thrown into jail
   4. Joseph is placed in charge of Egypt
   5. Joseph and his brothers meet in Egypt
   6. Jacob's family moves to Egypt
   7. Jacob and Joseph die in Egypt

Through Joseph, we learn that suffering, no matter how unfair, can develop in us a strong character.

God can turn even our greatest defeats into victory.

MEGATHEMES

THEME	EXPLANATION	IMPORTANCE
Beginnings	Genesis explains how many important realities began: the universe, earth, people, sin, and God's plan of salvation.	Genesis teaches us that the earth is well made and good. Mankind is special to God and unique. God creates and sustains all life.
Disobedience	People are always facing great choices. Disobedience occurs when people choose not to follow God's plan of living.	Genesis explains why men are evil: they choose to do wrong. Even great Bible heroes failed God and disobeyed.
Sin	Sin ruins people's lives. It happens when we disobey God.	Living God's way makes life productive and fulfilling.
Promises	God makes promises to help and protect mankind. This kind of promise is called a "covenant."	God kept his promises then, and he keeps them now. He promises to love us, accept us, forgive us.
Obedience	The opposite of sin is obedience. Obeying God restores our relationship to him.	The only way to enjoy the benefits of God's promises is to obey him.

Prosperity	Prosperity is deeper than mere material wealth. True prosperity and fulfillment come as a result of obeying God.	When people obey God, they find peace with him, with others, and with themselves.
Israel	God started the nation of Israel in order to have a dedicated people who would (1) keep his ways alive in the world, (2) proclaim to the world what he is really like, and (3) prepare the world for the birth of Christ.	God is looking for people today to follow him. We are to proclaim God's truth and love to all nations, not just our own.

KEY PLACES IN GENESIS

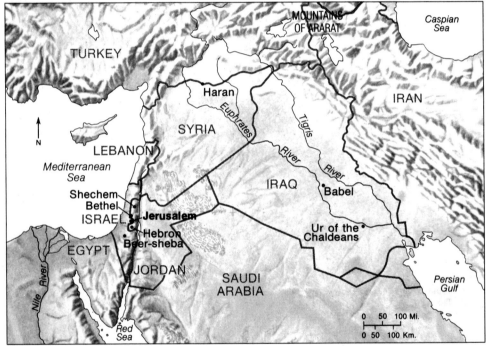

Modern names and boundaries are shown in gray.

God created the universe and the earth. Then he made man and woman, giving them a home in a beautiful garden. Unfortunately, Adam and Eve disobeyed God and were expelled from the garden (3:24).

1 Mountains of Ararat Adam and Eve's sin brought sin into the human race. Years later, sin had run rampant and God decided to destroy the earth with a great flood. But Noah, his family, and two of each animal were safe in a huge boat. When the floods receded, the boat rested on the Mountains of Ararat (8:4).

2 Babel People never learn. Again sin abounded and the pride of the people led them to build a huge tower as a monument to their own greatness—obviously they had no thought of God. As punishment, God scattered the people by giving them different languages (11:8, 9).

3 Ur of the Chaldeans Abram, a descendant of Shem, was born in this great city (11:27).

4 Haran Terah, Lot, Abram, and Sarai left Ur and, following the fertile crescent of the Euphrates River, headed toward the land of Canaan. Along the way, they settled in the city of Haran for a while (11:31).

5 Shechem God urged Abram to leave Haran and go to a place where he would become the father of a great nation (12:1, 2). So Abram, Lot, and Sarai traveled to the land of Canaan and settled near a city called Shechem (12:6).

6 Hebron Abraham moved on to Hebron, by the "oaks at Moreh," where he put down his deepest roots. Abraham, Isaac, and Jacob all lived and were buried there.

7 Beer-sheba A well was dug here as a sign of an oath between Abraham and the army of King Abimelech (21:31). Years later, as Isaac was moving from place to place, God appeared to him here and passed on to him the covenant he had made with his father, Abraham (26:23–25).

8 Bethel   After deceiving his brother out of both his birthright and his blessing, Jacob left Beer-sheba and fled to Haran (#4) to find a wife. Along the way God revealed himself to Jacob in a dream and again passed on the covenant he had made with Abraham and Isaac (28:10–22). Jacob lived in Haran, worked for Laban and married Leah and Rachel (29:15–28). After a tense meeting with his brother Esau, Jacob returned to Bethel.

9 Egypt   Jacob had 12 sons, including Joseph, Jacob's favorite. The other brothers grew jealous, until one day, out in the fields, the brothers sold him to Ishmaelite traders who were going to Egypt. Eventually, Joseph rose from Egyptian slave to Pharaoh's "right hand man," saving Egypt and the surrounding country from famine. His entire family moved from Canaan to Egypt and settled there during the severe famine.

A. THE STORY OF CREATION (1:1—2:3)

We sometimes wonder how our world came to be. But here we find the answer. God created the earth and everything in it, and made man like himself. Although we may not understand the complexity of just how he did it, it is clear that God did create all life. This shows not only God's authority over humanity, but his deep love for all people.

1:1
Ps 33:6; 89:11
Isa 42:5; 48:13
Jn 1:1-3
1:2
Job 26:13
Ps 104:30
1:3
Ps 33:9; 104:2
2 Cor 4:6
1:4,5
Ps 74:16

1 When God began creating the heavens and the earth, ²the earth was a shapeless, chaotic mass, with the Spirit of God brooding over the dark vapors. ³Then God said, "Let there be light." And light appeared. ⁴, ⁵And God was pleased with it, and divided the light from the darkness. He called the light "daytime," and the darkness "nighttime." Together they formed the first day.

⁶And God said, "Let the vapors separate to form the sky above and the oceans below." ⁷, ⁸So God made the sky, dividing the vapor above from the water below. This all happened on the second day.

1:1 *When God began creating,* or, "In the beginning God created . . ." **1:2** *The earth was,* or, "The earth became . . ."* a shapeless, chaotic mass, or, "shapeless and void." *over the dark vapors,* or, "over the cloud of darkness," or, "over the darkness and waters," or even, "over the dark gaseous mass." There is no "right" way to translate these words. **1:4, 5** *Together they formed the first day,* literally, "And there was evening and there was morning, one day (or, 'period of time')." **1:6** *Let the vapors separate,* literally, "Let there be a dome to divide the waters." **1:7, 8** *This all happened on the second day,* literally, "There was evening and there was morning, a second day (or, 'period of time')."

1:1   The simple statement that God created the heavens and the earth is one of the most challenging concepts confronting the modern mind. The vast galaxy we live in is spinning at the incredible speed of 490,000 miles an hour.

But even at this breakneck speed, our galaxy still needs 200 million years to make one rotation. And there are over one billion other galaxies just like ours.

Some scientists say that the number of stars in creation is equal to all the grains of all the sands on all the beaches of the world. Yet this complex sea of spinning stars functions with remarkable order and efficiency. To say that the universe "just happened" or "evolved" requires more faith than to believe that God is behind these amazing statistics. God did create a wonderful universe.

God did not *need* to create the universe; he *chose* to create it. Why? God is love, and love is best expressed toward something or someone else—so God created the world and people as an expression of his love. We should avoid reducing God's creation to only scientific terms while forgetting that God created the universe because he loved us.

1:1ff   The creation story teaches us much about God and ourselves. First, we learn about God: (1) he is creative; (2) as the Creator he is distinct from his creation; (3) he is eternal and in control of the world. We also learn about ourselves: (1) since God chose to create us, we are valuable in his eyes; (2) we are given a place above the animals.

●**1:1ff**   Did God create the world? If so, just how did he do it? This is still a subject of great debate. Some say there was a sudden explosion and the universe appeared. Others say God got it all started and the rest evolved over billions of years. Almost every ancient religion has its own story to explain how the world came to be. And almost every scientist has an opinion on the origin of the universe. But only the Bible shows one supreme God creating the earth out of his great love and giving all people a special place in it.

We will never know all the answers to how God created the world. But the Bible tells us that God did create it. That fact alone brings worth and dignity to all people.

1:2   Who created God? To ask that question, we have to assume there was another creator before God. At some time, however, we are forced to stop asking that question and realize that there had to be a Being who has always existed.

God is that infinite Being who has always been and who was created by no one. This is difficult to understand, for finite minds cannot comprehend what is infinite. For example, what is the highest number? It doesn't even exist and there is no point in trying to discover it. Likewise, we must stop thinking of the infinite God in finite terms.

1:2   The statement "the earth was a shapeless, chaotic mass" can also be translated "the earth was formless and void." This statement provides the setting for the creation narrative that follows. During the second and third days of creation, God gave *form* to the universe; during the next three days, God *filled* the earth with living beings. And the light that was created on the first day dispelled the darkness.

1:2   The image of the Spirit of God brooding over the dark vapors (or, over the surface of the deep waters) likens God's Spirit to a bird caring for and protecting its young (see Deuteronomy 32:11; Isaiah 31:5). God's Spirit was actively involved in the creation of the world (see Job 33:4; Psalm 104:30).

1:3—2:7   How long did it take God to create the world? There are two basic views about the days of creation: (1) each day was a literal 24-hour period; (2) each day represents an indefinite period of time (even millions of years).

The Bible does not mention which theory is true. But the real question is not how long God took, but how he did it. God created the world in an orderly fashion (he did not make plants before light); and he created men and women as unique beings capable of communication with him. No other part of creation can claim that remarkable privilege. The important point is not how long it took God to create the world—a few days or a few billion years. The point, Scripture says, is that he created it just the way he wanted.

9, 10Then God said, "Let the water beneath the sky be gathered into oceans so that the dry land will emerge." And so it was. Then God named the dry land "earth," and the water "seas." And God was pleased. 11, 12And he said, "Let the earth burst forth with every sort of grass and seed-bearing plant, and fruit trees with seeds inside the fruit, so that these seeds will produce the kinds of plants and fruits they came from." And so it was, and God was pleased. 13This all occurred on the third day.

14, 15Then God said, "Let bright lights appear in the sky to give light to the earth and to identify the day and the night; they shall bring about the seasons on the earth, and mark the days and years." And so it was. 16For God had made two huge lights, the sun and moon, to shine down upon the earth—the larger one, the sun, to preside over the day and the smaller one, the moon, to preside through the night; he had also made the stars. 17And God set them in the sky to light the earth, 18and to preside over the day and night, and to divide the light from the darkness. And God was pleased. 19This all happened on the fourth day.

20Then God said, "Let the waters teem with fish and other life, and let the skies be filled with birds of every kind." 21, 22So God created great sea animals, and every sort of fish and every kind of bird. And God looked at them with pleasure, and blessed them all. "Multiply and stock the oceans," he told them, and to the birds he said, "Let your numbers increase. Fill the earth!" 23That ended the fifth day.

24And God said, "Let the earth bring forth every kind of animal—cattle and reptiles and wildlife of every kind." And so it was. 25God made all sorts of wild animals and cattle and reptiles. And God was pleased with what he had done.

26Then God said, "Let us make a man—someone like ourselves, to be the master of all life upon the earth and in the skies and in the seas."

1:9	Job 26:7; Ps 24:1-2; 95:5
	Prov 8:9; Jer 5:22; 2 Pet 3:5
1:10	Gen 1:4; Gen 1:12
1:14,15	Gen 8:22; Deut 4:19; Ps 74:16; 104:19
1:16	Ps 8:3; 19:1-6; Ps 136:7-9; 1 Cor 15:41; Rev 21:23
1:18	Jer 31:35
1:20	Gen 8:17; Ps 104:24,25; Ps 148:7
1:21,22	Gen 6:20; 8:17,19; 35:11; Lev 26:9
1:25	Gen 2:19,20; Job 12:7-9; Jer 27:5
1:26	Gen 5:1; 9:6; Ps 8:6-8; Eph 4:24; Col 3:10; Jas 3:9

1:13 *This all occurred on the third day,* literally, "And there was evening and there was morning, a third day (or, 'period of time')." **1:19** *This all happened on the fourth day,* literally, "And there was evening and there was morning, a fourth day (or, 'period of time')." **1:23** *That ended the fifth day,* literally, "And there was evening and there was morning, a fifth day (or, 'period of time')." **1:26** *a man,* literally, "men." *someone like ourselves,* literally, "Let us make man in our image, in our likeness."

The Bible does not discuss the subject of evolution. Rather, its world view assumes God created the world. The biblical view of creation is not in conflict with science or with various evolutionary theories; it is in conflict with any world view that starts with no creator.

Equally committed and sincere Christians have struggled with the subject of beginnings and come to differing conclusions. This, of course, is to be expected since the evidence is very old and, due to the ravages of the ages, quite fragmented. Students of the Bible and of science should avoid polarizations and black/white thinking. Students of the Bible must be careful not to make the Bible say things it doesn't say, and students of science must not make science say things it doesn't say.

The most important aspect of the continuing discussion is not the *process* of creation, but the *origin* of creation. The world is not a product of blind chance and probability; God created it.

The Bible not only tells us that the world was created by God; more important, it tells us who this God is. It reveals God's personality, his character, and his plan for his creation. It also reveals God's deepest desire: to relate to and fellowship with the people he created. God took the ultimate step toward fellowship with us through his historic visit to this planet in the person of his Son, Jesus Christ. We can know this God who created the universe in a very personal way.

The heavens and the earth are here. We are here. God created all that we see and experience. The book of Genesis begins, "God began creating the heavens and the earth."

Here we begin the most exciting and fulfilling journey imaginable.

BEGINNINGS

●**1:25** The fact that "God was pleased" indicates his capacity for pleasure. People sometimes feel guilty for having a good time or for feeling good about an accomplishment. This need not be so. Just as God was pleased with his work, we can be pleased with ours. However, we cannot be pleased with our work if God would not be pleased with it. What are you doing that makes both you *and* God happy?

●**1:26** Why does God use the plural form when he says, "Let *us* make man . . . like *ourselves*"? One view says this is a reference to the Trinity—God, the Father; Jesus Christ, his Son; and the Holy Spirit—all of whom are God. It is difficult to prove (and understand) the existence of the Trinity in Genesis. But see John 14:26 where God, Jesus, and the Holy Spirit are all represented in one verse. Another view states that the plural wording is used to denote

1:27
Mt 19:4
1 Cor 11:8,9

27So God made man like his Maker.
Like God did God make man;
Man and maid did he make them.

1:29
Gen 9:3
Ps 115:16
Ps 136:25;
145:15
1:30
Ps 104:14
1:31
Ps 19:1; 104:24

28And God blessed them and told them, "Multiply and fill the earth and subdue it; you are masters of the fish and birds and all the animals. 29And look! I have given you the seed-bearing plants throughout the earth, and all the fruit trees for your food. 30And I've given all the grass and plants to the animals and birds for their food." 31Then God looked over all that he had made, and it was excellent in every way. This ended the sixth day.

2:1
Ps 136:5-9
Isa 42:5
2:2
Ex 31:17
Heb 4:4

2 Now at last the heavens and earth were successfully completed, with all that they contained. 2So on the seventh day, having finished his task, God ceased from this work he had been doing, 3and God blessed the seventh day and declared it holy, because it was the day when he ceased this work of creation.

B. THE STORY OF ADAM (2:4—5:32)

Learning about our ancestors often helps us understand ourselves. Adam and Eve, our first ancestors, were the highlight of God's creation—the very reason God made the world. But they didn't always live the way God intended. Through their mistakes, we can learn important lessons on how to live rightly. Adam and Eve teach us much about the nature of sin and its consequences.

1. Adam and Eve

2:4
Gen 1:3-31; 5:1;
6:9
Gen 10:1

4Here is a summary of the events in the creation of the heavens and earth when the Lord God made them.
5There were no plants or grain sprouting up across the earth at first, for the Lord

1:31 *This ended the sixth day,* literally, "And there was evening and there was morning, a sixth day (or, 'period of time')."

DAYS OF CREATION

First Day	Light (so there was light and darkness)	
Second Day	Sky and water (vapors separated)	
Third Day	Sea and earth (waters gathered)	
Fourth Day	Sun, moon, and stars (to preside over day and night, to bring about the seasons, and mark days and years)	
Fifth Day	Fish and birds (to fill the waters and the sky)	
Sixth Day	Animals (to fill the earth)	
	Man and woman (to care for the earth and commune with God)	
Seventh Day	God rested and was pleased	

---

majesty—today many kings still use the plural form in speaking of themselves.

1:26 How are we made like God? The phrase "Let us make man . . . like ourselves" does not mean that God created us exactly like himself, especially in a physical sense. Instead, we are reflections of God's glory. God is sinless, eternal, and unlimited. Although we are given the potential to be sinless and eternal, we are also given the choice to fall short. We will never be totally like God, because he is our supreme Creator. Our best hope is to reflect his character in our love, patience, forgiveness, kindness, and faithfulness.

We are made like God and therefore share many of his characteristics and emotions. Knowing this provides the basis for self-worth. Self-worth is not defined by possessions, achievements, physical attractiveness, or public acclaim. Self-worth is knowing that God created us in his likeness. Criticizing or downgrading ourselves is criticizing what God has made. Because we are like God we can feel positive about ourselves and our abilities. Knowing that you are a person of infinite worth gives you the freedom to love God, know him personally, and make a valuable contribution to those around you.

1:27 God made both man and woman in his image. Neither man nor woman is made more in the image of God than the other. From

the beginning we see the Bible placing both men and women at the pinnacle of God's creation. Neither is depreciated.

●**1:28** God worked like a master craftsman in creating the earth. Now he watches over his creation like a loving master. Just as God "masters" the earth with his loving care, we too are to "master" it. God's charge to man to subdue the earth implies responsibility to the environment and to the other creatures that share our planet. God was careful how he made this earth. We must not be careless about how we take care of it.

●**1:31** God was pleased with all he created, for it was excellent in every way. You are part of God's creation,and he is pleased with how he made you. At times you may feel worthless or of little value. Remember that God made you for a good reason. You are valuable to him.

2:2, 3 We live in a world that is action-oriented! Yet God demonstrated that rest is appropriate and right. If God himself rested from his work, then it should not amaze us that we need rest as well. Jesus demonstrated this principle in the New Testament when he and the disciples left in a boat to get away from the press of the crowd (see Mark 6:31, 32). Our times of rest refresh us for times of service.

God hadn't sent any rain; nor was there anyone to farm the soil. 6(However, water welled up from the ground at certain places and flowed across the land.)

7The time came when the Lord God formed a man's body from the dust of the ground and breathed into it the breath of life. And man became a living person.

2:7
Gen 3:19,23
Job 33:4
Ps 103:14
Ezek 37:5
Jn 20:22

The Garden of Eden

8Then the Lord God planted a garden in Eden, to the east, and placed in the garden the man he had formed. 9The Lord God planted all sorts of beautiful trees there in the garden, trees producing the choicest of fruit. At the center of the garden he placed the Tree of Life, and also the Tree of Conscience, giving knowledge of Good and Bad. 10A river from the land of Eden flowed through the garden to water it; afterwards the river divided into four branches. 11, 12One of these was named the Pishon; it winds across the entire length of the land of Havilah, where nuggets of pure gold are found, also beautiful bdellium and even lapis lazuli. 13The second branch is called the Gihon, crossing the entire length of the land of Cush. 14The third branch is the Tigris, which flows to the east of the city of Asher. And the fourth is the Euphrates.

2:8
Gen 3:23; 13:10
Isa 51:3
Ezek 28:13
Joel 2:3

2:9
Gen 3:22
Ezek 47:12
Rev 2:7
22:2,14

2:10
Rev 22:1,17

2:14
Gen 15:18
Deut 1:7
Dan 10:4

15The Lord God placed the man in the Garden of Eden as its gardener, to tend and care for it. 16, 17But the Lord God gave the man this warning: "You may eat any fruit in the garden except fruit from the Tree of Conscience—for its fruit will open your eyes to make you aware of right and wrong, good and bad. If you eat its fruit, you will be doomed to die."

2:16
Deut 30:15,19
2:17
Gen 3:1,16,17
Rom 5:2; 6:23
Jas 1:15

Eve is created

18And the Lord God said, "It isn't good for man to be alone; I will make a companion for him, a helper suited to his needs." 19, 20So the Lord God formed from the soil every kind of animal and bird, and brought them to the man to see what he would call them; and whatever he called them, that was their name. But still there was no proper helper for the man. 21Then the Lord God caused the man to fall into a deep sleep, and took one of his ribs and closed up the place from which

2:18
Gen 3:12
Prov 18:22

2:19
Gen 1:20-25
6:20

2:7 *from the dust of the ground*, or, "from a lump of soil," or, "from clods in the soil," or, "from a clod of clay."

2:7 "From the dust of the ground" implies that there is nothing specially good about the chemical elements from which we are made. Water, dirt, a little protein—there is really not much to our physical bodies. The body is a lifeless shell until God brings it alive with his "breath of life." When God removes his life-giving breath, our bodies once again return to dust. Therefore, man's life and worth come from God's Spirit. This graphically portrays our need for God. Many boast of their significant achievements, only to fail soon after. Others have no achievements to boast about. But the reality is that life and worth come from the God of the universe, and he chose to give you that mysterious and miraculous gift. Value it, as he does.

2:8-14 The Garden of Eden was a showcase of the magnificent beauty God intended for his creation. Eden was no accident. It was a place to be fully enjoyed.

2:9 Other translations call the "Tree of Conscience" the "Tree of the Knowledge of Good and Evil." The name of this tree implies that evil had already occurred, if not in the garden, then at the time of Satan's fall.

●**2:9, 16, 17** Were the Tree of Life and the Tree of Conscience real trees? Two different views are often expressed:
(1) *The trees were real, but symbolic.* Eternal life with God was symbolized by eating from the Tree of Life.
(2) *The trees were real, possessing special properties.* By eating the fruit from the Tree of Life, Adam and Eve could have had eternal life, enjoying a permanent relationship as children of God.
In either case, Adam and Eve's sin separated them from the Tree of Life and thus kept them from obtaining eternal life. Interestingly, the Tree of Life again appears in Revelation 22 where people will enjoy eternal life with God.

●**2:15-17** God gave Adam responsibility for the garden and told him not to eat from the Tree of Conscience. Rather than physically preventing him from eating, God gave Adam a choice, even though Adam might choose wrongly. God still gives us choices today, and we, too, often choose wrongly. These wrong choices may cause us pain and irritation, but they can help us learn and grow and make better choices in the future. Living with the consequences of our choices is one of the best ways to become more responsible.

2:16, 17 Why would God place a tree in the garden and then forbid Adam to eat from it? God wanted Adam to obey, but he gave him the freedom to choose. Without choice, Adam would have been a prisoner forced to obey. The two trees presented an exercise in choice, with rewards for choosing to obey or consequences for choosing to disobey.

2:18-24 God's creative work was not complete until he made woman. He could have made her from the dust of the ground, as he made man. He chose, however, to make her from the man's bone and flesh. In so doing, he illustrated for us that in marriage man and woman symbolically become one flesh. This is a mystical union of the couple's hearts and lives. Throughout the Bible, God treats this special union seriously. If you are married or planning to be married, are you willing to keep the commitment which, in fact, makes the two of you one? The goal in marriage should be more than friendship; it should be oneness.

2:21-23 God styles and equips men and women for various tasks, but all lead to the same goal—honoring God. Man gives life to woman; woman gives life to the world. Each role carries exclusive privileges that should eliminate any attitudes about an inferior or superior sex.

2:22
1 Cor 11:8
1 Tim 2:13
2:23
Gen 29:14
Eph 5:28-30
2:24
Mt 19:5
Eph 5:31

he had removed it, 22and made the rib into a woman, and brought her to the man. 23"This is it!" Adam exclaimed. "She is part of my own bone and flesh! Her name is 'woman' because she was taken out of a man." 24This explains why a man leaves his father and mother and is joined to his wife in such a way that the two become one person. 25Now although the man and his wife were both naked, neither of them was embarrassed or ashamed.

Adam and Eve sin

3:1
1 Chron 21:1
Ezek 28:12-17
Mt 4:3,6,9
Rev 12:9; 20:2
3:2,3
Gen 2:16
Ex 19:12

3 The serpent was the craftiest of all the creatures the Lord God had made. So the serpent came to the woman. "Really?" he asked. *"None* of the fruit in the garden? God says you mustn't eat *any* of it?"

2, 3"Of course we may eat it," the woman told him. "It's only the fruit from the tree at the *center* of the garden that we are not to eat. God says we mustn't eat it or even touch it, or we will die."

2:24 *the two become one person,* literally, "one flesh."

WHAT THE BIBLE SAYS ABOUT MARRIAGE	Genesis 2:18–24	Marriage is God's idea
	Genesis 24:58–60	Commitment is essential to a successful marriage
	Genesis 29:10, 11	Romance is important
	Jeremiah 7:34	Marriage holds times of great joy
	Malachi 2:14, 15	Marriage creates the best environment for raising children
	Matthew 5:32	Unfaithfulness breaks the bond of trust, the foundation of all relationships
	Matthew 19:6	Marriage is permanent
	Romans 7:2, 3	Ideally, only death should dissolve marriage
	Ephesians 5:21–33	Marriage is based on the principled practice of love, not on feelings
	Ephesians 5:23, 32	Marriage is a living symbol of Christ and the church
	Hebrews 13:4	Marriage is good and honorable

2:24 God gave marriage as a gift to Adam and Eve. They were perfectly created for each other. Marriage was not just for convenience, nor was it brought about by any culture. It was instituted by God and has three basic aspects: (1) the man "leaves" his father and mother and, in a public act, promises himself to his wife; (2) the man and woman are joined together by taking responsibility for each other's welfare and loving their mate above all others; (3) the two become "one person" or "one flesh" in the intimacy and commitment of sexual union which is reserved for marriage. Strong marriages today include all three of these aspects.

2:25 Have you ever noticed how a little child can run naked through a room full of strangers without embarrassment? He is not aware of his nakedness, just as Adam and Eve were not embarrassed in their innocence. But after Adam and Eve sinned, embarrassment, shame, and awkwardness followed—creating barriers between themselves and God. We often experience these same barriers in marriage. Ideally, a husband and wife should have no barriers, feeling no shame exposing themselves to each other or to God. Like Adam and Eve (3:7), we put on fig leaves (barriers) because we have areas we don't want our spouse (or God) to know about. Then we hide—just as Adam and Eve hid from God. In marriage, lack of spiritual, emotional, and intellectual intimacy usually precedes a breakdown of physical intimacy. In the same way, when we fail to expose our sins and secret thoughts to God, we shut down the lines of communication we have with him.

●**3:1** Disguised as a crafty serpent, Satan came to tempt Eve.

Satan at one time was an angelic being who rebelled against God and was thrown out of heaven. God makes it clear that Satan is a created being and thus has limitations. Although Satan is trying to tempt everyone away from God, he will not be the final victor—in Genesis 3:14, 15 God promises that Satan will be crushed.

●**3:1–6** Why does Satan tempt us? Temptation is Satan's invitation to give in to his kind of life and give up on God's kind of life. Satan tempted Eve and succeeded in getting her to sin. He's been busy getting people to sin ever since—he even tempted Jesus (Matthew 4:11).

How could Eve have resisted temptation? By following the same guidelines we can follow. First, we must realize that *being tempted* is not a sin. We have not sinned until we *give in* to the temptation. Then, to resist temptation, we must: (1) pray for strength to resist, (2) run (sometimes literally), and (3) say no when confronted with what we know is wrong. James 1:12 tells of the blessings and rewards for those who don't give in when tempted.

●**3:2–6** The serpent (Satan) tempted Eve by getting her to doubt God's goodness. He suggested that God was strict, stingy, and selfish for not wanting Eve to share his knowledge of good and evil. Satan made Eve forget all that God had given her and focus on the one thing she couldn't have. We fall into trouble, too, when we focus on the few things we don't have rather than on the countless things God has given us. The next time you are feeling sorry for yourself over what you don't have, consider all you do have and thank God.

4"That's a lie!" the serpent hissed. "You'll not die! 5God knows very well that the instant you eat it you will become like him, for your eyes will be opened—you will be able to distinguish good from evil!"

3:4
Jn 8:44
2 Cor 2:11
11:3

6The woman was convinced. How lovely and fresh looking it was! And it would make her so wise! So she ate some of the fruit and gave some to her husband, and he ate it too. 7And as they ate it, suddenly they became aware of their nakedness, and were embarrassed. So they strung fig leaves together to cover themselves around the hips.

3:5
Gen 2:17
3:22

3:6
2 Cor 11:3
1 Tim 2:14
Jas 1:14
1 Jn 2:16

8That evening they heard the sound of the Lord God walking in the garden; and they hid themselves among the trees. 9The Lord God called to Adam, "Why are you hiding?"

3:8
Lev 26:12
Deut 23:14
Job 31:33

3:9 *Why are you hiding?*, or, "Where are you?"

		SATAN'S PLAN
Doubt	Makes you question God's Word and his goodness	
Discouragement	Makes you look at your problems rather than at God	
Diversion	Makes the wrong things seem attractive so you will want them more than the right things	
Defeat	Makes you feel like a failure, so you don't even try	
Delay	Makes you put off doing something so it never gets done	

3:5 Adam and Eve got what they wanted: an intimate knowledge of both good and evil. But they got it in a distorted and painful way. Satan had twisted their thinking by telling them they could know the difference between good and evil by *doing* evil. We sometimes have the illusion that "freedom" is doing anything we want. God says true freedom comes from obedience and knowing what *not* to do. The restrictions he gives us are for our good, showing us how to avoid evil. We have the freedom to walk in front of a speeding car, but we don't need to be hit to realize it would be a foolish thing to do. Don't listen to Satan's temptations to experience evil in order to learn more about life.

●**3:5** Satan used a sincere motive to tempt Eve—'You will become like God!" To become more like God is the highest goal of humanity. It is what we are supposed to do. But Satan misled Eve on the right way to accomplish this goal. He told her that you become more like God by defying God's authority, by taking God's place and deciding for yourself what is best for your life. You become your own "god."

But Scripture clearly states that to become like God is not to be God himself. Rather, it is to reflect his characteristics and recognize his authority over your life. Like Eve, we often have a worthy goal but try to achieve it the wrong way. It's like paying off an election judge to be voted into office. Serving the people is no longer the highest goal.

The ultimate goal of self-exaltation is rebellion against God. As soon as we begin to leave God out of our plans, we are placing ourselves above him, which is exactly what Satan wants us to do.

●**3:6** Satan tried to show Eve that sin is "lovely." A knowledge of both good and evil seemed desirable and harmless to Eve. People usually choose wrong things because they have become convinced that those things are good, at least for themselves. Our sins do not always appear ugly to us, and the "lovely" sins are the hardest to avoid. So prepare yourself for the attractive temptations that may come your way. First Corinthians 10:13 says that although we cannot always prevent temptation, we can always resist.

●**3:6, 7** Notice what Eve did: she looked, then took, then ate, then gave. The battle is often lost at the first look. Temptation often begins by simply seeing something we want. Are you struggling with temptation because you have not learned that looking is the first step toward sin? We would win over temptation more often if we followed Paul's advice to run from those things that produce evil thoughts (2 Timothy 2:22).

3:6, 7 One of the realities of sin is that its effect spreads. After Eve sinned, she involved Adam in her wrongdoing. When we do something wrong, often our first relief from guilt comes by involving someone else. Like poison spilled in a river, sin swiftly spreads and becomes impossible to recapture. Recognize and confess your sin to God before you are tempted to pollute those around you.

●**3:7** Adam and Eve chose their course of action (disobedience), and now God chose his. As a holy God, he could respond only in a way that was consistent with his perfect moral nature. He could not allow sin to go unchecked; he had to punish it. If the consequences of Adam and Eve's sin seem extreme, remember that their sin set in motion the world's constant tendency toward disobeying God. That is why we sin today: every human being ever born has inherited the sinful nature of Adam and Eve (Romans 5:12–21). Adam and Eve's punishment (3:16-24) reflects how seriously God views sin of any kind.

3:7, 8 After sinning, Adam and Eve felt guilt and embarrassment over their nakedness. Their guilty feelings made them run from God and try to hide. Guilt (or a guilty conscience) is a warning signal God placed inside you that goes off when you've done wrong. The worst thing we could do is to eliminate the guilty feelings without eliminating the cause. That is like using a pain killer but not addressing the disease. Be glad those guilty feelings are there—they make you aware of your sin so you can ask God to forgive you and correct your wrongdoing.

●**3:8** After sinning, Adam and Eve tried to hide from God. The thought of two humans covered with fig leaves trying to hide from an all-seeing, all-knowing God is humorous. How could they be so silly as to think they could actually hide? Yet we do the same when we try to hide things from God. Share all you do and think with him and don't try to hide—it can't be done.

3:8 This verse shows God's desire for our fellowship. It also shows why we are afraid to have fellowship with him. Adam and Eve hid from God when they heard him approaching. God wanted to be with them, but because of their sin, Adam and Eve were afraid to show themselves to him. Sin had broken their fellowship with God. Sin has broken our fellowship with God as well. But through Jesus Christ, God's Son, the way has been opened for us to renew our fellowship with him. God longs to be with us. He is actively offering us his unconditional love. Our natural response is fear, for we know we can't live up to his standards. But recognizing that he loves us, regardless of our faults, can help remove that dread.

3:10
Job 23:15
1 Jn 3:20

3:11
Gen 4:10

¹⁰And Adam replied, "I heard you coming and didn't want you to see me naked. So I hid."

¹¹"Who told you you were naked?" the Lord God asked. "Have you eaten fruit from the tree I warned you about?"

ADAM

We can hardly imagine what it must have been like to be the first and only person on earth. It's one thing for us to be lonely; it was another for Adam, who had never known another human being. He missed much that makes us who we are—he had no childhood, no parents, no family or friends. He had to learn to be human on his own. Fortunately, God didn't let him struggle too long before presenting him with an ideal companion and mate, Eve. Theirs was a complete, innocent, and open oneness, without a hint of shame.

One of Adam's first conversations with his delightful new companion must have been about the rules of the garden. Before God made Eve he had already given Adam complete freedom in the garden, with the responsibility to tend and care for it. But one tree was off limits, the Tree of Conscience. Adam would have told Eve all about this. She knew, when Satan approached her, that the tree's fruit was not to be eaten. However, she decided to eat the forbidden fruit. Then she offered some to Adam. At that moment, the fate of creation was on the line. Sadly, Adam didn't pause to consider the consequences. He went ahead and ate.

In that moment of small rebellion something large, beautiful, and free was shattered . . . the perfect creation of God. Man was separated from God by his desire to act on his own. The effect on a plate glass window is the same whether a pebble or a boulder is hurled at it—the thousands of fragments can never be regathered.

In the case of man's sin, however, God already had a plan in motion to overcome the effects of the rebellion. The entire Bible is the story of how that plan unfolds, ultimately leading to God's own visit to earth through his Son, Jesus. His sinless life and death made it possible for God to offer forgiveness to all who want it. Our small and large acts of rebellion prove that we are descendants of Adam. Only by asking forgiveness of Jesus Christ can we become children of God.

Strengths and accomplishments:
- The first zoologist—namer of animals
- The first landscape architect, placed in the garden to tend and care for it
- Father of the human race
- The first person made in the image of God, and the first human to share an intimate personal relationship with God

Weaknesses and mistakes:
- Avoided responsibility and blamed others; chose to hide rather than to confront; made excuses rather than admitting the truth
- Greatest mistake: teamed up with Eve to bring sin into the world

Lessons from his life:
- As Adam's descendants, we all reflect to some degree the image of God
- God wants people who are free to do wrong to choose instead to love him
- We should not blame others for our own faults
- We cannot hide from God

Vital statistics:
- Where: Garden of Eden
- Occupation: Caretaker, gardener, farmer
- Relatives: Wife: Eve. Sons: Cain, Abel, Seth. Numerous other children. The only man who never had an earthly mother or father.

Key verses:
"But it was the woman you gave me who brought me some, and I ate it" (Genesis 3:12).
"Everyone dies because all of us are related to Adam, being members of his sinful race, and wherever there is sin, death results. But all who are related to Christ will rise again" (1 Corinthians 15:22).

Adam's story is told in Genesis 1:26—4:26. He is also mentioned in 1 Chronicles 1:1; Job 31:33; Luke 3:38; Romans 5:14; 1 Corinthians 15:22, 45; 1 Timothy 2:13, 14.

3:11-13 Adam and Eve failed to heed God's warning in 2:16, 17. God's command not to eat from the Tree of Conscience showed the essential nature of obedience to God. Most commands of God are obviously for our own good. But more important, the reason for obeying God is that he tells us to, and that must be reason enough.

12"Yes," Adam admitted, "but it was the woman you gave me who brought me some, and I ate it."

13Then the Lord God asked the woman, "How could you do such a thing?" "The serpent tricked me," she replied.

3:13
2 Cor 11:3
1 Tim 2:14

14So the Lord God said to the serpent, "This is your punishment: You are singled out from among all the domestic and wild animals of the whole earth—to be cursed. You shall grovel in the dust as long as you live, crawling along on your belly. 15From now on you and the woman will be enemies, as will your offspring and hers. You will strike his heel, but he will crush your head."

3:14
Deut 28:15
Isa 65:25

3:15
Jn 8:44
Acts 13:10
Rom 16:20
Gal 4:4
1 Jn 3:8-10
Rev 12:7

16Then God said to the woman, "You shall bear children in intense pain and suffering; yet even so, you shall welcome your husband's affections, and he shall be your master."

3:16
Gen 35:16
1 Cor 7:4; 11:3
Eph 5:22
Tit 2:5

17And to Adam, God said, "Because you listened to your wife and ate the fruit when I told you not to, I have placed a curse upon the soil. All your life you will struggle to extract a living from it. 18It will grow thorns and thistles for you, and you shall eat its grasses. 19All your life you will sweat to master it, until your dying day. Then you will return to the ground from which you came. For you were made from the ground, and to the ground you will return."

3:17
Job 5:6,7
Rom 8:20-22

3:18
Heb 6:8

3:19
Gen 2:7
Ps 90:3; 104:29
Eccles 12:7
Rom 5:12
1 Cor 15:21,22

20The man named his wife Eve (meaning "The life-giving one"), for he said, "She shall become the mother of all mankind"; 21and the Lord God clothed Adam and his wife with garments made from skins of animals.

3:20
1 Tim 2:13

3:21
2 Cor 5:2,3

22Then the Lord God said, "Now that the man has become as we are, knowing good from bad, what if he eats the fruit of the Tree of Life and lives forever?" 23So the Lord God banished him forever from the Garden of Eden, and sent him out to farm the ground from which he had been taken. 24Thus God expelled him, and placed mighty angels at the east of the Garden of Eden, with a flaming sword to guard the entrance to the Tree of Life.

3:22
Jn 6:48

3:24
Rev 2:7; 22:2,14

2. Cain and Abel

Cain kills Abel

4 Then Adam had sexual intercourse with Eve his wife, and she conceived and gave birth to a son, Cain (meaning "I have created"). For, as she said, "With God's help, I have created a man!" 2Her next child was his brother, Abel.

4:2
Lk 11:50,51

●**3:12, 13** When God asked Adam about his sin, Adam blamed Eve. Then Eve blamed the serpent. How easy it is to excuse our sins by blaming someone else. We often fall into the trap of blaming others or circumstances for our personal failures. But God knows the truth! And he holds each of us responsible for what we do (see verses 14–19). Admit sin and apologize to God. Don't try to get away with sin by blaming someone else.

●**3:14-19** Adam and Eve learned by painful experience that since God is holy and hates sin, he must punish sinners. The rest of the book of Genesis recounts painful stories of lives ruined as a result of sin. Disobedience is sin and it breaks our fellowship with God. Fortunately, when we disobey, God can forgive us, restoring our relationship with him.

3:15 Satan is our enemy—he'll do anything he can to get us to follow his evil, deadly path. The phrase "You will strike at his heel" refers to Satan's repeated attempts to defeat Christ during his life on earth. "He shall strike you on your head" foreshadows Satan's defeat when Christ rose from the dead. A bruise on the heel is not deadly, but a strike on the head is. Already God was revealing his plan to defeat Satan and offer salvation to the world through his Son, Jesus Christ.

3:16-19 Adam and Eve's disobedience affected all of creation, including the environment. Years ago people thought nothing of polluting streams with chemical wastes and garbage. This seemed so insignificant, so small. Now we know that just two or three parts per million of certain chemicals can damage human health. Sin in

our lives is strangely similar to toxic wastes. Even small amounts are deadly.

3:22-24 Life in the Garden of Eden was like living in heaven. Everything was perfect.

When God first placed Adam and Eve in the garden, he made it clear that complete obedience would be rewarded by immortal life (living forever in the paradise of Eden). But after disobeying, Adam and Eve no longer deserved to live there. So God told them to leave. If they had continued to live in the garden, and if they had eaten from the Tree of Life, they would have lived forever. But eternal life in a state of sin would mean forever trying to hide from God. Like Adam and Eve, all of us have sinned and are separated from fellowship with God. God is preparing a new earth as the place of eternal paradise for all his people (Revelation 22).

3:24 This is how Adam and Eve broke their relationship with God: (1) they became convinced their way was better than God's; (2) they became self-conscious and hid; (3) they tried to excuse and defend themselves. To build a relationship with God, we must reverse those steps, doing the opposite of Adam and Eve: (1) drop our excuses and self-defenses; (2) stop trying to hide from God; (3) become convinced that God's way is better than our way.

4:2 No longer was everything provided for Adam and Eve as in the Garden of Eden. Although they worked to care for the garden, their tasks were probably fun and delightful. But now Adam and his family had to struggle to fight the elements in order to grow their own food and spin wool for their clothes. Adam's oldest son, Cain, became a farmer, while Abel, the younger, was a shepherd.

4:3
Lev 2:1
Num 18:12
4:4
Ex 13:12
Lev 3:15,16
Heb 11:4
4:5
Mt 20:15
4:7
Lk 11:35
Rom 6:12
Jas 1:15

Abel became a shepherd, while Cain was a farmer. ³At harvest time Cain brought the Lord a gift of his farm produce, ⁴and Abel brought the fatty cuts of meat from his best lambs, and presented them to the Lord. And the Lord accepted Abel's offering, ⁵but not Cain's. This made Cain both dejected and very angry, and his face grew dark with fury.

⁶"Why are you angry?" the Lord asked him. "Why is your face so dark with rage? ⁷It can be bright with joy if you will do what you should! But if you refuse to obey, watch out. Sin is waiting to attack you, longing to destroy you. But you can conquer it!"

We know very little about Eve, the first woman in the world, yet she is the mother of us all. She was the final piece in the intricate and amazing puzzle of God's creation. Adam now had another human being with whom to fellowship—someone with an equal share in God's image. Here was someone alike enough for companionship, yet different enough for relationship. Together, they were greater than either could have been alone.

Eve was approached by Satan in the Garden of Eden, where she and Adam lived. He questioned her contentment. How could she be happy when she was not allowed to eat from one of the fruit trees? Satan helped Eve shift her focus from all that God had done and given to the one thing he had withheld. And Eve was willing to accept Satan's viewpoint without checking with God.

Sound familiar? How often is our attention drawn from the much which is ours to the little that isn't? We get that "I've got to have it" feeling. Eve was typical of us all—and we consistently show we are her descendants by repeating her mistakes. Our desires, like Eve's, can be quite easily manipulated. They are not the best basis for actions. We need to keep God in our decision-making process always. His Word, the Bible, is our guidebook in decision-making.

Strengths and accomplishments:
• First wife and mother
• First female. As such she shared a special relationship with God, had co-responsibility with Adam over creation, and displayed certain characteristics of God

Weaknesses and mistakes:
• Allowed her contentment to be undermined by Satan
• Acted impulsively without talking either to God or to her mate
• Not only sinned, but shared her sin with her mate
• When confronted, blamed others

Lessons from her life:
• The female shares in the image of God (1:27)
• The necessary ingredients for a strong marriage are commitment to each other, companionship with each other, complete oneness, absence of shame (2:24, 25)
• The basic human tendency to sin goes back to the beginning of the human race

Vital statistics:
• Where: Garden of Eden
• Occupation: Wife/helper/companion/co-manager of Eden
• Relatives: Husband: Adam. Sons: Cain, Abel, Seth. Numerous other children.

Key verse:
"And the Lord God said, 'It isn't good for man to be alone; I will make a companion for him, a helper suited to his needs' " (Genesis 2:18).

Eve's story is told in Genesis 2:19—4:26. Her death is not mentioned in Scripture.

Farming and shepherding are the two oldest occupations on earth, and in the Middle East today their jobs have changed little over the centuries.

4:3, 4 We are not told why God rejected Cain's sacrifice. Perhaps Cain's attitude was improper, or perhaps his offering was not up to God's standards. God evaluates both our motives and the quality of what we offer him. When we give to God and others, we should have a joyful heart because of what we are able to give. When we give, we should not worry about how much we are giving up; for all things are God's in the first place. Instead, we should joyfully give

to God our best in time, money, possessions, and talents.

●**4:6, 7** How do you react when someone suggests you have done something wrong? Do you move to correct the mistake or deny that you need to correct it? After Cain's sacrifice was rejected, God gave him the chance to right his wrong and try again. God even encouraged him to do this! But Cain refused, and the rest of his life is a startling example of what happens to those who refuse to admit their mistakes. The next time someone suggests you are wrong, take an honest look at yourself and choose God's way instead of Cain's.

8One day Cain suggested to his brother, "Let's go out into the fields." And while they were together there, Cain attacked and killed his brother.

9But afterwards the Lord asked Cain, "Where is your brother? Where is Abel?" "How should I know?" Cain retorted. "Am I supposed to keep track of him wherever he goes?"

10But the Lord said, "Your brother's blood calls to me from the ground. What have you done? 11You are hereby banished from this ground which you have defiled with your brother's blood. 12No longer will it yield crops for you, even if you toil on it forever! From now on you will be a fugitive and a tramp upon the earth, wandering from place to place."

13Cain replied to the Lord, "My punishment is greater than I can bear. 14For you have banished me from my farm and from you, and made me a fugitive and a tramp; and everyone who sees me will try to kill me."

15The Lord replied, "They won't kill you, for I will give seven times your punishment to anyone who does." Then the Lord put an identifying mark on Cain as a warning not to kill him. 16So Cain went out from the presence of the Lord and settled in the land of Nod, east of Eden.

Cain's descendants

17Then Cain's wife conceived and presented him with a baby son named Enoch; so when Cain founded a city, he named it Enoch, after his son.

18Enoch was the father of Irad; Irad was the father of Mehujael; Mehujael was the father of Methusael; Methusael was the father of Lamech;

19Lamech married two wives—Adah and Zillah. 20To Adah was born a baby named Jabal. He became the first of the cattlemen and those living in tents. 21His brother's name was Jubal, the first musician—the inventor of the harp and flute. 22To Lamech's other wife, Zillah, was born Tubal-cain. He opened the first foundry forging instruments of bronze and iron.

23One day Lamech said to Adah and Zillah, "Listen to me, my wives. I have killed a youth who attacked and wounded me. 24If anyone who kills Cain will be punished seven times, anyone taking revenge against me for killing that youth should be punished seventy-seven times!"

3. Adam's descendants

25Later on Eve gave birth to another son and named him Seth (meaning "Granted"); for, as Eve put it, "God has granted me another son for the one Cain killed." 26When Seth grew up, he had a son and named him Enosh. It was during his lifetime that men first began to call themselves "the Lord's people."

4:8 Heb 12:24 / 1 Jn 3:12
4:9 Ps 9:12 / 10:13,14
4:10 Heb 12:24
4:11 Deut 27:15-26 / Gal 3:10
4:12 Lev 26:20 / Deut 20:15-24,
4:14 Gen 9:6 / Job 15:22
4:15 Rev 14:9
4:16 2 Kgs 13:23; 24:20 / Jer 23:39; 52:3
4:17 Ps 49:11
4:23 Lev 19:18 / Deut 32:35
4:25 Gen 4:8; 5:3 / 1 Chron 1:1 / Lk 3:38
4:26 Gen 12:8

4:18 or, "the ancestor of," and so also in the remainder of the verse. **4:21** *the inventor of,* literally, "He was the father of all such as handle the harp and pipe." **4:22** *He opened the first foundry,* literally, "He was the father of all metal workers in bronze and iron." **4:26** *men first began to call themselves "the Lord's people,"* literally, "This man was the first to invoke the name of Jehovah."

4:8-10 This is the first murder—taking a life by the shedding of human blood. Blood represents life (Leviticus 17:10-14). If blood is removed from a living person, he will die. Since God created life and gave it to man, only God should take life away.

●**4:8-10** Adam and Eve's disobedience brought sin into the human race. They may have thought their sin (eating a "harmless" piece of fruit) wasn't very bad, but notice how quickly their sinful nature developed in the lives of their children. Simple disobedience suddenly degenerated into outright murder. Adam and Eve acted only against God, but Cain acted against both God and man. A small sin has a way of growing out of control. Let God help you with your little sins before they turn into tragedies.

4:12-15 Cain was severely punished for this murder. God judges all sins and punishes appropriately, but not simply out of anger or vengeance. Rather, God's punishment is meant to correct us and restore our fellowship with him. When you're corrected, don't resent it, but renew your fellowship with God.

4:14 We have heard about only four people so far—Adam, Eve, Cain, and Abel. So two questions arise: (1) why was Cain worried about being killed by others, and (2) where did he get his wife?

Adam and Eve had numerous children—they had been told to "fill the earth" (1:28). Cain's guilt and fear over killing his brother were heavy, and he probably feared repercussions from his family. If he was capable of killing, so were they. The wife Cain chose may have been one of his sisters or a niece. The human race was still genetically pure and there was little fear of side effects from marrying relatives.

●**4:19-26** Unfortunately, when left to themselves, people tend to get worse instead of better. This short narrative about Lamech and his family shows us the variety of talent and ability God gives man. But it also presents the continuous development of sin as time passes. Another murder had occurred, presumably in self-defense. Violence is on the rise. Two distinct groups are now appearing: (1) those who show indifference to sin and evil, and (2) those who are called "people of God" (the descendants of Seth, 4:26). Seth will take Abel's place as leader of a line of God's faithful people.

5:1
Gen 1:26; 6:9
5:2
Gen 1:27
Mk 10:6
5:3
Gen 4:25
5:4
1 Chron 1:1
5:5
Gen 3:19
Heb 9:27
5:6
1 Chron 1:1
Lk 3:38
5:9
1 Chron 1:1
Lk 3:37
5:12
1 Chron 1:1
Lk 3:37

5 Here is a list of some of the descendants of Adam—the man who was like God from the day of his creation. ²God created man and woman and blessed them, and called them Man from the start.

3, 4, 5*Adam:* Adam was 130 years old when his son Seth was born, the very image of his father in every way. After Seth was born, Adam lived another 800 years, producing sons and daughters, and died at the age of 930.

6, 7, 8*Seth:* Seth was 105 years old when his son Enosh was born. Afterwards he lived another 807 years, producing sons and daughters, and died at the age of 912.

9, 10, 11*Enosh:* Enosh was ninety years old when his son Kenan was born. Afterwards he lived another 815 years, producing sons and daughters, and died at the age of 905.

12, 13, 14*Kenan:* Kenan was seventy years old when his son Mahalalel was born. Afterwards he lived another 840 years, producing sons and daughters, and died at the age of 910.

15, 16, 17*Mahalalel:* Mahalalel was sixty-five years old when his son Jared was

5:1 *Here is a list of some of the descendants of Adam,* literally, "This is the roll of Adam's descendants." *the man who was like God,* literally, "in the likeness of God." **5:3-5** *when his son,* or, by Hebrew usage, "When his son, the ancestor (of Seth) was born."* So also in verses 6, 9, 15, 18, 21, 25, 28, 32. *the very image of his father in every way,* literally, "In his own likeness, after his image." *After Seth was born,* or, by Hebrew usage, "After this ancestor of Seth was born."

Abel was the second child born into the world, but the first one to obey God. All we know about this man is that his parents were Adam and Eve, he was a shepherd, he presented pleasing sacrifices to God, and his short life was ended at the hands of his jealous older brother, Cain.

The Bible doesn't tell us why God liked Abel's gift and disliked Cain's, but both Cain and Abel knew what God expected. Only Abel obeyed. Throughout history, Abel is remembered for his obedience and faith (Hebrews 11:4), and he is called "righteous" (Matthew 23:35).

The Bible is filled with God's general guidelines and expectations for our lives. It is also filled with more specific directions. Like Abel, we must obey regardless of the cost, and trust God to make things right.

Strengths and accomplishments:
● First member of the Hall of Faith in Hebrews 11:4
● First shepherd
● First martyr for truth (Matthew 23:35)

Lessons from his life:
● God hears those who come to him
● God recognizes the innocent person, and sooner or later judges the guilty

Vital statistics:
● Where: Just outside of Eden
● Occupation: Shepherd
● Relatives: Parents: Adam and Eve. Brother: Cain.

Key verse:
"God accepted Abel and proved it by accepting his gift; and though Abel is long dead, we can still learn lessons from him about trusting God" (Hebrews 11:4).

Abel's story is told in Genesis 4:1–8. He is also mentioned in Matthew 23:35; Luke 11:51; Hebrews 11:4 and 12:24.

5:1ff The Bible contains several lists of ancestors, called *genealogies.* There are two basic views concerning these lists: (1) they are complete, recording the entire history of a family, tribe, or nation; or (2) they are not intended to be exhaustive and may include only famous people or the heads of families. In the original Hebrew genealogies, the phrase "was the son of" can also mean "was the descendant of."

Why are genealogies included in the Bible? The Hebrews carried on their beliefs through oral tradition. Writing was still primitive and, in many places, nonexistent. Stories were told to children, who passed them on to their children. Genealogies gave a skeletal outline that helped people remember the stories. For centuries these genealogies were added to and passed down from family to family. Even more important than family tradition,

genealogies were included to confirm the Bible's promise that the coming Messiah, Jesus Christ, would be born into the line of Abraham.

Genealogies point out an interesting characteristic of God. People are important to him as individuals, not just as masses. Therefore God refers to people by name, mentioning their lifespan and descendants. The next time you feel overwhelmed in a vast crowd, remember that the focus of God's attention and love is on the individual.

5:3–5 In the most general sense, all human beings are related, going back to Adam and Eve. Actually, we are a family of mankind, sharing one flesh and blood. Remember this when prejudice enters your mind or hatred invades your feelings. Each person is a valuable and unique creation of God, just like you.

born. Afterwards he lived 830 years, producing sons and daughters, and died at the age of 895.

18, 19, 20*Jared:* Jared was 162 years old when his son Enoch was born. Afterwards he lived another 800 years, producing sons and daughters, and died at the age of 962.

21-24*Enoch:* Enoch was sixty-five years old when his son Methuselah was born. Afterwards he lived another 300 years in fellowship with God, and produced sons and daughters; then, when he was 365, and in constant touch with God, he disappeared, for God took him!

25, 26, 27*Methuselah:* Methuselah was 187 years old when his son Lamech was born; afterwards he lived another 782 years, producing sons and daughters, and died at the age of 969.

28-31*Lamech:* Lamech was 182 years old when his son Noah was born. Lamech named him Noah (meaning "Relief") because he said, "He will bring us relief from the hard work of farming this ground which God has cursed." Afterwards Lamech lived 595 years, producing sons and daughters, and died at the age of 777.

32*Noah:* Noah was 500 years old and had three sons, Shem, Ham, and Japheth.

5:18
1 Chron. 1:1
Lk 3:37
Jude 14

5:22
Gen 6:9; 24:20; 48:15
Heb 11:5
Jude 14

5:24
2 Kgs 2:11
Ps 49:5; 73:24

5:29
Gen 3:17; 8:21
Rom 8:20

5:32
Gen 7:6
Gen 9:18

C. THE STORY OF NOAH (6:1—11:32)

Earth was no longer the perfect paradise that God had intended. It is frightening to see how quickly all of humanity forgot about God. Incredibly, in all the world, only one man and his family still worshiped God. That man was Noah. Because of his faithfulness and obedience, God saved him and his family from a vast flood that destroyed every other human being on earth. This section shows us how God hates sin and judges those who enjoy it.

1. The great flood

6 Now a population explosion took place upon the earth. It was at this time that beings from the spirit world looked upon the beautiful earth women and took any they desired to be their wives. 3Then Jehovah said, "My Spirit must not forever be disgraced in man, wholly evil as he is. I will give him 120 years to mend his ways."

4In those days, and even afterwards, when the evil beings from the spirit world were sexually involved with human women, their children became giants, of whom so many legends are told. 5When the Lord God saw the extent of human wickedness, and that the trend and direction of men's lives were only towards evil, 6he was sorry he had made them. It broke his heart.

6:1, 2 *beings from the spirit world,* literally, "sons of God."

6:1
Gen 1:28
6:2
2 Pet 2:14
6:3
Ps 78:39
1 Pet 3:20

6:4
Num 13:33
6:5
Ps 14:2,3
6:6
Ex 32:14
Num 23:19

5:25–27 How did these people live for so long? Some believe that the ages listed were lengths of family dynasties rather than ages of individual men. Those who believe these were actual ages state three main possibilities. (1) The human race was genetically purer in this early time period so there was less disease to shorten the lifespan. (2) No rain had yet fallen on the earth and the "vapor above" (1:7, 8) kept out harmful cosmic rays. Thus, the environmental factors that cause aging were less pronounced. (3) God gave people longer lives so they would have time to "fill the earth" (1:28) and make a significant impact for God.

●**6:1–4** The "beings from the spirit world," more literally, "the sons of God," were probably not angels, because angels cannot marry or reproduce (Matthew 22:30; Mark 12:25). Some experts believe that this phrase refers to the sons of Seth (called "the Lord's people" in 4:26), but they were no longer godly. Therefore, these verses tell of intermarriage between Seth's godly descendants and Cain's evil descendants. This would have weakened the godly line and increased moral depravity in the world. The resulting population explosion brought an explosion of evil.

●**6:3** What patience God showed, allowing the people of Noah's day a great deal of time (120 years) to change their sinful ways. God demonstrates his great patience with us as well. He is giving

us time to quit living our way and begin living his way, the way he shows us in his Word. While 120 years may seem like a long time for God to wait, time did run out one day, and the flood waters swept across the earth. Your time also may be running out. Turn to God to forgive your sins. You can't see the stopwatch of God's patience, and there is no bargaining for additional time.

6:4 The giants mentioned here were probably large people sometimes reaching nine or ten feet in height. These may have been the same people mentioned in Numbers 13:33. Goliath, a man nine feet tall, appears in 1 Samuel 17. They used their physical advantage to oppress the people around them.

6:6, 7 Does this mean God was sorry for creating humanity? Was he admitting he had made a mistake? No, God does not change his mind (1 Samuel 15:29). Instead, this was God's expression of sorrow for what the people had done to themselves—the same feeling a parent might have over a rebellious child. God was sorry that the people chose sin and death instead of a relationship with him.

●**6:6–8** The sin of the people "broke God's heart." Our sins break God's heart as much as sin did in Noah's day. Noah, however, was a pleasure to God. Although we are far from perfect, we can follow Noah's example and be a pleasure to God in the midst of the sin that surrounds us.

6:7
Deut 29:19,20

6:9
Ezek 14:14

6:11
Deut 31:29
Judg 2:19
Ezek 8:17

6:12
Gen 8:21
Ps 14:1-3;
53:2,3
Rom 3:23

6:13
Isa 34:1-4
Ezek 7:2,3

6:14
Ex 2:3

7And he said, "I will blot out from the face of the earth all mankind that I created. Yes, and the animals too, and the reptiles and the birds. For I am sorry I made them."

8But Noah was a pleasure to the Lord. Here is the story of Noah: 9, 10He was the only truly righteous man living on the earth at that time. He tried always to conduct his affairs according to God's will. And he had three sons—Shem, Ham, and Japheth.

11Meanwhile, the crime rate was rising rapidly across the earth, and, as seen by God, the world was rotten to the core.

12, 13As God observed how bad it was, and saw that all mankind was vicious and depraved, he said to Noah, "I have decided to destroy all mankind; for the earth is filled with crime because of man. Yes, I will destroy mankind from the earth. 14Make a boat from resinous wood, sealing it with tar; and construct decks and

In spite of parents' efforts and worries, conflicts between children in a family seem inevitable. Sibling relationships allow both competition and cooperation. In most cases, the mixture of loving and fighting eventually creates a strong bond between brothers and sisters. It isn't unusual, though, to hear parents say, "They fight so much I hope they don't kill each other before they grow up"' In Cain's case, the troubling potential became a tragedy. And while we don't know many details of this first child's life, his story can still teach us.

Cain got angry. Furious. Both he and his brother Abel had made sacrifices to God, and his had been rejected. Cain's reaction gives us a clue that his attitude was probably wrong from the start. Cain had a choice to make. He could correct his attitude about his sacrifice to God, or he could take out his anger on his brother. His decision is a clear reminder of how often we are aware of opposite choices, yet choose the wrong just as Cain did. We may not be choosing to murder, but we are still intentionally choosing what we shouldn't.

The feelings motivating our behavior can't always be changed by simple thought-power. But here we can begin to experience God's willingness to help. Asking for his help to do what is right can prevent us from setting into motion actions which we will later regret.

Strengths and accomplishments:
● First human child
● First to follow in father's profession, farming

Weaknesses and mistakes:
● When disappointed, reacted out of anger and discouragement
● Took the negative option even when a positive possibility was offered
● Was the first murderer

Lessons from his life:
● Anger is not the sin. It is what we get angry about or actions motivated by anger that can be sinful. Anger must be the energy behind good action, not evil action.
● What we offer to God must be from the heart—the best we are and have
● The consequences of sin are sometimes for life

Vital statistics:
● Where: Near Eden, which was probably located in the present-day countries of Iraq or Iran
● Occupation: Farmer at first, later nomad
● Relatives: Parents: Adam and Eve. Brothers: Abel, Seth, and others not mentioned by name.

Key verse:
"Your face . . . can be bright with joy if you will do what you should! But if you refuse to obey, watch out. Sin is waiting to attack you, longing to destroy you. But you can conquer it!" (Genesis 4:7).

Cain's story is told in Genesis 4:1–17. He is also mentioned in Hebrews 11:4; 1 John 3:12; Jude 11.

6:9, 10 Although Noah lived among evil people, he tried to do what pleased God by conducting his affairs according to God's will. For a lifetime he walked step by step in faith, a living example to his generation. Like Noah, we live in a world filled with evil. Are we being an influence on others, or are we being influenced? Either the two- or three-foot space around us is becoming more like us, or we are becoming more like it.

stalls throughout the ship. ¹⁵Make it 450 feet long, 75 feet wide, and 45 feet high. ¹⁶Construct a skylight all the way around the ship, eighteen inches below the roof; and make three decks inside the boat—a bottom, middle, and upper deck—and put a door in the side.

¹⁷"Look! I am going to cover the earth with a flood and destroy every living being—everything in which there is the breath of life. All will die. ¹⁸But I promise to keep you safe in the ship, with your wife and your sons and their wives. ¹⁹, ²⁰Bring a pair of every animal—a male and a female—into the boat with you, to keep them alive through the flood. Bring in a pair of each kind of bird and animal and reptile. ²¹Store away in the boat all the food that they and you will need." ²²And Noah did everything as God commanded him.

6:17
Lev 26:28
Ps 29:10
Isa 54:9
2 Pet 2:5
6:21
Gen 1:29
6:22
Gen 7:5
Ex 40:16

7 Finally the day came when the Lord said to Noah, "Go into the boat with all your family, for among all the people of the earth, I consider you alone to be righteous. ²Bring in the animals, too—a pair of each, except those kinds I have chosen for eating and for sacrifice: take seven pairs of each of them, ³and seven pairs of every kind of bird. Thus there will be every kind of life reproducing again after the flood has ended. ⁴One week from today I will begin forty days and nights of rain; and all the animals and birds and reptiles I have made will die."

7:1
Job 5:19
Prov 11:8
Isa 26:20
Mt 24:38
Lk 17:26
Heb 11:17
1 Pet 3:20
7:2
Lev 11:2-47
Deut·14:3-20
Ezek 44:23

⁵So Noah did everything the Lord commanded him. ⁶He was 600 years old when the flood came. ⁷He boarded the boat with his wife and sons and their wives, to escape the flood. ⁸, ⁹With him were all the various kinds of animals—those for eating and sacrifice, and those that were not, and the birds and reptiles. They came into the boat in pairs, male and female, just as God commanded Noah.

7:11
Ps 78:23
Ezek 26:19
Mal 3:10

¹⁰, ¹¹, ¹²One week later, when Noah was 600 years, two months, and seventeen days old, the rain came down in mighty torrents from the sky, and the subterranean waters burst forth upon the earth for forty days and nights. ¹³But Noah had gone into the boat that very day with his wife and his sons, Shem, Ham, and Japheth, and their wives. ¹⁴, ¹⁵With them in the boat were pairs of every kind of animal—domestic and wild—and reptiles and birds of every sort. ¹⁶Two by two they came, male and female, just as God had commanded. Then the Lord God closed the door and shut them in.

7:12
Ex 24:18
Deut 9:9
1 Kgs 19:8
Mt 4:2
7:13
Heb 11:7
1 Pet 3:20
2 Pet 2:5
7:15
Gen 6:19; 7:8

¹⁷For forty days the roaring floods prevailed, covering the ground and lifting the boat high above the earth. ¹⁸As the water rose higher and higher above the ground, the boat floated safely upon it; ¹⁹until finally the water covered all the high mountains under the whole heaven, ²⁰standing twenty-two feet and more above the highest peaks. ²¹And all living things upon the earth perished—birds, domestic and wild animals, and reptiles and all mankind— ²²everything that breathed and lived upon dry land. ²³All existence on the earth was blotted out—man and animals alike, and reptiles and birds. God destroyed them all, leaving only Noah alive, and those with him in the boat. ²⁴And the water covered the earth 150 days.

7:18
Ex 14:28
Ps 69:14,15
7:19
Ps 46:2,3
2 Pet 3:6
7:20
Ps 104:6
7:23
Mt 24:37-39
1 Pet 3:20
2 Pet 2:5
7:24
Gen 7:11; 8:4

8 God didn't forget about Noah and all the animals in the boat! He sent a wind to blow across the waters, and the floods began to disappear, ²for the subterranean water sources ceased their gushing, and the torrential rains subsided. ³, ⁴So the flood gradually receded until, 150 days after it began, the boat came to rest

8:1
a) Ex 2:24
2 Pet 2:5
b) Ex 14:21
8:4
Isa 37:38

7:3 *seven pairs,* literally, "the male and female."   **7:16** *the Lord God,* literally, "Jehovah."

6:15 The boat Noah built was no canoe! Picture yourself building a boat the length of one and a half football fields and as high as a four-story building. The "ark" (as it is commonly called) was exactly six times longer than it was wide—the same ratio used by modern shipbuilders. This huge boat was probably built miles from any body of water by only a few faithful men who trusted God and believed his promises.

●**6:18** Noah got right to work when God told him to build the ark. The other people must have been warned about the coming disaster (1 Peter 3:20), but apparently they did not expect it to

happen. Today things haven't changed much. Each day thousands of people are warned of God's inevitable judgment, yet most of them don't really believe it will happen. Don't expect people to welcome or accept your message of God's coming judgment on sin. Those who don't believe in God will deny his judgment and try to get you to deny God as well. But remember God's promise to Noah to keep him safe. This can inspire you to trust God for deliverance in the judgment that is sure to come.

7:1 Pairs of every animal joined Noah in the ark; seven pairs were taken of those animals used for sacrifice. Many scholars estimate that almost 45,000 animals could have fit into the ark.

upon the mountains of Ararat. ⁵Three months later, as the waters continued to go down, other mountain peaks appeared.

⁶After another forty days, Noah opened a porthole ⁷and released a raven that flew back and forth until the earth was dry. ⁸Meanwhile he sent out a dove to see if it could find dry ground, ⁹but the dove found no place to light, and returned to Noah, for the water was still too high. So Noah held out his hand and drew the dove back into the boat.

¹⁰Seven days later Noah released the dove again, ¹¹and this time, towards evening, the bird returned to him with an olive leaf in her beak. So Noah knew that

8:6
Gen 6:16

8:7
Lev 11:15
Deut 14:14
1 Kgs 17:4
Lk 12:24

8:8
Isa 60:8
Hos 11:11
Mt 10:16

8:5 *three months later,* literally, "on the first day of the tenth month."

NOAH

The story of Noah's life involved not one, but two great and tragic floods. The world in Noah's day was flooded with evil. The number of those who remembered the God of creation, perfection, and love had dwindled to one. Of God's people, only Noah was left. God's response to the severe situation was a 120-year-long last chance, during which he had Noah build a graphic illustration of the message of his life. Nothing like a huge boat, built on dry land, to make a point! For Noah, obedience meant a long-term commitment to a project.

Many of us have trouble sticking to any project, whether or not it is directed by God. It is interesting that the length of Noah's obedience was greater than today's expected lifetime. Our only comparable long-term project is our very lives. But perhaps this is one great challenge Noah's life gives us: to live, in acceptance of God's grace, an entire lifetime of obedience and gratitude.

Strengths and accomplishments:
- Only follower of God left in his generation
- Second father of the human race
- Man of patience, consistence, and obedience
- First major shipbuilder in history

Lessons from his life:
- God is faithful to those who obey him
- God does not always protect us from trouble, but cares for us in spite of trouble
- Obedience is a long-term commitment
- A man may be faithful, but his sinful nature always travels with him

Vital statistics:
- Where: We're not told how far from the Garden of Eden location people had settled
- Occupation: Farmer, shipbuilder, preacher
- Relatives: Grandfather: Methuselah. Father: Lamech. Sons: Ham, Shem, and Japheth.

Key verse:
"Noah did everything as God commanded him" (Genesis 6:22).

Noah's story is told in Genesis 5:29—10:32. He is also mentioned in 1 Chronicles 1:4; Isaiah 54:9; Ezekiel 14:14, 20; Matthew 24:37, 38; Luke 3:36; 17:26, 27; Hebrews 11:7; 1 Peter 3:20; 2 Peter 2:5.

7:16 Many have wondered how this animal kingdom roundup happened. Did Noah and his sons spend years collecting them? In reality, the creation, along with Noah, was doing just as God had commanded. There seemed to be no problem gathering the animals—God took care of the details of that job while Noah was doing his part, building the ark. Often we do just the opposite of Noah. We worry about details in our lives over which we have no control, while neglecting specific areas that *are* under our control (like attitudes, relationships, responsibilities). Try to be more like Noah, concentrating on those things God has given you to do, and leaving the rest to him.

●**7:17–21** Was the flood a local event, or did it cover the entire earth? A universal flood was certainly possible. There is enough water on the earth to cover all dry land (the earth began that way in Genesis 1:9, 10). Afterwards, God promised never again to destroy the earth with a flood. Thus, this flood must either have covered the entire earth or destroyed all the inhabited parts of the earth. Remember, God's reason for sending the flood was to destroy all the earth's wickedness. It would have taken a major flood to accomplish this.

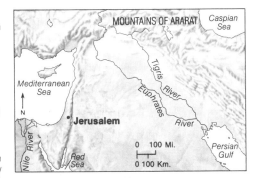

MOUNTAINS OF ARARAT The boat touched land in the Mountains of Ararat located in present-day Turkey near the Russian border. There it rested for almost eight months before Noah, his family, and the animals stepped onto dry land.

the water was almost gone. ¹²A week later he released the dove again, and this time she didn't come back.

¹³Twenty-nine days after that, Noah opened the door to look, and the water was gone. ¹⁴Eight more weeks went by. Then at last the earth was dry. ¹⁵, ¹⁶Then God told Noah, "You may all go out. ¹⁷Release all the animals, birds, and reptiles, so that they will breed abundantly and reproduce in great numbers." ¹⁸, ¹⁹So the boat was soon empty. Noah, his wife, and his sons and their wives all disembarked, along with all the animals, reptiles, and birds—all left the ark in pairs and groups.

²⁰Then Noah built an altar and sacrificed on it some of the animals and birds God had designated for that purpose. ²¹And Jehovah was pleased with the sacrifice and said to himself, "I will never do it again—I will never again curse the earth, destroying all living things, even though man's bent is always toward evil from his earliest youth, and even though he does such wicked things. ²²As long as the earth remains, there will be springtime and harvest, cold and heat, winter and summer, day and night."

8:13 Gen 7:11
8:15 Gen 6:13; 7:1
8:17 Gen 7:8,14
8:19 Gen 7:2,3,8,9
8:20 Gen 4:4; 12:7 13:18, 22.2
8:21 Gen 3:17; 5:29 Lev 1:9 Isa 54:9
8:22 Gen 45:6 Ps 74:16,17

2. Repopulating the earth

9 God blessed Noah and his sons and told them to have many children and to repopulate the earth.

²,³"All wild animals and birds and fish will be afraid of you," God told him; "for I have placed them in your power, and they are yours to use for food, in addition to grain and vegetables. ⁴But never eat animals unless their life-blood has been drained off. ⁵,⁶And murder is forbidden. Man-killing animals must die, and any man who murders shall be killed; for to kill a man is to kill one made like God. ⁷Yes, have many children and repopulate the earth and subdue it."

9:2 Gen 1:26 Ps 8:6-8
9:4 Lev 3:17 7:26,27; 17:10
9:5 Ex 21:12,28,29 Lev 19:17
9:6 Ex 20:13

The rainbow

⁸Then God told Noah and his sons, ⁹, ¹⁰, ¹¹"I solemnly promise you and your children and the animals you brought with you—all these birds and cattle and wild animals—that I will never again send another flood to destroy the earth. ¹²And I seal this promise with this sign: ¹³I have placed my rainbow in the clouds as a sign of my promise until the end of time, to you and to all the earth. ¹⁴When I send clouds over the earth, the rainbow will be seen in the clouds, ¹⁵and I will remember my promise to you and to every being, that never again will the floods come and destroy all life. ¹⁶, ¹⁷For I will see the rainbow in the cloud and remember my eternal promise to every living being on the earth."

9:11 Isa 54:9 2 Pet 3:6
9:12 Gen 17:11 Mt 26:26-28
9:13 Ezek 1:28
9:15 Gen 6:18 8:21,22 Deut 7:9

Noah's descendants

¹⁸The names of Noah's three sons were Shem, Ham, and Japheth. (Ham is the

8:13 *Twenty-nine days after that,* literally, "in the 601st year, in the first month, the first day of the month."
8:20 *some of the animals and birds God had designated,* literally, "Clean," i.e., ritually approved by God.
8:21 *Jehovah was pleased with the sacrifice,* literally, "and Jehovah smelled the delicious odor and said . . ."
9:9-11 *promise you and your children,* literally, "your seed."

8:15, 16 Noah occasionally tested the earth to see if it was dry, but he didn't get out of the ark until God told him to. He was waiting for God's timing. God knew that even though the water was gone, the earth was not dry enough for Noah and his family to venture out. What patience Noah showed, especially after spending an entire year inside his boat! We, like Noah, must trust God to give us patience during those difficult times when we must wait.

●**8:21, 22** Countless times throughout the Bible, we see God showing his love and patience toward men and women in order to save them. And even though God realizes that people are "bent" toward doing wrong, he continues to do his part to reach them. When we sin or fall away from God, we surely deserve to be destroyed by his judgment. But God has now promised never again to destroy everything on earth with a curse of judgment until the day Jesus Christ returns to destroy evil forever. Now every change of season is a reminder of his promise.

9:5, 6 Here God explains why murder is so wrong: to kill a person is to kill one made like God. Since all people are made like God, all people possess the qualities that differentiate us from the animals—morality, reason, creativity, and self-worth. When we interact with others, we are interacting with beings made like God, beings who will live eternally. God intended for us to recognize these special qualities in all people.

9:8–13 Noah stepped out of the ark onto an earth deserted of human life. But God gave him a reassuring promise. This promise, or covenant, had three parts: (1) never again will a flood do such destruction; (2) as long as the earth remains, the seasons of the year will always come as expected; (3) a rainbow will shine when it rains as a sign to all that God will keep his promises. To this day, God has kept his promises. The earth's order and seasons are still preserved, and rainbows still remind us of his faithfulness to his Word.

ancestor of the Canaanites.) ¹⁹From these three sons of Noah came all the nations of the earth.

²⁰, ²¹Noah became a farmer and planted a vineyard, and he made wine. One day as he was drunk and lay naked in his tent, ²²Ham, the father of Canaan, saw his father's nakedness and went outside and told his two brothers. ²³Then Shem and Japheth took a robe and held it over their shoulders and, walking backwards into the tent, let it fall across their father to cover his nakedness as they looked the other way. ²⁴, ²⁵When Noah awoke from his drunken stupor, and learned what had happened and what Ham, his younger son, had done, he cursed Ham's descendants:

"A curse upon the Canaanites," he swore.
"May they be the lowest of slaves
To the descendants of Shem and Japheth."

²⁶, ²⁷Then he said,

"God bless Shem,
And may Canaan be his slave.
God bless Japheth,
And let him share the prosperity of Shem,
And let Canaan be his slave."

²⁸Noah lived another 350 years after the flood, ²⁹and was 950 years old at his death.

10 These are the families of Shem, Ham, and Japheth, who were the three sons of Noah; for sons were born to them after the flood.

²The sons of Japheth were: Gomer, Magog, Madai, Javan, Tubal, Meshech, Tiras.

³The sons of Gomer: Ashkenaz, Riphath, Togarmah.

⁴The sons of Javan: Elishah, Tarshish, Kittim, Dodanim.

⁵Their descendants became the maritime nations in various lands, each with a separate language.

⁶The sons of Ham were: Cush, Mizraim, Put, Canaan.

⁷The sons of Cush were: Seba, Havilah, Sabtah, Raamah, Sabteca. The sons of Raamah were: Sheba, Dedan.

⁸One of the descendants of Cush was Nimrod, who became the first of the kings. ⁹He was a mighty hunter, blessed of God, and his name became proverbial. People would speak of someone as being "like Nimrod—a mighty hunter, blessed of

9:20,21 Gen 19:32 Prov 20:1
9:22 Prov 30:17 Heb 2:15
9:23 Ex 20:12
9:24 Deut 27:16
9:25 Judg 1:28
9:26 Gen 14:20; 27:40
9:27 Gen 10:2-5 Isa 66:19
9:29 Gen 5:32; 7:11
10:1 Gen 6:9; 9:18 1 Chron 1:4
10:2 1 Chron 1:5-7 Isa 66:19 Ezek 27:13 38:2,3,6
10:3 Jer 51:27 Ezek 27:14
10:4 1 Chron 1:6,7
10:6 1 Chron 1:8,9
10:7 Isa 43:3 Ezek 27:15,20, 22

9:24, 25 *he cursed Ham's descendants*, literally, "cursed be Canaan." **9:26, 27** *God bless Shem, and may Canaan be his slave*, or, "Blessed be Jehovah, the God of Shem . . . and may the Canaanites be Shem's slaves." **10:2** *The sons*, or, "descendants." **10:8** *One of the descendants*, or, "the son of Cush." **10:9** *a mighty hunter, blessed of God*, or, "a mighty hunter against the Lord."

BIBLE NATIONS DESCENDED FROM NOAH'S SONS			
Shem	*Ham*	*Japheth*	Shem's descendants were called Semites. Abraham, David, and Jesus descended from Shem. Ham's descendants settled in Canaan, Egypt, and the rest of Africa. Japheth's descendants settled for the most part in Europe and Asia Minor.
Hebrews	Canaanites	Greeks	
Chaldeans	Egyptians	Thracians	
Assyrians	Philistines	Scythians	
Persians	Hittites		
Syrians	Amorites		

9:20–27 Noah, the great hero of faith, was drunk—a poor example of godliness to his sons. Perhaps this story is included to show us that even godly men can sin and that their bad influence affects their families. Though the wicked people on the earth had been killed, the possibility of evil still existed in the hearts of Noah and his family. Ham's mocking attitude revealed a severe lack of respect for his father and for God.

9:25 This verse has been used by many to support racial prejudice and even slavery. Noah's curse wasn't directed toward any particular race of people, but rather at the Canaanite nation (a nation that God knew would become wicked and evil). The curse

was fulfilled when the Israelites entered the Promised Land and drove the Canaanites out (see the book of Joshua).

10:8–12 Who was Nimrod? Not much is known about him except that he was a mighty, powerful man and "blessed of God." But people given great blessings can let their gifts go to their heads. This is probably what happened to Nimrod. Although he was called "blessed of God," he is also considered by some to be the founder of the great, godless Babylonian Empire. The Bible mentions some of his building projects (10:11, 12). Perhaps Nimrod realized that religion could unify people for his own political purposes.

God." 10The heart of his empire included Babel, Erech, Accad, and Calneh in the land of Shinar. 11, 12From there he extended his reign to Assyria. He built Nineveh, Rehoboth-Ir, Calah, and Resen (which is located between Nineveh and Calah), the main city of the empire.

13, 14Mizraim was the ancestor of the people inhabiting these areas: Ludim, Anamim, Lehabim, Naphtuhim, Pathrusim, Casluhim (from whom came the Philistines), and Caphtorim.

15-19Canaan's oldest son was Sidon, and he was also the father of Heth; from Canaan descended these nations: Jebusites, Amorites, Girgashites, Hivites, Arkites, Sinites, Arvadites, Zemarites, Hamathites. Eventually the descendants of Canaan spread from Sidon all the way to Gerar, in the Gaza strip; and to Sodom, Gomorrah, Admah, and Zeboiim, near Lasha.

20These, then, were the descendants of Ham, spread abroad in many lands and nations, with many languages.

21Eber descended from Shem, the oldest brother of Japheth. 22Here is a list of Shem's other descendants: Elam, Asshur, Arpachshad, Lud, Aram.

23Aram's sons were: Uz, Hul, Gether, Mash.

24Arpachshad's son was Shelah, and Shelah's son was Eber.

25Two sons were born to Eber: Peleg (meaning "Division," for during his lifetime the people of the world were separated and dispersed), and Joktan (Peleg's brother).

26-30Joktan was the father of Almodad, Sheleph, Hazarmaveth, Jerah, Hadoram, Uzal, Diklah, Obal, Abima-el, Sheba, Ophir, Havi-lah, Jobab. These descendants of Joktan lived all the way from Mesha to the eastern hills of Sephar.

31These, then, were the descendants of Shem, classified according to their political groupings, languages, and geographical locations.

32All of the men listed above descended from Noah, through many generations, living in the various nations that developed after the flood.

3. The tower of Babel

11 At that time all mankind spoke a single language. 2As the population grew and spread eastward, a plain was discovered in the land of Babylon, and was soon thickly populated. 3, 4The people who lived there began to talk about building a great city, with a temple-tower reaching to the skies—a proud, eternal monument to themselves.

"This will weld us together," they said, "and keep us from scattering all over the world." So they made great piles of hardburned brick, and collected bitumen to use as mortar.

5But when God came down to see the city and the tower mankind was making, 6he said, "Look! If they are able to accomplish all this when they have just *begun* to exploit their linguistic and political unity, just think of what they will do later! Nothing will be unattainable for them! 7Come, let us go down and give them different languages, so that they won't understand each other's words!"

8So, in that way, God scattered them all over the earth; and that ended the building of the city. 9That is why the city was called Babel (meaning "confusion"),

10:13, 14 *ancestor,* or, "father." 10:23 *sons,* or, "descendants." 10:26-30 *father,* or "ancestor." 11:2 *the land of Babylon,* literally, "the land of Shinar," located at the mouth of the Persian Gulf. *and was soon thickly populated,* literally, "and they settled there."

10:10
Gen 11:9
10:11
a)Mic 5:6
b)Num 4:22,24
Ezra 4:2
10:13
1 Chron 1:11,12
Jer 46:9
10:15
Gen 15:19-21;
23:3
1 Chron 1:13
Jer 47:4
10:16
Gen 15:19-21
10:19
Gen 14:2,3
10:22
Gen 11:10-26
2 Kgs 15:29
1 Chron 1:17-23
Isa 66:19
10:23
Job 1:1
Jer 25:30
10:24
Lk 3:35

10:32
Gen 9:19; 10:1

11:2
Gen 10:10; 14:1
Isa 11:11
Dan 1:2
Zech 5:11
11:3
Gen 14:10
11:4
2 Sam 8:13
Ps 49:11-13
11:5
Gen 18:21
Ex 19:11
11:6
Gen 9:19; 11:1
11:7
Gen 1:26; 3:22
Job 5:12
11:8
Gen 10:25,32
11:9
Gen 10:10
1 Cor 14:23

11:3, 4 This tower of Babel was most likely a ziggurat, a common structure in the area at this time. Most often built as temples, they looked like pyramids with steps or ramps leading up the sides. Ziggurats stood as high as 300 feet and were often just as wide, making them the focal point of the city. The people of this story built their tower as a monument to their own greatness, something for the whole world to see.

11:4 The tower of Babel was a great human achievement—a wonder of the world. But it was a monument to the people themselves rather than to God. We often build monuments to ourselves (expensive clothes, big house, fancy car, important job) to call attention to our achievements. These may not be wrong in themselves, but when we use them to give us identity and self-worth, they take God's place in our lives.

because it was there that Jehovah confused them by giving them many languages, thus widely scattering them across the face of the earth.

Shem's descendants

11:10
Gen 10:22-25

10, 11Shem's line of descendants included Arpachshad, born two years after the flood when Shem was 100 years old; after that he lived another 500 years, and had many sons and daughters.

12, 13When Arpachshad was thirty-five years old, his son Shelah was born, and

11:13
1 Chron 1:17

after that he lived another 403 years, and had many sons and daughters.

14, 15Shelah was thirty years old when his son Eber was born, living 403 years after that, and had many sons and daughters.

16, 17Eber was thirty-four years old when his son Peleg was born. He lived another 430 years afterwards, and had many sons and daughters.

18, 19Peleg was thirty years old when his son Reu was born. He lived another 209 years afterwards, and had many sons and daughters.

20, 21Reu was thirty-two years old when Serug was born. He lived 207 years after that, with many sons and daughters.

22, 23Serug was thirty years old when his son Nahor was born. He lived 200 years afterwards, with many sons and daughters.

11:24
Josh 24:2

24, 25Nahor was twenty-nine years old at the birth of his son Terah. He lived 119 years afterwards, and had sons and daughters.

11:26
Gen 22:20
1 Chron 1:26,27

26By the time Terah was seventy years old, he had three sons, Abram, Nahor, and Haran.

11:29
Gen 17:15
20:12; 22:20
31:53

27And Haran had a son named Lot. 28But Haran died young, in the land where he was born (in Ur of the Chaldeans), and was survived by his father.

11:30
Gen 15:2; 16:1
18:11; 25:21
1 Sam 1:5
Luke 1:7

29Meanwhile, Abram married his half-sister Sarai, while his brother Nahor married their orphaned niece Milcah, who was the daughter of their brother Haran; and she had a sister named Iscah. 30But Sarai was barren; she had no children.

11:31
Gen 27:43
Josh 24:2
Heb 11:8
Acts 7:2

31Then Terah took his son Abram, his grandson Lot (his son Haran's child), and his daughter-in-law Sarai, and left Ur of the Chaldeans to go to the land of Canaan; but they stopped instead at the city of Haran and settled there. 32And there Terah died at the age of 205.

11:12, 13 *his son,* or, by Hebrew usage, "there was born to him the ancestor of Shelah, and after that . . ." So also throughout the remainder of the chapter.   **11:29** *half-sister,* implied. (See 20:12.) *orphaned niece Milcah,* implied. **11:32** *age of 205,* implied. The Samaritan Pentateuch says that Terah died when he was 145 years old, so that his death occurred in the year of Abraham's departure from Haran. This is more consistent with 11:26 and 12:4. See also Acts 7:4.

THE TOWER OF BABEL The plain between the Tigris and Euphrates rivers offered a perfect location for the "temple-tower reaching to the skies."

11:26–28 Abram grew up in Ur of the Chaldeans—an important city in the ancient world. Archeologists have discovered evidence of a flourishing civilization there in Abram's day. The city carried on an extensive trade with its neighbors and had a vast library. Growing up in Ur, Abram was probably well educated.

11:10-27 In Genesis 9:24-27 we read Noah's curse of Ham's descendants and his blessing on Shem and Japheth's descendants. Note the beginning of the fulfillment of Noah's words: one of Ham's sons is Canaan (10:6). Shem's descendants are listed here and in 10:22-31. The curse was on Ham's descendants who became the evil Canaanites; a blessing was on Shem's descendants from whom came Abram and the entire Jewish nation which would eventually conquer the land of Canaan in the days of Joshua.

11:31 Terah left Ur to go to Canaan, but settled in Haran instead. Why did he stop half way? It may have been his health, the climate, or even fear. But this did not change Abram's calling ("God had told Abram"—12:1). He had respect for his father's leadership, but when Terah died, Abram moved on to Canaan. God's will may come in stages. As the time in Haran was a transition period for Abram, so God may give us transition periods and times of waiting to help us depend on him and trust his timing. If we patiently do his will during the transition times, we will be better prepared to serve him as we should when he calls us.

D. THE STORY OF ABRAHAM (12:1—25:18)

Despite God's swift judgment of sin, most people ignored him and continued to sin. But a handful of people really tried to follow him. One of these was Abraham. God appeared to Abraham one day and promised to make his descendants into a great nation. Abraham's part of the agreement was to obey God. Through sharp testing and an incident that almost destroyed his family, Abraham remained faithful to God. Throughout this section we discover how to live a life of faith.

1. God promises a nation to Abraham

12 God had told Abram, "Leave your own country behind you, and your own people, and go to the land I will guide you to. ²If you do, I will cause you to become the father of a great nation; I will bless you and make your name famous, and you will be a blessing to many others. ³I will bless those who bless you and curse those who curse you; and the entire world will be blessed because of you."

⁴So Abram departed as the Lord had instructed him, and Lot went too; Abram was seventy-five years old at that time. ⁵He took his wife Sarai, his nephew Lot, and all his wealth—the cattle and slaves he had gotten in Haran—and finally arrived in Canaan. ⁶Traveling through Canaan, they came to a place near Shechem, and set up camp beside the oak at Moreh. (This area was inhabited by Canaanites at that time.)

⁷Then Jehovah appeared to Abram and said, "I am going to give this land to your descendants." And Abram built an altar there to commemorate Jehovah's visit. ⁸Afterwards Abram left that place and traveled southward to the hilly country between Bethel on the west and Ai on the east. There he made camp, and made an altar to the Lord and prayed to him. ⁹Thus he continued slowly southward to the Negeb, pausing frequently.

¹⁰There was at that time a terrible famine in the land: and so Abram went on down to Egypt to live. ¹¹, ¹², ¹³But as he was approaching the borders of Egypt, he asked Sarai his wife to tell everyone that she was his sister! "You are very

12:1 Gen 15:7 Acts 7:3 Heb 11:8

12:2 Gen 13:16 15:5; 17:5 18:18; 22:17 Zech 8:13

12:3 Gen 22:18 26:4; 27:29 Ex 23:22 Acts 3:25 Gal 3:8

12:7 Gen 13:15 17:1; 18:1 Isa 41:8; 44:3 Gal 3:16

12:8 Gen 4:26; 8:20 22:9

12:9 Gen 13:1; 20:1

12:10 Gen 26:1; 42:5

12:11 Gen 26:7; 29:17

12:2 *you will be a blessing to many others,* or, "I will make your name so famous that it will be used to pronounce blessings on others." **12:3** *the entire world will be blessed because of you,* or, "the nations will bless themselves because of you." **12:8** *traveled southward,* implied.

●**12:1-3** Abram moved out in faith from Ur to Haran and finally to Canaan. God then established a covenant with Abram, telling him that he would be the founder of a great nation. Not only would this great nation be blessed, God said, but the other nations of the world would be blessed too—all because of Abram.

Israel, the nation that would come from Abram, was to be a people who followed God and influenced those with whom it came in contact. We, too, are to extend God's love to all nations, not just our own. Through Abram's family tree, Jesus Christ was born to save humanity. Through Christ, all people and all nations can have a personal relationship with God and be blessed beyond measure. As you read the rest of the book of Genesis, notice how people (Esau, Laban, Lot) and nations (Egypt) were blessed because of their association with those in Abram's direct line of descendants.

●**12:2** God promised to bless Abram and make him great. But there was one condition. Abram had to do what God wanted him to do. This meant leaving his home and friends and traveling to a new land where God promised to build a great nation from Abram's family. Abram obeyed, walking away from his home for God's promise of even greater things in the future. God may be trying to lead you to a place of greater service and usefulness for him. Don't let the comfort and security of your present position make you miss God's plan for you.

12:5 God planned to develop a nation of people he would call his own. He called Abram from the godless, man-centered city of Ur to a fertile region called Canaan, where a God-centered, moral nation could be established. Though small in dimension, the land of Canaan was the focal point for most of the history of Israel as well as for the rise of Christianity. This small land given to one man, Abram, has had a tremendous impact on world history.

●**12:7** Abram built an altar to God. Altars of worship were used in

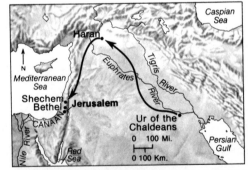

ABRAM'S JOURNEY TO CANAAN Abram, Sarai, and Lot traveled from Ur of the Chaldeans to Canaan by way of Haran. Though indirect, this route followed the rivers rather than attempting to cross the vast desert.

many religions. But for the people of God, altars were more than places of sacrifice. Altars symbolized communion with God and commemorated notable encounters with him. Built of rough stones and earth, they often remained in place for years as continual reminders of God's protection and promises.

Abram regularly built altars to God for two reasons: (1) for prayer and worship, and (2) to remember God's promise to bless him. He couldn't survive spiritually without regularly renewing his love and loyalty to God. These occasions of altar-building helped Abram remember that God was at the center of his life. Without regular worship, it is difficult to remember what God desires and even more difficult to obey.

beautiful," he told her, "and when the Egyptians see you they will say, 'This is his wife. Let's kill him and then we can have her!' But if you say you are my sister, then the Egyptians will treat me well because of you, and spare my life!" 14And sure enough, when they arrived in Egypt everyone spoke of her beauty. 15When the palace aides saw her, they praised her to their king, the Pharaoh, and she was taken into his harem. 16Then Pharaoh gave Abram many gifts because of her—sheep, oxen, donkeys, men and women slaves, and camels.

17But the Lord sent a terrible plague upon Pharaoh's household on account of her being there. 18Then Pharaoh called Abram before him and accused him sharply. "What is this you have done to me?" he demanded. "Why didn't you tell me she was your wife? 19Why were you willing to let me marry her, saying she was your sister? Here, take her and be gone!" 20And Pharaoh sent them out of the country under armed escort—Abram, his wife, and all his household and possessions.

2. Abraham and Lot
Abraham and Lot separate

13 So they left Egypt and traveled north into the Negeb—Abram with his wife, and Lot, and all that they owned, for Abram was very rich in livestock, silver, and gold. 3, 4Then they continued northward toward Bethel where he had camped before, between Bethel and Ai—to the place where he had built the altar. And there he again worshiped the Lord.

5Lot too was very wealthy, with sheep and cattle and many servants. 6But the land could not support both Abram and Lot with all their flocks and herds. There were too many animals for the available pasture. 7So fights broke out between the

12:15 *she was taken into his harem*, literally, "into the household of Pharaoh." **13:5** *many servants*, implied. Literally, "many tents." **13:7** *despite the danger they all faced*, implied.

12:12
Gen 20:11
12:13
Gen 20:2,12
12:16
Gen 13:2
20:14; 24:35
12:17
1 Chron 16:21
Ps 105:14
12:18
Gen 3:13; 4:10
20:9

13:1
Gen 12:9; 20:1
13:2
Gen 12:16
20:14; 24:35
13:3
Gen 12:8; 28:19
13:5
Gen 12:4,5
13:6
Gen 36:6,7

ABRAM'S JOURNEY TO EGYPT
A famine could cause the loss of a shepherd's wealth. So Abram traveled through the Negeb Desert to Egypt, where there was plenty of food and good land for his flocks.

they knew the truth, they would kill him to get Sarai. Sarai would have been a desirable addition to Pharaoh's harem because of her wealth, beauty, and potential for political alliance. As her brother, Abram would have been given a place of honor. As her husband, however, his life would be in danger, for Sarai could not enter Pharaoh's harem unless Abram were dead. So Abram told only half the truth and showed a lack of faith in God's protection, even after all God had promised him. This is also a lesson in how lying compounds the effects of sin. When he lied, Abram's problem didn't become easier, but more complex.

13:1, 2 In Abram's day, shepherds could acquire great wealth. Abram was a shepherd. His wealth included not only money, but also sheep. Sheep were a valuable commodity used for food, clothing, tent material, and sacrifices. Sheep were often traded for other goods and services. Abram was able to watch his wealth grow and multiply daily.

13:5–9 Facing a potential conflict with his nephew Lot, Abram took the initiative in settling the dispute. He gave Lot first choice, even though Abram, being older, had the right to choose first. Abram also showed a willingness to risk being cheated. Abram's example shows us how to respond to difficult family situations: (1) take the initiative in resolving conflicts; (2) let others have first choice, even if that means not getting what we want; (3) put family peace above personal desires.

12:10 When famine struck, Abram continued to Egypt where there was food. Why would there be a famine in the land to which God had just called Abram? This was a test of Abram's faith. Abram didn't question God's leading when he faced this difficulty. Many believers find that when they determine to follow God, they immediately encounter great obstacles. The next time you face such a test, don't try to second-guess what God is doing. Use the intelligence God gave you (as Abram did when he temporarily moved to Egypt, a land with plenty of food) and wait for new opportunities.

12:11–13 Abram, acting out of fear, asked Sarai to tell a half-truth by saying she was his sister. She *was* Abram's half sister, but she was also his wife (11:29).

Abram's intent was to deceive the Egyptians. He feared that if

13:7, 8 Surrounded by hostile neighbors, the herdsmen of Abram and Lot should have pulled together. Instead, they let petty jealousy tear them apart. A similar situation exists today. Many Christian people argue and fight, while Satan is at work all around them.

Rivalries, arguments, and disagreements among believers can be destructive in three ways: (1) they damage good will, trust, and peace—the foundations of human relationships; (2) they hamper progress toward important goals; (3) they make us self-centered rather than love-centered. Jesus understood how destructive this could be. In his final prayer before being betrayed and arrested, Jesus asked God that his followers be "of one heart and mind" (John 17:21).

herdsmen of Abram and Lot, despite the danger they all faced from the tribes of Canaanites and Perizzites present in the land. 8Then Abram talked it over with Lot. "This fighting between our men has got to stop," he said. "We can't afford to let a rift develop between our clans. Close relatives such as we are must present a united front! 9I'll tell you what we'll do. Take your choice of any section of the land you want, and we will separate. If you want that part over there to the east, then I'll stay here in the western section. Or, if you want the west, then I'll go over there to the east."

10Lot took a long look at the fertile plains of the Jordan River, well watered everywhere (this was before Jehovah destroyed Sodom and Gomorrah); the whole section was like the Garden of Eden, or like the beautiful countryside around Zoar in Egypt. 11So that is what Lot chose—the Jordan valley to the east of them. He went there with his flocks and servants, and thus he and Abram parted company. 12For Abram stayed in the land of Canaan, while Lot lived among the cities of the plain, settling at a place near the city of Sodom. 13The men of this area were unusually wicked, and sinned greatly against Jehovah.

14After Lot was gone, the Lord said to Abram, "Look as far as you can see in every direction, 15for I am going to give it all to you and your descendants. 16And I am going to give you so many descendants that, like dust, they can't be counted! 17Hike in all directions and explore the new possessions I am giving you." 18Then Abram moved his tent to the oaks of Mamre, near Hebron, and built an altar to Jehovah there.

Abraham rescues Lot

14 Now war filled the land—Amraphel, king of Shinar, Arioch, king of Ellasar, Ched-or-laomer, king of Elam, and Tidal, king of Goiim 2Fought against: Bera, king of Sodom, Birsha, king of Gomorrah, Shinab, king of Admah, Shemeber, king of Zeboiim, and The king of Bela (later called Zoar).

3These kings (of Sodom, Gomorrah, Admah, Zeboiim, and Bela) mobilized their armies in Siddim Valley (that is, the valley of the Dead Sea). 4For twelve years they had all been subject to King Ched-or-laomer, but now in the thirteenth year, they rebelled.

5, 6One year later, Ched-or-laomer and his allies arrived and the slaughter began. For they were victorious over the following tribes at the places indicated:

The Rephaim in Ashteroth-karnaim; The Zuzim in Ham; The Emim in the plain of Kiriathaim; The Horites in Mount Seir, as far as El-paran at the edge of the desert. 7Then they swung around to Enmishpat (later called Kadesh) and destroyed the Amalekites, and also the Amorites living in Hazazan-tamar.

13:10 *Garden of Eden,* literally, "the Garden of Jehovah."

13:8	Mt 5:9 / Heb 12:14
13:9	Gen 20:15
13:10	Gen 2:8 / 14:2,8 / 19:22,30 / Deut 34:3
13:13	Gen 18:20 / Deut 32:32 / Isa 1:9; 3:9 / Rom 9:29 / 2 Pet 2:7
13:14	Gen 28:14 / Deut 3:27 / 34:1-4
13:15	Gen 12:2,7 / 15:18; 17:7,8
13:16	Gen 15:5; 28:14 / Num 23:10
13:17	Num 13:17-24
13:18	Gen 8:20; 12:7 / 14:13; 18:1
14:1	Jer 48:34 / Dan 8:2 / Acts 2:9
14:2	13:10; 19:24 / Deut 29:23
14:3	Num 34:12 / Deut 3:17 / Josh 3:16
14:5	Deut 1:4 / 2:10,20; 3:11 / Josh 13:19
14:7	Gen 16:14; 20:1 / Num 13:26 / Deut 1:19 / 2 Chron 20:2

13:10, 11 Lot's character is revealed by the nature of his choices. He took the best share of the land even though it meant living near Sodom, a city known for its sin. He was greedy for the best, without thinking about his uncle Abram's needs or what was fair.

Our lives are a series of choices. We too can choose the best while ignoring the needs and feelings of others. This kind of choice, as Lot's life shows, leads to problems. When we stop making choices in God's direction, all that is left is to make choices in the wrong direction.

13:12 Good pasture and available water seemed like a wise choice to Lot at first. But he failed to recognize that the wicked influence of Sodom could provide temptations strong enough to destroy his family. Have you chosen to live or work in a "Sodom"? Even though you may be strong enough to resist the temptations, other members of your family may not. While we are commanded by Scripture to reach people in the "Sodom" near us, we must be careful that we don't become the very people we are trying to reach.

14:4–16 Who was Ched-or-laomer, and why was he important? In Abram's time, most cities had their own kings. Wars and rivalries were common. A conquered city paid tribute to the victorious king. Nothing is known about Ched-or-laomer except what we read in the Bible. Apparently he was quite powerful. Five cities including Sodom had paid tribute (taxes) to him for twelve years. The five cities formed an alliance and rebelled by withholding tribute. Ched-or-laomer reacted swiftly and reconquered them all. When he defeated Sodom, he captured Lot, his family, and his possessions. Abram, with only 318 men, chased Ched-or-laomer's army and attacked him near Damascus. With God's help, he defeated them and recovered Lot, his family, and their possessions.

14:8
Gen 13:10; 14:2

8, 9But now the other army, that of the kings of Sodom, Gomorrah, Admah, Zeboiim, and Bela (Zoar), unsuccessfully attacked Ched-or-laomer and his allies as they were in the Dead Sea Valley (four kings against five). 10As it happened, the valley was full of asphalt pits. And as the army of the kings of Sodom and Gomorrah fled, some slipped into the pits, and the remainder fled to the mountains.

14:12
Gen 11:27
13:6,12

11Then the victors plundered Sodom and Gomorrah and carried off all their wealth and food, and went on their homeward way, 12taking with them Lot—Abram's nephew who lived in Sodom—and all he owned. 13One of the men who escaped

14:13
Gen 10:16
13:18; 39:14

came and told Abram the Hebrew, who was camping among the oaks belonging to Mamre the Amorite (brother of Eshcol and Aner, Abram's allies).

14:8, 9 *unsuccessfully,* implied.   **14:11** *the victors plundered,* implied.   **14:12** *Abram's nephew,* literally, "Abram's brother's son."

Some people simply drift through life. Their choices, when they can muster the will to choose, tend to follow the course of least resistance. Lot, Abram's nephew, was such a person.

While still young, Lot lost his father. Although this must have been hard on him, he was not left without strong role models in his grandfather Terah and his uncle Abram, who raised him. Still, Lot's life shows his pattern of being tentative in his actions, so caught up in the present moment that he seems to have been incapable of seeing the consequences of his actions. It is hard to imagine what his life would have been like without Abram's careful attention and God's intervention.

By the time Lot drifted out of the picture, his life had taken an ugly turn. He had so blended into the sinful culture of his day that he did not want to leave it. Then his daughters committed incest with him. His drifting finally led him in a very specific direction—destruction.

Lot, however, is called good in the New Testament (2 Peter 2:7). Ruth, the descendant of Moab, was an ancestor of Jesus Christ, even though Moab was a result of Lot's incestuous relationship with one of his daughters.

This gives hope to us that God forgives and often brings about positive circumstances from evil.

What is the direction of your life? Are you headed toward God or away from him? If you're a drifter, the choice for God may seem difficult, but it is the one choice that puts all other choices in a different light.

Strengths and accomplishments:
• He was a successful businessman
• Peter calls him a good man (2 Peter 2:7, 8)

Weaknesses and mistakes:
• When faced with decisions, he tended to put off deciding, then chose the easiest course of action
• When given a choice, his first reaction was to think of himself

Lesson from his life:
• God wants us to do more than drift through life. He wants people to be an influence for him.

Vital statistics:
• Where: Lived first in Ur of the Chaldeans, then moved to Canaan with Abram. Eventually, he moved to the wicked city of Sodom.
• Occupation: Wealthy sheep and cattle rancher. Also a city official.
• Relatives: Father: Haran. Adopted by Abram when his father died. The name of his wife, who turned into a pillar of salt, is not mentioned.

Key verse:
"When Lot still hesitated, the angels seized his hand" (Genesis 19:16).

Lot's story is told in Genesis 11—14; 19. He is also mentioned in Deuteronomy 2:9; Luke 17:28–32; 2 Peter 2:7.

14:12 Lot's greed for the best of everything led him into sinful surroundings. His burning desire for possessions and success cost him his freedom and enjoyment. As a captive to King Ched-or-laomer, he faced torture, slavery, or death. In much the same way, we can be enticed into doing something or going somewhere we shouldn't. The prosperity we long for is captivating: it can both entice us and enslave us if our motives are not in line with God's desires.

¹⁴When Abram learned that Lot had been captured, he called together the men born into his household, 318 of them in all, and chased after the retiring army as far as Dan. ¹⁵He divided his men and attacked during the night from several directions, and pursued the fleeing army to Hobah, north of Damascus, ¹⁶and recovered everything—the loot that had been taken, his relative Lot, and all of Lot's possessions, including the women and other captives.

¹⁷As Abram returned from his strike against Ched-or-laomer and the other kings at the Valley of Shaveh (later called King's Valley), the king of Sodom came out to meet him, ¹⁸and Melchizedek, the king of Salem (Jerusalem), who was a priest of the God of Highest Heaven, brought him bread and wine. ¹⁹, ²⁰Then Melchizedek blessed Abram with this blessing:

"The blessing of the supreme God, Creator of heaven and earth, be upon you, Abram; and blessed be God, who has delivered your enemies over to you."

Then Abram gave Melchizedek a tenth of all the loot.

²¹The king of Sodom told him, "Just give me back my people who were captured; keep for yourself the booty stolen from my city."

²²But Abram replied, "I have solemnly promised Jehovah, the supreme God, Creator of heaven and earth, ²³that I will not take so much as a single thread from you, lest you say, 'Abram is rich because of what I gave him!' ²⁴All I'll accept is what these young men of mine have eaten; but give a share of the loot to Aner, Eshcol, and Mamre, my allies."

14:14
Gen 12:5
Deut 34:1

14:15
Gen 15:2
1 Kgs 15:8
Acts 9:2

14:16
Gen 14:12,14

14:17
Gen 14:5
2 Sam 18:18

14:18
Po 7:17; 60:14
76:2; 110:4
Heb 5:6,10; 7:1

14:19
Gen 27:25; 48:9
Mk 10:16

14:20
Gen 9:26; 24:27
Ps 44:3
72:17-19
Heb 7:4,6

14:22
Gen 1:1

14:23
2 Kgs 5:16

14:24
Gen 14:13

3. God promises a son to Abraham

15 Afterwards Jehovah spoke to Abram in a vision, and this is what he told him: "Don't be fearful, Abram, for I will defend you. And I will give you great blessings."

15:1
Gen 21:17
26:24; 46:2
Num 12:6

LOT'S RESCUE
Having conquered Sodom, Ched-or-laomer left for his home country, taking many captives with him. Abram learned what had happened and chased Ched-or-laomer past Dan and beyond Damascus. There he defeated the king and rescued the captives, among them Lot.

Mediterranean Sea

Damascus

•Dan

Sea of Galilee

Jordan River

N

Jerusalem

Dead Sea

Hebron•

0   20 Mi.

0   20 Km.

Possible location of **Sodom and Gomorrah**

14:14–16 These incidents portray two of Abram's characteristics: (1) He had courage that came from God. He faced a powerful foe and attacked. (2) He was prepared. He had taken time to train his men for a potential conflict. We never know when we will be called upon to complete difficult tasks. Like Abram, we should prepare for those times and then take courage from God when they come.

14:14–16 When Abram learned that Lot was a prisoner, he immediately tried to help his nephew. It is easier and safer not to become involved. But with Lot in serious trouble, Abram acted at once. Sometimes we must get involved in a messy or painful

situation in order to help others. We should be willing to act immediately when others need our help.

14:18 Who was Melchizedek? He was obviously a godly man, for his name means "king of justice" and "king of peace" (Hebrews 7:2). He was a priest of "the God of highest heaven." He recognized God as Creator of heaven and earth. What else is known about him? Four main theories have been suggested. (1) Melchizedek was a respected king of that region. Abram was simply showing him the respect he deserved. (2) The name Melchizedek may have been a standing title for all the kings of Salem (Jerusalem). (3) Melchizedek was a "type" of Christ (Hebrews 7:3). A type is an Old Testament event or teaching that is so closely related to what Christ did that it illustrates a lesson about Christ. Hebrews 7 calls Melchizedek a type of Christ and discusses him in more detail. (4) Melchizedek was the appearance on earth of the pre-incarnate Christ in a temporary bodily form. Many scholars support this view.

14:20 Abram gave one-tenth of the booty to Melchizedek. Even in some pagan religions, it was traditional to give a tenth of one's "earnings" to the gods. Abram followed accepted tradition. However, Abram refused to take any booty from the king of Sodom. Even though this huge amount would significantly increase what he could have given to God, he chose to reject it for more important reasons—he didn't want the ungodly people of Sodom to say, "Look what we have done to make Abram great." Instead, Abram wanted them to look at his life and say, "Look what *God* has done for Abram." In this case, accepting the gifts would have focused everyone's attention on Abram rather than on God, who really won the victory. When people look at us, they need to see what God has accomplished in our lives.

●**15:1** God told Abram not to be afraid. Why would Abram be afraid? Perhaps he feared revenge from the kings he had just defeated (14:15). God then gave Abram two good reasons for courage: (1) he promised to defend Abram and be at his side

15:3
Gen 14:14

15:4
Gen 17:16
Gal 4:28

15:5
Gen 12:2
22:17; 32:12
Rom 4:18

2, 3But Abram replied, "O Lord Jehovah, what good are all your blessings when I have no son? For without a son, some other member of my household will inherit all my wealth."

4Then Jehovah told him, "No, no one else will be your heir, for you will have a son to inherit everything you own."

5Then God brought Abram outside beneath the nighttime sky and told him, "Look up into the heavens and count the stars if you can. Your descendants will be

15:2, 3 *some other member of my household* was Eliezer of Damascus.

Do you like a good mystery? History is full of them! They usually involve people. One of the most mysterious people in the Bible is the King of Peace, Melchizedek. He appeared one day in the life of Abraham (then Abram) and was never heard from again. What happened that day, however, was to be remembered throughout history and eventually became a subject of a New Testament letter (Hebrews).

This meeting between Abram and Melchizedek was most unusual. Though the two men were strangers and foreigners to each other, they shared a most important characteristic: both worshiped and served the one God who made heaven and earth. This was a great moment of triumph for Abram. He had just defeated an army and regained the freedom of a large group of captives. If there was any doubt in his mind about whose victory it was, Melchizedek set the record straight by reminding Abram, "Blessed be God, who has delivered your enemies over to you." Abram recognized that this man worshiped the same God he did.

Melchizedek was one of a small group of godly people throughout the Old Testament who came in contact with the Jews (Israelites), but were not Jews themselves. This seems to indicate that the requirement to be a follower of God is not genetic (a Jew, an Israelite). Instead, it means faithfully obeying his teachings and recognizing his greatness.

Do you let God speak to you through other people? Does your evaluation of others place a high priority on where God fits into their lives? Are you more aware of the little differences between you or the big similarities you share? Do you know the God of the Bible well enough to know if you truly worship him? Allow Melchizedek, Abraham, David, and Jesus, along with many other persons in the Bible, to tell you about and show you this great God, Creator of heaven and earth. He wants you to know how much he loves you; he wants you to know him personally.

Strengths and accomplishments:
- The first priest/king of Scripture—a leader with a heart tuned to God
- Good at encouraging others to serve God wholeheartedly
- A man whose character obviously reflected his love for God
- A person in the Old Testament who reminds us of Jesus and who some believe really was Jesus

Lessons from his life:
- Live for God and you're likely to be at the right place at the right time. To see if you can serve God, his first test is to examine your heart. To whom or what is your greatest loyalty? If you answered *God,* you pass the test and all other factors are unimportant.

Vital statistics:
- Where: Ruled in Salem, site of the future Jerusalem
- Occupation: King of Salem and Priest of the Most High God

Key verse:
"This Melchizedek was king of the city of Salem, and also a priest of the Most High God" (Hebrews 7:1).

Melchizedek's story is told in Genesis 14:17–20. He is also mentioned in Psalm 110:4; Hebrews 5—7.

---

during difficulties, and (2) he promised to give Abram "great blessings." When you fear what lies ahead, remember that God won't desert you in difficult times and has promised you great blessings.

15:2, 3 Eliezer was Abram's most trusted servant, maybe acting as household administrator (Genesis 24). According to custom, if Abram were to die without a son of his own, his eldest servant would become his heir. Though Abram loved his servant, he wanted a son of his own to carry on the family line.

●**15:5** Abram wasn't promised wealth or fame—he already had that. Instead God promised descendants that would be like the stars in the sky—"too many to count." To appreciate the vast number of stars scattered through the sky, you need to be, like Abram, away from any interfering lights or buildings. Or pick up a handful of sand and try to count the grains—it can't be done! Just when Abram was despairing over having no heir, God promised descendants too numerous to imagine!

like that—too many to count!" 6And Abram believed God; then God considered him righteous on account of his faith.

7And he told him, "I am Jehovah who brought you out of the city of Ur of the Chaldeans, to give you this land."

8But Abram replied, "O Lord Jehovah, how can I be sure that you will give it to me?" 9Then Jehovah told him to take a three-year-old heifer, a three-year-old female goat, a three-year-old ram, a turtledove and a young pigeon, 10and to slay them and to cut them apart down the middle, and to separate the halves, but not to divide the birds. 11And when the vultures came down upon the carcasses, Abram shooed them away.

12That evening as the sun was going down, a deep sleep fell upon Abram, and a vision of terrible foreboding, darkness, and horror.

13Then Jehovah told Abram, "Your descendants will be oppressed as slaves in a foreign land for 400 years. 14But I will punish the nation that enslaves them, and at the end they will come away with great wealth. 15(But you will die in peace, at a ripe old age.) 16After four generations they will return here to this land; for the wickedness of the Amorite nations living here now will not be ready for punishment until then."

17As the sun went down and it was dark, Abram saw a smoking fire-pot and a flaming torch that passed between the halves of the carcasses. 18So that day Jehovah made this covenant with Abram: "I have given this land to your descendants from the Wadi-el-Arish to the Euphrates River. 19, 20, 21And I give to them these nations: Kenites, Kenizzites, Kadmonites, Hittites, Perizzites, Rephaim, Amorites, Canaanites, Girgashites, Jebusites."

Abraham's second wife

16 But Sarai and Abram had no children. So Sarai took her maid, an Egyptian girl named Hagar, 2, 3and gave her to Abram to be his second wife.

"Since the Lord has given me no children," Sarai said, "you may sleep with my servant girl, and her children shall be mine."

And Abram agreed. (This took place ten years after Abram had first arrived in the land of Canaan.) 4So he slept with Hagar, and she conceived; and when she

15:16 *Amorite nations living here now,* implied.   **15:18** *Wadi-el-Arish,* literally, "River of Egypt," at the southern border of Judah.

15:6
Ps 106:31
Rom 4:3
Gal 3:6

15:7
Gen 12:1; 13:15
Acts 7:2-4

15:8
Judg 6:17
Lk 1:18

15:9
Lev 1:2

15:12
Gen 2:21; 28:11
1 Sam 26:12

15:13
Ex 12:40
Acts 7:6
Gal 3:17

15:14
Ex 6:5

15:15
Gen 25:7,8

15:16
Ex 33:2

15:18
Num 34:1-15
Deut 1:7,8

15:19
Num 24:21

15:21
Gen 10:15
Ex 23:23,28

16:1
Gen 11:30
15:2; 21:9
Gal 4:24,25

16:2
Gen 30:3
Ex 21:4

16:3
Gen 13:1

●**15:6** Although Abram had been demonstrating his faith through his actions, it was faith, not actions, that made Abram right with God (Romans 4:1–5). We too can have a right relationship with God by trusting him with our lives. Our outward actions—church attendance, prayer, good deeds—will not by themselves make us right with God. A right relationship is based on faith—the confidence that God is who he says he is and does what he says he will do. Right actions follow naturally as a by-product.

15:6 We have read of Abram's mistakes, and we know he was only human. How could God call him righteous? Though human and sinful, Abram believed and trusted in God. It was faith, not perfection, that made him right in God's eyes. This same principle holds for all of us. Our first response must be to believe in God. When we do, he declares us "righteous."

15:13, 14 The book of Exodus tells the story of this incredible journey.

15:16 The Amorites were one of the nations living in Canaan, the land God promised to Abram. God knew the people would grow more wicked and would someday need to be punished. Part of that punishment would involve taking away their land and giving it to Abram's descendants. God, in his mercy, was giving the Amorites plenty of time to repent, but he already knew they would not. At the right time, they would be "ready for punishment." Everything God does is true to his character. He is merciful, knows all, and acts justly—and his timing is perfect.

●**15:17** Why did God send this strange vision to Abram? God's covenant with Abram was serious business. It represented an incredible promise from God and a huge responsibility for Abram. To confirm his promise, God gave Abram a sign—the smoking fire-pot and flaming torch. God took the initiative, gave the confirmation, and followed through on his promises. The sign to Abram was a visible assurance to him that the covenant God had made was real.

●**16:1–3** Sarai gave Hagar to Abram as a substitute wife, a common practice of that time. A married woman who could not have children was shamed by her peers and was often required to give a female servant to her husband in order to produce heirs. The children born to the servant woman were considered the children of the wife. Abram was acting in line with the custom of the day. But his action showed a lack of faith in God to fulfill his promise that Abram and *Sarai* would have a child (15:4).

●**16:3** Sarai took matters into her own hands by giving Hagar to Abram. Like Abram, she had trouble believing God's promise, which was apparently directed specifically toward Abram and Sarai. Out of this lack of faith came a series of problems. This invariably happens when we take over for God, trying to make a promise of his come true through efforts that are not in line with God's specific directions. In this case, time was the greatest test of Abram and Sarai's willingness to allow God to supply their needs. Sometimes we too must simply wait. When we ask God for something, and it is clear that we must wait, the temptation increases to do something ourselves to make it happen in the wrong way.

realized she was pregnant, she became very proud and arrogant toward her mistress Sarai.

16:5
Gen 31:53

⁵Then Sarai said to Abram, "It's all your fault. For now this servant girl of mine despises me, though I myself gave her the privilege of being your wife. May the Lord judge you for doing this to me!"

⁶"You have my permission to punish the girl as you see fit," Abram replied. So Sarai beat her and she ran away.

16:7
Gen 21:17
22:11

⁷The Angel of the Lord found her beside a desert spring along the road to Shur.

16:5 *May the Lord judge you for doing this to me,* literally, "Let the Lord judge between me and you."

ISHMAEL

Have you ever wondered if you were born into the wrong family? We don't know much about how Ishmael viewed life, but that question must have haunted him at times. His life, his name, and his position were bound up in a conflict between two jealous women. Sarah, impatient with God's timetable, had taken matters into her own hands, deciding to have a child through another woman. Hagar, servant that she was, submitted to being used this way. But her pregnancy gave birth to strong feelings of superiority toward Sarah. Into this tense atmosphere, Ishmael was born.

For 16 years, Abraham thought Ishmael's birth had fulfilled God's promise. He was surprised to hear God say that the child he would work through would be Abraham and Sarah's very own. Sarah's pregnancy and Isaac's birth must have had a devastating impact on Ishmael. Until then he had been treated as a son, but this latest arrival made his future uncertain. During Isaac's weaning celebration, Sarah caught Ishmael teasing his half brother. As a result, Hagar and Ishmael were permanently expelled from Abraham's family.

Much of what happened throughout his life cannot be blamed on Ishmael. He was caught in a process much bigger than himself. However, his own actions showed that he had chosen to become part of the problem and not part of the solution. He chose to live out his circumstances instead of living above them.

The choice he made is one we all must make. There are circumstances over which we have no control (heredity, for instance), but there are others over which we do have control (decisions we make). At the heart of the matter is the sin-oriented nature we have all inherited. It can be partly controlled, although not overcome, by human effort. In the context of history, Ishmael's life represents the mess we make when we don't try to change those things that we can change. The God of the Bible has offered a solution. His answer is not control, but a changed life freely given by God. To have a changed life, turn to God, trust him to forgive your sinful past, and begin to change your attitude toward him and others.

Strengths and accomplishments:
- One of the first to experience the physical sign of God's covenant, circumcision
- Known for his ability as an archer and hunter
- Fathered twelve sons who became leaders of warrior tribes

Weakness and mistake:
- Failed to recognize the place of his half brother, Isaac, and mocked him

Lesson from his life:
- God's plans incorporate people's mistakes

Vital statistics:
- Where: Canaan and Egypt
- Occupation: Archer/Hunter/Warrior
- Relatives: Parents: Hagar and Abraham. Half brother: Isaac.

Key verses:
"Hagar, what's wrong? Don't be afraid! For God has heard the lad's cries as he is lying there. Go and get the boy and comfort him, for I will make a great nation from his descendants" (Genesis 21:17, 18).

Ishmael's story is told in Genesis 16—17, 25—28, and 36. He is also mentioned in 1 Chronicles 1:28–31; Galatians 4:28, 29.

16:5 Sarai arranged for Hagar to have a child by Abram and then blamed Abram for going along with the plan. Sarai blamed someone else for her situation just as Adam and Eve did in Genesis 3:12, 13. It is easier to strikeout in frustration and point the finger at someone else than to admit an error and ask forgiveness.

16:6 Did Sarai really beat Hagar? After Sarai blamed Abram for her problems, he gave her authority to punish Hagar as she pleased. Sarai took out her anger against Abram and herself on Hagar. Although Sarai may not literally have beaten her, the treatment was harsh enough to cause Hagar to run away. Anger, especially when it arises out of our own shortcomings, can be dangerous.

⁸*The Angel:* "Hagar, Sarai's maid, where have you come from, and where are you going?"

Hagar: "I am running away from my mistress."

⁹⁻¹²*The Angel:* "Return to your mistress and act as you should, for I will make you into a great nation. Yes, you are pregnant and your baby will be a son, and you are to name him Ishmael ('God hears'), because God has heard your woes. This son of yours will be a wild one—free and untamed as a wild ass!
He will be against everyone, and everyone will feel the same towards him. But he will live near the rest of his kin."

¹³Thereafter Hagar spoke of Jehovah—for it was he who appeared to her—as "the God who looked upon me," for she thought, "I saw God and lived to tell it."

¹⁴Later that well was named "The Well of the Living One Who Sees Me." It lies between Kadesh and Bered.

¹⁵So Hagar gave Abram a son, and Abram named him Ishmael. ¹⁶(Abram was eighty-six years old at this time.)

The terms of the promise

17 When Abram was ninety-nine years old, God appeared to him and told him, "I am the Almighty; obey me and live as you should. ², ³, ⁴I will prepare a contract between us, guaranteeing to make you into a mighty nation. In fact you shall be the father of not only one nation, but a multitude of nations!" Abram fell face downward in the dust as God talked with him.

⁵"What's more," God told him, "I am changing your name. It is no longer 'Abram' ('Exalted Father'), but 'Abraham' ('Father of Nations')—for that is what you will be. I have declared it. ⁶I will give you millions of descendants who will form many nations! Kings shall be among your descendants! ⁷, ⁸And I will continue this agreement between us generation after generation, forever, for it shall be between me and your children as well. It is a contract that I shall be your God and the God of your posterity. And I will give all this land of Canaan to you and them, forever. And I will be your God.

16:13 *Thereafter,* implied.

16:8
Gen 3:9; 4:9
16:9
Gen 21:12
Eccles 10:4
Eph 6:5
Tit 2:9
16:10
Gen 17:20
16:11
Gen 16:15
Ex 3:7,8
16:12
Gen 21.20
Job 39:5-8
16:13
Gen 12:8; 32:30
16:14
Gen 14:7
16:15
Gen 21:9; 25:12
16:16
Gen 12:4; 16:3

17:1
Gen 12:7; 28:3
17:2
Gen 13:16
15:5; 17:2
17:3
Gen 17:17; 18:2
Ex 3:6
17:5
Neh 9:7
Rom 4:17
17:6
Gen 35:11
17:7
Gen 12:7; 13:15
Lev 11:45; 26:12
Ps 105:8-11

16:8 Hagar was running away from her mistress and her problem. The Angel of the Lord gave her this advice: (1) to return and face Sarai, the cause of her problem, and (2) to act as she should. This suggests that she needed to work on her attitude toward Sarai, no matter how justified it may have been. Running from our problems rarely solves them. With Hagar we learn that it is wise to return to our problems, face them squarely, accept God's promise of help, correct our attitudes, and act as we should, not as we would like to.

16:9–12 The statement that Ishmael would be "free and untamed as a wild ass" was actually a compliment, something Hagar could take pride in. In Abram's culture, the ass or donkey was a highly valued animal.

16:13 We have watched three people make serious mistakes: (1) Sarai, who took matters into her own hands and gave her servant girl to Abram; (2) Abram, who went along with the plan but who, when things began to go wrong, refused to get involved in solving the problem; and (3) Hagar, who ran away from the problem. In spite of this messy situation, God demonstrates how he is not limited by the complications in our lives. He can bring good out of any situation. Sarai and Abram still received the son they so desperately wanted, and God solved Hagar's problem despite Abram's refusal to get involved. No problem in your life is too complicated for God if you are willing to allow him to help you.

17:1 The Lord told Abram: "I am God; therefore obey me and live as you should." God has the same message for us today. We are to obey him because he is God. That is reason enough. If you don't think the benefits are worth it, consider first who God is—the only one who has the power and ability to meet your every need.

●**17:2–4** Why did God repeat his covenant to Abram? Twice before, God had mentioned this agreement (Genesis 12 and 15). Now, however, God was bringing it into focus and preparing to carry it out. God now revealed to Abram several specific parts of his covenant: (1) God would make Abram the father of a mighty nation; (2) many nations and kings would come from his descendants; (3) God would continue to reveal himself to those descending from Abraham; (4) God would give Abram's descendants the land of Canaan.

●**17:5** God changes Abram's name to Abraham to reflect his new position as the father of a nation. From this point on he is always referred to as Abraham.

●**17:5–8** God was making an agreement, or contract, between himself and Abraham. The terms were very simple. Abraham's part was to believe in God and obey him. God's part was to give him heirs, property, power, and wealth. Most contracts we make with others are even trades. We give something and in return receive something of equal value. But when we make the agreement to become part of God's family, the blessings far outweigh what we must give up.

17:9
Ex 19:5; 26:5
Ps 25:10

17:10
Acts 7:8

17:11
Ex 12:48
Deut 10:16

17:12
Gen 21:4
Lev 12:3
Lk 1:59; 2:21
Phil 3:5

17:13
Ex 12:44

17:14
Ex 30:33
Lev 7:20

17:16
Gen 18:10

9, 10"Your part of the contract," God told him, "is to obey its terms. You personally and all your posterity have this continual responsibility: that every male among you shall be circumcised; 11the foreskin of his penis shall be cut off. This will be the proof that you and they accept this covenant. 12Every male shall be circumcised on the eighth day after birth. This applies to every foreign-born slave as well as to everyone born in your household. This is a permanent part of this contract, and it applies to all your posterity. 13All must be circumcised. Your bodies will thus be marked as participants in my everlasting covenant. 14Anyone who refuses these terms shall be cut off from his people; for he has violated my contract."

15Then God added, "Regarding Sarai your wife—her name is no longer 'Sarai' but 'Sarah' ('Princess'). 16And I will bless her and give you a son from her! Yes, I will bless her richly, and make her the mother of nations! Many kings shall be among your posterity."

ABRAHAM

We all know that there are consequences to any action we take. What we do can set into motion a series of events that may still be going on long after we're gone. Unfortunately, when we are making a decision most of us think only of the immediate consequences. These are often misleading because they are short-lived.

Abraham had a choice to make. His decision was between setting out with his family and belongings for parts unknown or staying right where he was. He had to decide between the security of what he already had and the uncertainty of traveling under God's direction. All he had to go on was God's promise to guide and bless him. Abraham could hardly have been expected to visualize how much of the future was resting on his decision of whether to go or to stay. But his obedience affected the history of the world. His decision to follow God set into motion the development of the nation that God would eventually use as his own when he visited earth himself. When Jesus Christ came to earth, God's promise was fulfilled: through Abraham the entire world was blessed.

You probably don't know the long-term effects of most decisions you make. But shouldn't the fact that there will be long-term results cause you to think carefully and seek God's guidance as you make choices and take action today?

Strengths and accomplishments:
- His faith pleased God
- Became the founder of the Jewish nation
- Was respected by others and courageous in defending his family at any cost
- Was not only a caring father to his own family, but practiced hospitality to others
- Was a successful and wealthy rancher
- He usually avoided conflicts, but when they were unavoidable, he allowed his opponent to set the rules for settling the disputes

Weakness and mistake:
- Under direct pressure, he distorted the truth

Lessons from his life:
- God desires dependence, trust, and faith in him—not faith in our ability to please him
- God's plan from the beginning has been to make himself known to all people

Vital statistics:
- Where: Born in Ur of the Chaldeans; spent most of his life in the land of Canaan
- Occupation: Wealthy livestock owner
- Relatives: Brothers: Nahor and Haran. Father: Terah. Wife: Sarah. Nephew: Lot. Sons: Ishmael and Isaac.
- Contemporaries: Abimelech, Melchizedek

Key verse:
"And Abram believed God; then God considered him righteous on account of his faith" (Genesis 15:6).

Abraham's story is told in Genesis 11—25. He is also mentioned in Exodus 2:24; Acts 7:2–8; Romans 4; Galatians 3; Hebrews 6, 7, 11.

●**17:9, 10** Why did God require circumcision? (1) As a sign of obedience to him in all matters. (2) As a sign of belonging to his covenant people. Once circumcised, there was no turning back. The man would be identified as a Jew forever. (3) As a symbol of "cutting off" the old life of sin, purifying one's heart toward God, and dedicating oneself to God and his promises. (4) Possibly as a health measure.

Circumcision more than any other practice tended to separate God's people from their heathen neighbors. In Abraham's day, this was essential to develop the pure worship of the one true God.

¹⁷Then Abraham threw himself down in worship before the Lord, but inside he was laughing in disbelief! "Me, be a father?" he said in amusement. "Me—100 years old? And Sarah, to have a baby at 90?"

¹⁸And Abraham said to God, "Yes, do bless Ishmael!"

¹⁹"No," God replied, "that isn't what I said. *Sarah* shall bear you a son; and you are to name him Isaac ('Laughter'), and I will sign my covenant with him forever, and with his descendants. ²⁰As for Ishmael, all right, I will bless him also, just as you have asked me to. I will cause him to multiply and become a great nation. Twelve princes shall be among his posterity. ²¹But my contract is with Isaac, who will be born to you and Sarah next year at about this time."

²²That ended the conversation and God left. ²³Then, that very day, Abraham took Ishmael his son and every other male—born in his household or bought from outside—and cut off their foreskins, just as God had told him to. ²⁴⁻²⁷Abraham was ninety-nine years old at that time, and Ishmael was thirteen. Both were circumcised the same day, along with all the other men and boys of the household, whether born there or bought as slaves.

17:17
Gen 17:3; 18:13

17:19
Gen 21:1,2
26:3-5

17:20
Gen 21:13
25:16

17:21
Gen 17:7,19

17:22
Gen 18:33
35:13

17:23
Gen 14:14

17:24
Gen 16:16; 17:1
Rom 4:11

17:25
Gen 16:16

4. Sodom and Gomorrah
Three angels visit Abraham

18 The Lord appeared again to Abraham while he was living in the oak grove at Mamre. This is the way it happened: One hot summer afternoon as he was sitting in the opening of his tent, ²he suddenly noticed three men coming toward him. He sprang up and ran to meet them and welcomed them.

³, ⁴"Sirs," he said, "please don't go any further. Stop awhile and rest here in the shade of this tree while I get water to refresh your feet, ⁵and a bite to eat to strengthen you. Do stay awhile before continuing your journey."

"All right," they said, "do as you have said."

⁶Then Abraham ran back to the tent and said to Sarah, "Quick! Mix up some pancakes! Use your best flour, and make enough for the three of them!" ⁷Then he ran out to the herd and selected a fat calf and told a servant to hurry and butcher it. ⁸Soon, taking them cheese and milk and the roast veal, he set it before the men and stood beneath the trees beside them as they ate.

⁹"Where is Sarah, your wife?" they asked him.

"In the tent," Abraham replied.

¹⁰Then the Lord said, "Next year I will give you and Sarah a son!" (Sarah was listening from the tent door behind him.) ¹¹Now Abraham and Sarah were both very old, and Sarah was long since past the time when she could have a baby. ¹²So Sarah laughed silently. "A woman my age have a baby?" she scoffed to herself. "And with a husband as old as mine?"

¹³Then God said to Abraham, "Why did Sarah laugh? Why did she say 'Can an old woman like me have a baby?' ¹⁴Is anything too hard for God? Next year, just as I told you, I will certainly see to it that Sarah has a son."

18:1
Gen 12:7; 13:18
Gen 14:13

18:2
Gen 19:1; 23:7
33:3,6,7
Josh 5:13-15

18:3
Gen 19:2; 24:31

18:5
Judg 6:18; 13:15,
16

18:7
Judg 13:15

18:8
Deut 32:14

18:10
Gen 22:15
Judg 13:3
Rom 9:9

18:11
Gen 17:17

18:12
1 Pet 3:6

18:14
Gen 18:10
Jer 32:17,27
Lk 1:37

17:17 *inside he was laughing in disbelief,* implied.   **18:6** *pancakes,* probably some sort of *tortilla.*   **18:10** *next year,* literally, "when life would be due."

●**17:17–27** How could Abraham doubt God? Abraham, the man God considered "righteous" because of his faith, had trouble believing God's promise to him. However, in spite of his doubts, Abraham proceeded to follow God's commands (17:22–27). Even those of great faith may have doubts. When God seems to want the impossible and you begin to doubt his leading, be like Abraham. Focus on God's commitment to fulfill his promises to you, and then continue to obey.

18:2–5 Abraham was eager to show hospitality to these men, as was Lot in Genesis 19:2. In Abraham's day, a person's reputation was largely connected to his hospitality—the sharing of home and food. Even strangers were to be treated as highly honored guests.

Meeting another's need for food or shelter was and still is one of the most immediate and practical ways to obey God and do his will. It is also a time-honored relationship-builder. Hebrews 13:2 suggests that we, like Abraham, might actually entertain angels. This thought should be on our minds the next time we have the opportunity to meet the needs of any stranger.

18:14 "Is anything too hard for God?" This question reveals much about God. Make it a habit to insert your specific needs into this question. "Is this day in my life too hard for God?" "Is this habit I'm trying to break too hard for God?" "Is the communication problem I'm having too hard for God?" Asking the question in this way reminds you that God is personally involved in your life and offers his power to help you.

¹⁵But Sarah denied it. "I didn't laugh," she lied, for she was afraid.

18:16
Gen 18:22; 19:1

¹⁶Then the men stood up from their meal and started on toward Sodom; and Abraham went with them part of the way.

18:17
Gen 19:24

¹⁷"Should I hide my plan from Abraham?" God asked. ¹⁸"For Abraham shall

18:18
Gen 12:2,3
Gal 3:18

become a mighty nation, and he will be a source of blessing for all the nations of the earth. ¹⁹And I have picked him out to have godly descendants and a godly

18:19
Neh 9:7

household—men who are just and good—so that I can do for him all I have promised."

SARAH

There probably isn't anything harder to do than to wait, whether we are expecting something good, something bad, or an unknown.

One way we often cope with a long wait (or even a short one) is to begin helping God get his plan into action. Sarah tried this approach. She was too old to expect to have a child of her own, so she thought God must have something else in mind. From Sarah's limited point of view this could only be to give Abraham a son through another woman—a common practice in her day. The plan seemed harmless enough. Abraham would sleep with Sarah's slave girl who would then give birth to a child. Sarah would take the child as her own. The plan worked beautifully—at first. But as you read about the events that followed, you will be struck by how often Sarah must have regretted the day she decided to push God's timetable ahead.

Another way we cope with a long wait is to gradually conclude that what we're waiting for is never going to happen. Sarah waited ninety years for a baby! When God told her she would finally have one of her own, she laughed, not so much from a lack of faith in what God could do, but from doubt about what he could do *through her*. When confronted about her laughter, she lied—as she had seen her husband do from time to time. She probably didn't want her true feelings to be known.

What parts of your life seem to be "on hold" right now? Do you understand that this may be part of God's plan for you? The Bible has more than enough clear direction to keep us busy while we're waiting for some particular part of life to move ahead.

Strengths and accomplishments:
• Was intensely loyal to her own child
• Became the mother of a nation and an ancestor of Jesus
• Was a woman of faith. She is the first woman listed in the Hall of Faith in Hebrews 11.

Weaknesses and mistakes:
• Had trouble believing God's promises to her
• Attempted to work problems out on her own, without consulting God
• Tried to cover her own faults by blaming others

Lessons from her life:
• God responds to faith even in the midst of failures
• God is not bound by what usually happens. He can stretch the limits and cause unheard-of events to occur.

Vital statistics:
• Where: Married Abram in Ur of the Chaldeans, then moved with him to Canaan
• Occupation: Wife, mother, household manager
• Relatives: Father: Terah. Husband: Abraham. Brothers: Nahor and Haran. Nephew: Lot. Son: Isaac.

Key verse:
"Sarah, too, had faith, and because of this she was able to become a mother in spite of her old age, for she realized that God, who gave her his promise, would certainly do what he said" (Hebrews 11:11).

Sarah's story is told in Genesis 11—25. She is also mentioned in Isaiah 51:2; Romans 4:19; 9:9; Hebrews 11:11; 1 Peter 3:6.

●**18:15** Sarah lied because she was afraid of being discovered. Fear is the most common motive for lying. We are afraid that our inner thoughts and emotions will be exposed or our wrongdoings discovered. But lying causes greater complications than telling the truth. If God can't be trusted with our innermost thoughts and fears, we are in greater trouble than we first imagined.

Abraham prays for Sodom

20So the Lord told Abraham, "I have heard that the people of Sodom and Gomorrah are utterly evil, and that everything they do is wicked. 21I am going down to see whether these reports are true or not. Then I will know."

22, 23So the other two went on toward Sodom, but the Lord remained with Abraham a while. Then Abraham approached him and said, "Will you kill good and bad alike? 24Suppose you find fifty godly people there within the city—will you destroy it, and not spare it for their sakes? 25That wouldn't be right! Surely you wouldn't do such a thing, to kill the godly with the wicked! Why, you would be treating godly and wicked exactly the same! Surely you wouldn't do that! Should not the Judge of all the earth be fair?"

26And God replied, "If I find fifty godly people there, I will spare the entire city for their sake."

27Then Abraham spoke again. "Since I have begun, let me go on and speak further to the Lord, though I am but dust and ashes. 28*Suppose there are only forty-five? Will you destroy the city for lack of five?*"

And God said, "I will not destroy it if I find forty-five."

29Then Abraham went further with his request. *"Suppose there are only forty?"*

And God replied, "I won't destroy it if there are forty."

30"Please don't be angry," Abraham pleaded. "Let me speak: *suppose only thirty are found there?*"

And God replied, "I won't do it if there are thirty there."

31Then Abraham said, "Since I have dared to speak to God, let me continue—*Suppose there are only twenty?*"

And God said, "Then I won't destroy it for the sake of the twenty."

32Finally, Abraham said, "Oh, let not the Lord be angry; I will speak but this once more! *Suppose only ten are found?*"

And God said, "Then, for the sake of the ten, I won't destroy it."

33And the Lord went on his way when he had finished his conversation with Abraham. And Abraham returned to his tent.

God rescues Lot

19 That evening the two angels came to the entrance of the city of Sodom, and Lot was sitting there as they arrived. When he saw them he stood up to meet them, and welcomed them.

18:20
Gen 13:13
19:13
18:21
Gen 11:5
Ex 3:8
18:22
Gen 18:16; 19:1
18:23
Ex 23:7
18:25
Deut 1:16; 32:4
Ps 58:11
18:26
Isa 65:8
Jer 5:1
18:27
Ezra 9:6
Isa 6:5
Lk 18:1
18:30
Ex 32:32
18:33
Gen 17:22; 35:13
19:1
Gen 18:2

18:20-33 Did Abraham change God's mind? Of course not. The more likely answer is that God changed Abraham's mind. Abraham knew that God is just and that he punishes sin. But he may have wondered about God's mercy. Abraham seemed to be probing God's mind to see how merciful he really was. He left his conversation with God convinced that God was both kind and fair. Our prayers may not change God's mind, but they may change ours just as Abraham's prayer changed his. Prayer is the means through which we can better comprehend the mind of God.

18:20-33 Why did God let Abraham question his justice and intercede for a wicked city? Abraham knew God must punish sin, but he also knew from experience that God is merciful to sinners. God knew there were not ten righteous people in the city, but he was merciful enough to allow Abraham to intercede. He was also merciful enough to help Lot, Abraham's nephew, get out of Sodom before it was destroyed. God does not take pleasure in destroying the wicked, but he must punish sin. He is both just and merciful. We must be thankful that God's mercy extends to us.

18:21 God gave a fair test to the men of Sodom. He was not ignorant of all the wicked things going on, but, in his fairness and long-suffering, gave the people of Sodom one last chance to turn to him. God is still waiting with the hope that all people will turn to him (2 Peter 3:9). The wise will turn to him before his patience wears out.

●**18:25** Was God being unfair to the people of Sodom? Did he really plan to destroy the good with the wicked? On the contrary, God's fairness stood out: (1) he agreed to spare the entire city if only ten godly people lived there; (2) he showed great mercy toward Lot, apparently the only man in the city who had any kind of relationship with him (and even that was questionable). God went so far as to almost force Lot to leave Sodom before it was destroyed. Remember God's patience when you are tempted to think he is unfair. Even the most godly people deserve his justice. We should be glad God doesn't direct his justice toward us as he did toward Sodom.

18:33 God showed Abraham that asking for anything is allowed, with the understanding that God's answers come from God's perspective. They are not always in harmony with our expectations, for only he knows the whole story. Are you missing God's answer to a prayer of yours because you haven't considered any possible answer other than the one you expect?

●**19:1** The city gate was the meeting place for city officials and others to discuss current events and transact business. It was a place of authority and status where you could see and be seen. Evidently Lot held an important position in the government or associated with those who did, for the angels found him at the city gate when they arrived. Perhaps this is why Lot was so reluctant to leave (19:16, 18-22).

²"Sirs," he said, "come.to my home as my guests for the night; you can get up as early as you like and be on your way again."

"Oh, no thanks," they said, "we'll just stretch out here along the street."

³But he was very urgent, until at last they went home with him, and he set a great feast before them, complete with freshly baked unleavened bread. After the meal, ⁴as they were preparing to retire for the night, the men of the city—yes, Sodomites, young and old from all over the city—surrounded the house ⁵and shouted to Lot, "Bring out those men to us so we can rape them."

⁶Lot stepped outside to talk to them, shutting the door behind him. ⁷"Please, fellows," he begged, "don't do such a wicked thing. ⁸Look—I have two virgin daughters, and I'll surrender them to you to do with as you wish. But leave these men alone, for they are under my protection."

⁹"Stand back," they yelled. "Who do you think you are? We let this fellow settle among us and now he tries to tell us what to do! We'll deal with you far worse than with those other men." And they lunged at Lot and began breaking down the door.

¹⁰But the two men reached out and pulled Lot in and bolted the door, ¹¹and temporarily blinded the men of Sodom so that they couldn't find the door.

¹²"What relatives do you have here in the city?" the men asked. "Get them out of this place—sons-in-law, sons, daughters, or anyone else. ¹³For we will destroy the city completely. The stench of the place has reached to heaven and God has sent us to destroy it."

¹⁴So Lot rushed out to tell his daughters' fiancés, "Quick, get out of the city, for the Lord is going to destroy it." But the young men looked at him as though he had lost his senses.

¹⁵At dawn the next morning the angels became urgent. "Hurry," they said to Lot, "take your wife and your two daughters who are here and get out while you can, or you will be caught in the destruction of the city."

¹⁶When Lot still hesitated, the angels seized his hand and the hands of his wife and two daughters and rushed them to safety, outside the city, for the Lord was merciful.

¹⁷"Flee for your lives," the angels told him. *"And don't look back.* Escape to the mountains. Don't stay down here on the plain or you will die."

¹⁸, ¹⁹, ²⁰"Oh no, sirs, please," Lot begged, "since you've been so kind to me and saved my life, and you've granted me such mercy, let me flee to that little village over there instead of into the mountains, for I fear disaster in the mountain. See, the village is close by and it is just a small one. Please, please, let me go there instead. Don't you see how small it is? And my life will be saved."

²¹"All right," the angel said, "I accept your proposition and won't destroy that

---

●**19:8** How could any father give his daughters to be savaged by a mob of perverts, just to protect two strangers? Possibly Lot was scheming to save both the girls and the visitors, hoping the girls' fiances (19:14) would rescue them or that the homosexual men would be uninterested in the girls and simply go away. Although it was the custom of the day to protect your guests at *any* cost, this terrible suggestion reveals how deeply sin had been absorbed into Lot's life. He had become hardened to evil acts in an evil city. Whatever Lot's motives were, we see here an illustration of Sodom's terrible wickedness—a wickedness so great that God had to destroy the entire city.

19:13 God promised to spare Sodom if only ten godly people lived there (18:32). Obviously not even ten could be found, for the angels arrived to destroy the city. Archeological evidence points to an advanced civilization in this area during Abraham's day. Most researchers also confirm some kind of sudden and devastating destruction. It is now widely thought that the buried city lies covered beneath the waters of the southern end of the Dead Sea. The sins of Sodom reveal that the people of Lot's day had to deal with the same kinds of repulsive sins the world faces today.

●**19:14** Lot had lived so long and so contented among ungodly

people that he was no longer a believable witness for God. He had allowed his environment to shape him, rather than shaping his environment. Do those who know you see you as a witness for God, or are you just one of the crowd, blending in unnoticed? Lot had compromised to the point that he had become almost useless to God. When he finally did make a stand, no one listened. Have you, too, become useless to God because you are too much like your environment? To make a difference, you first must decide to be different.

●**19:16** Lot hesitated and the angel seized his hand and rushed him to safety. He did not want to abandon the wealth and comfort he enjoyed in Sodom. It is easy to criticize Lot for being hypnotized by his attraction to Sodom when the choice seems so clear to us. To be wiser than Lot, we must see that our hesitation to obey stems from the false attractions of the pleasures of our culture.

19:16, 29 Notice how God's mercy toward Abraham extended to Lot and his family. Because Abraham pleaded for Lot, God was merciful and saved Lot from the fiery death that engulfed Sodom. A godly person can often affect others for good. James says the prayer of a godly person is powerful (James 5:16). All Christians should follow Abraham's example and pray for others to be saved.

little city. 22But hurry! For I can do nothing until you are there." (From that time on that village was named Zoar, meaning "Little City.")

23The sun was rising as Lot reached the village. 24Then the Lord rained down fire and flaming tar from heaven upon Sodom and Gomorrah, 25and utterly destroyed them, along with the other cities and villages of the plain, eliminating all life—people, plants, and animals alike. 26But Lot's wife looked back as she was following along behind him, and became a pillar of salt.

27That morning Abraham was up early and hurried out to the place where he had stood before the Lord. 28He looked out across the plain to Sodom and Gomorrah and saw columns of smoke and fumes, as from a furnace, rising from the cities there. 29So God heeded Abraham's plea and kept Lot safe, removing him from the maelstrom of death that engulfed the cities.

The sin of Lot's daughters

30Afterwards Lot left Zoar, fearful of the people there, and went to live in a cave in the mountains with his two daughters. 31One day the older girl said to her sister, "There isn't a man anywhere in this entire area that our father would let us marry. And our father will soon be too old for having children. 32Come, let's fill him with wine and then we will sleep with him, so that our clan will not come to an end." 33So they got him drunk that night, and the older girl went in and had sexual intercourse with her father; but he was unaware of her lying down or getting up again.

34The next morning she said to her younger sister, "I slept with my father last night. Let's fill him with wine again tonight, and you go in and lie with him, so that our family line will continue." 35So they got him drunk again that night, and the younger girl went in and lay with him, and, as before, he didn't know that anyone was there. 36And so it was that both girls became pregnant from their father. 37The older girl's baby was named Moab; he became the ancestor of the nation of the Moabites. 38The name of the younger girl's baby was Benammi; he became the ancestor of the nation of the Ammonites.

Abraham deceives the king

20 Now Abraham moved south to the Negeb, and settled between Kadesh and Shur. One day, when visiting the city of Gerar, 2he declared that Sarah was his sister! Then King Abimelech sent for her, and had her brought to him at his palace.

19:22
Gen 13:10
19:30
Isa 15:5

19:24
Lk 17:29
2 Pet 2:6
Jude 7

19:25
Deut 29:23
Isa 3:9; 13:19
2 Pet 2:6

19:26
Gen 19:17
Lk 17:32

19:29
2 Pet 2:7,8

19:30
Gen 13:10
1 Sam 22:1
1 Kgs 18:4

19:31
Gen 19:14
Gen 38:8,9,18

19:32
Prov 23:31-33
Hab 2:15

19:33
Gen 9:21
Lev 18:6
Prov 20:1

19:37
Gen 36:35
Ex 15:15
Num 21:29
Deut 2:9
Ruth 1:1

19:38
Num 21:24
Deut 2:19

20:1
Gen 13:1; 14:7
26:1

20:2
Gen 12:13
20:12; 26:7

19:24 In the story of Sodom and Gomorrah, we see two facets of God's character: his great patience (considering sparing a wicked city for ten good men) and his fierce anger (destroying both cities). As we grow spiritually, we should find ourselves developing both a deeper fear of God (because of his anger toward sin) and a deeper love for God (because of his patience when we sin).

●**19:26** Lot's wife turned back to look at the smoldering city of Sodom. Clinging to the comforts of the past, she was unwilling to turn completely from sin. Are you looking back longingly at sin while trying to move forward with God? You can't make progress with God as long as you are holding onto pieces of your old life. Jesus said it this way in Matthew 6:24: "You cannot serve two masters."

●**19:30–38** In this pitiful sequel to the story of the destruction of Sodom, we see two women compelled to preserve their family line. They were not driven by lust, but by desperation—they feared they would never marry. Lot's tendency to compromise and refusal to act reached its peak. He should have found right partners for his daughters long before this—Abraham's family wasn't far away. Now the two daughters stooped to incest, showing their acceptance of the morals learned in Sodom. When we are desperate for what we feel we must have, we are most likely to sin.

●**19:30–38** Why doesn't the Bible openly condemn these sisters for what they did? In many cases, the Bible does not judge people for

their actions. It simply reports the events. However, incest is clearly condemned in other parts of Scripture (Leviticus 18:6–18; 20:11, 12, 17, 19–21; Deuteronomy 22:30; 27:20–23; Ezekiel 22:11; 1 Corinthians 5:1). Perhaps the consequence of their actions (Moab and Ammon became enemies of Israel) was God's way of judging their sin.

19:37, 38 Moab and Benammi were the products of incest. They became the fathers of two of Israel's greatest enemies, the Moabites and Ammonites. These nations settled east of the Jordan River, and Israel never conquered them. Because of the family connection, Moses was forbidden to attack them (Deuteronomy 2:9). Ruth, great-grandmother of King David and an ancestor of Jesus, was from Moab.

20:2 Abraham had used this same trick before to protect himself and Sarah (12:11–13). Though Abraham is one of our heroes of faith, he did not learn his lesson well enough the first time. In fact, by giving in to the temptation again he risked turning a sinful act into a sinful pattern—lying whenever he suspected his life was in danger.

However godly we may be, certain temptations are especially difficult to resist. These are the vulnerable spots in our spiritual armor. As we struggle with these weaknesses, we can be encouraged to know that God is watching out for us just as he did with Abraham.

20:3
Gen 28:12
31:24,37:5

20:4
Gen 18:23-25

20:5
Gen 12:17
1 Kgs 9:4
Ps 7:8; 26:6

20:6
Gen 15:1; 31:7
Ps 84:11

20:7
Ex 7:1
1 Sam 7:5
Job 42:8

20:9
Gen 12:18

20:11
Gen 12:12
22:12; 42:18

20:13
Gen 11:31; 12:1

20:14
Gen 12:16

20:15
Gen 47:6

20:16
Gen 23:15

20:17
Num 12:13; 21:7

20:18
Gen 12:17

21:1
Gen 17:16,21

21:5
Rom 4:19

21:6
Gen 18:12

21:7
Gen 18:14
Lk 1:37

3But that night God came to him in a dream and told him, "You are a dead man, for that woman you took is married."

4But Abimelech hadn't slept with her yet, so he said, "Lord, will you slay an innocent man? 5He told me, 'She is my sister,' and she herself said, 'Yes, he is my brother.' I hadn't the slightest intention of doing anything wrong."

6"Yes, I know," the Lord replied. "That is why I held you back from sinning against me; that is why I didn't let you touch her. 7Now restore her to her husband, and he will pray for you (for he is a prophet) and you shall live. But if you don't return her to him, you are doomed to death along with all your household."

8The king was up early the next morning, and hastily called a meeting of all the palace personnel and told them what had happened. And great fear swept through the crowd.

9, 10Then the king called for Abraham. "What is this you've done to us?" he demanded. "What have I done that deserves treatment like this, to make me and my kingdom guilty of this great sin? Who would suspect that you would do a thing like this to me? Whatever made you think of this vile deed?"

11, 12"Well," Abraham said, "I figured this to be a godless place. 'They will want my wife and will kill me to get her,' I thought. And besides, she is my sister—or at least a half-sister (we both have the same father)—and I married her. 13And when God sent me traveling far from my childhood home, I told her, 'Have the kindness to mention, wherever we come, that you are my sister.' "

14Then King Abimelech took sheep and oxen and servants—both men and women—and gave them to Abraham, and returned Sarah his wife to him.

15"Look my kingdom over, and choose the place where you want to live," the king told him. 16Then he turned to Sarah. "Look," he said, "I am giving your 'brother' a thousand silver pieces as damages for what I did, to compensate for any embarrassment and to settle any claim against me regarding this matter. Now justice has been done."

17Then Abraham prayed, asking God to cure the king and queen and the other women of the household, so that they could have children; 18for God had stricken all the women with barrenness to punish Abimelech for taking Abraham's wife.

5. Birth and near sacrifice of Isaac

21 Then God did as he had promised, and Sarah became pregnant and gave Abraham a baby son in his old age, at the time God had said; 3and Abraham named him Isaac (meaning "Laughter!"). 4, 5Eight days after he was born, Abraham circumcised him, as God required. (Abraham was 100 years old at that time.)

6And Sarah declared, "God has brought me laughter! All who hear about this shall rejoice with me. 7For who would have dreamed that I would ever have a baby? Yet I have given Abraham a child in his old age!"

20:6 Abimelech had unknowingly taken a married woman to his wife and was about to commit adultery. But God somehow prevented him from touching Sarah and held him back from sinning. What mercy on God's part. How many times has God done the same for us, holding us back from sin in ways we can't even detect? We have no way of knowing—we just know from this story that he can. God works just as often in ways we can't see as in ways we can.

20:11, 12 Abraham *assumed* that Abimelech was a wicked and ungodly man. He made a quick judgment based on an assumption that may not have been true. Abraham then resorted to a half-truth, deceiving Abimelech instead of trusting God to work in the king's life. Don't assume that God will not work in a situation that has potential problems. He may intervene when you least expect it.

20:17, 18 Why did God condemn Abimelech when it was Abraham who told the lie? Two reasons are suggested. (1) Abimelech was politically motivated to ally himself with

Abraham. To place Sarah in his harem would strengthen Abimelech's international position. (2) God was telling Abimelech that he wouldn't be punished if he simply did what was right. God was giving him the chance to prevent an unwarranted alliance and a sinful sexual relationship.

21:1–7 Who could believe Abraham would have a son at 100 years of age—and live to raise him to adulthood? But doing the impossible is everyday business for God. Our big problems may not seem so impossible if we let God handle them.

21:7 "Who would have dreamed!" After several promises, a visit by two angels, and the appearance of the Lord himself, Sarah finally cried out with surprise and joy at the birth of her son. Because of her doubt, worry, and fear, she had forfeited the peace she could have felt in God's wonderful promise to her. The way to bring peace to a troubled heart and mind is to focus on the promises of God. Trust him to do what he says.

Hagar and Ishmael sent away

⁸Time went by and the child grew and was weaned; and Abraham gave a party to celebrate the happy occasion. ⁹But when Sarah noticed Ishmael—the son of Abraham and the Egyptian girl Hagar—teasing Isaac, ¹⁰she turned upon Abraham and demanded, "Get rid of that slave girl and her son. He is not going to share your property with my son. I won't have it."

¹¹This upset Abraham very much, for after all, Ishmael too was his son.

¹²But God told Abraham, "Don't be upset over the boy or your slave-girl wife; do as Sarah says, for Isaac is the son through whom my promise will be fulfilled. ¹³And I will make a nation of the descendants of the slave-girl's son, too, because he also is yours."

¹⁴So Abraham got up early the next morning, prepared food for the journey, and strapped a canteen of water to Hagar's shoulders and sent her away with their son. She walked out into the wilderness of Beersheba, wandering aimlessly.

¹⁵When the water was gone she left the youth in the shade of a bush ¹⁶and went off and sat down a hundred yards or so away. "I don't want to watch him die," she said, and burst into tears, sobbing wildly.

¹⁷Then God heard the boy crying, and the Angel of God called to Hagar from the sky, "Hagar, what's wrong? Don't be afraid! For God has heard the lad's cries as he is lying there. ¹⁸Go and get him and comfort him, for I will make a great nation from his descendants."

¹⁹Then God opened her eyes and she saw a well; so she refilled the canteen and gave the lad a drink. ²⁰, ²¹And God blessed the boy and he grew up in the wilderness of Paran, and became an expert archer. And his mother arranged a marriage for him with a girl from Egypt.

A treaty by a well

²²About this time King Abimelech, and Phicol, commander of his troops, came to Abraham and said to him, "It is evident that God helps you in everything you do; ²³swear to me by God's name that you won't defraud me or my son or my grandson, but that you will be on friendly terms with my country, as I have been toward you."

²⁴Abraham replied, "All right, I swear to it!" ²⁵Then Abraham complained to the king about a well the king's servants had taken violently away from Abraham's servants.

²⁶"This is the first I've heard of it," the king exclaimed, "and I have no idea who is responsible. Why didn't you tell me before?"

²⁷Then Abraham gave sheep and oxen to the king, as sacrifices to seal their pact. ²⁸, ²⁹But when he took seven ewe lambs and set them off by themselves, the king inquired, "Why are you doing that?"

³⁰And Abraham replied, "They are my gift to you as a public confirmation that this well is mine."

³¹So from that time on the well was called Beer-sheba ("Well of the Oath"), because that was the place where they made their covenant. ³²Then King Abimelech, and Phicol, commander of his army, returned home again. ³³And Abraham planted a tamarisk tree beside the well, and prayed there to the Lord, calling upon the Eternal God. ³⁴And Abraham lived in the Philistine country for a long time.

21:9 *teasing,* or "mocking," whether in innocent fun or otherwise is not clear in the text.

21:18 What happened to Ishmael, and who were his descendants? Ishmael became the ruler of a large tribe or nation. The Ishmaelites were nomads living in the wilderness of Sinai and Paran (south of Israel). One of Ishmael's daughters married Esau, Ishmael's nephew (28:9). The Bible pictures them as hostile to Israel and to God (Psalm 83:6).

21:31 Beer-sheba, the southernmost city of Israel, lay on the edge of a vast wilderness that stretched as far as Egypt to the southwest and Mount Sinai to the south. The phrase "from Dan to Beer-sheba" was often used to describe the traditional boundaries of the Promised Land (2 Samuel 17:11). Beer-sheba's southern location and the presence of several wells in the area may explain why Abraham settled there. Beer-sheba was also the home of Isaac, Abraham's son.

Cross-references (margin):

21:8 1 Sam 1:22
21:9 Gal 4:29
21:10 Gen 16:4,5; Gal 4:30
21:12 Rom 9:7; Heb 11:18
21:13 Gen 16:10; 21:18; Gen 25:12-18
21:14 Gen 16:7
21:16 Jer 6:26
21:17 Ex 3:7; Deut 26:7; Ps 6:8
21:18 Gen 16:1-12; 25:12
21:19 Isa 48:15
21:20 Gen 28:15
21:21 Gen 14:6; 25:18
21:22 Gen 26:26
21:23 Gen 24:2
21:24 Gen 14:22
21:25 Gen 13:7; 26:15
21:27 Gen 26:31; Prov 18:16
21:14
21:30 Gen 31:44
21:31 Gen 21:14; 26:33; Josh 15:28
21:33 1 Sam 22:6; 31:13; Ps 90:2; Isa 9:6; 40:28
21:34 Gen 22:19

God tests Abraham's obedience

22:1
Ex 15:25; 16:4
Deut 8:2
Prov 17:3

22 Later on, God tested Abraham's [faith and obedience].
"Abraham!" God called.
"Yes, Lord?" he replied.

22:1 *faith and obedience,* implied.

A name carries great authority. It sets you apart. It triggers memories. The sound of it calls you to attention anywhere.

Many Bible names accomplished even more. They were often descriptions of important facts about one's past and hopes for the future. The choice of the name *Isaac,* "laughter," for Abraham and Sarah's son must have created a variety of feelings in them each time it was spoken. At times it must have recalled their shocked laughter at God's announcement that they would be parents in their old age. At other times, it must have brought back joyful feelings of receiving their long-awaited answer to prayer for a child. Most important, it was a testimony to God's power in making his promise a reality.

In a family of forceful initiators, Isaac was the quiet, "mind-my-own-business" type unless he was specifically called on to take action. He was the protected only child from the time Sarah got rid of Ishmael until Abraham arranged his marriage to Rebekah.

In his own family, Isaac had the patriarchal position, but Rebekah had the power. Rather than stand his ground, Isaac found it easier to compromise or lie to avoid confrontations.

In spite of these shortcomings, Isaac was part of God's plan. The model his father gave him included a great gift of faith in the one true God. God's promise to create a great nation through which he would bless the world was passed on by Isaac to his twin sons.

It is usually not hard to identify with Isaac in his weaknesses. But consider for a moment that God works through people in spite of their shortcomings and, often, through them. As you pray, put into words your desire to be available to God. You will discover that his willingness to use you is even greater than your desire to be used.

Strengths and accomplishments:
* He was the miracle child born to Sarah when she was 90 years old and Abraham when he was 100 years old
* He was the first descendant in fulfillment of God's promise to Abraham
* He seems to have been a caring and consistent husband, at least until his sons were born
* He demonstrated great patience

Weaknesses and mistakes:
* Under pressure he tended to imitate his father and lie
* In conflict he sought to avoid confrontation
* He played favorites between his sons and alienated his wife

Lessons from his life:
* Patience often brings rewards
* Both God's plans and his promises are larger than people
* God keeps his promises! He remains faithful though we are often faithless
* Playing favorites is sure to bring family conflict

Vital statistics:
* Where: The area called Negeb, in the southern part of Palestine, between Kadesh and Shur (Genesis 20:1)
* Occupation: Wealthy livestock owner
* Relatives: Parents: Abraham and Sarah. Half brother: Ishmael. Wife: Rebekah. Sons: Jacob and Esau.

Key verse:
"Sarah shall bear you a son; and you are to name him Isaac ('Laughter'), and I will sign my covenant with him forever, and with his descendants" (Genesis 17:19).

Isaac's story is told in Genesis 17:15—35:29. He is also mentioned in Romans 9:7, 8; Hebrews 11:17–20; James 2:21–24.

●**22:1** God gave Abraham a test. The purpose of this test was not to trip Abraham and watch him fall. Rather, God's real purpose was to deepen Abraham's capacity to obey God, and thus to develop his character. Just as fire refines ore to extract precious metals, God refines us through difficult circumstances. When we are tested we can complain, or we can try to see how God is stretching us to develop our character.

²"Take with you your only son—yes, Isaac whom you love so much—and go to the land of Moriah and sacrifice him there as a burnt offering upon one of the mountains which I'll point out to you!"

22:2
2 Kgs 3:27
2 Chron 3:1
Jn 3:16

³The next morning Abraham got up early, chopped wood for a fire upon the altar, saddled his donkey, and took with him his son Isaac and two young men who were his servants, and started off to the place where God had told him to go. ⁴On the third day of the journey Abraham saw the place in the distance.

22:3
Mt 10:37

⁵"Stay here with the donkey," Abraham told the young men, "and the lad and I will travel yonder and worship, and then come right back."

⁶Abraham placed the wood for the burnt offering upon Isaac's shoulders, while he himself carried the knife and the flint for striking a fire. So the two of them went on together.

22:7
Gen 8:20
Ex 29:38
Jn 1:29
Rev 13:7

⁷"Father," Isaac asked, "we have the wood and the flint to make the fire, but where is the lamb for the sacrifice?"

22:8
Gen 18:14
Mt 19:26
1 Pet 1:19
Rev 5:6

⁸"God will see to it, my son," Abraham replied. And they went on.

⁹When they arrived at the place where God had told Abraham to go, he built an altar and placed the wood in order, ready for the fire, and then tied Isaac and laid him on the altar over the wood. ¹⁰And Abraham took the knife and lifted it up to plunge it into his son, to slay him.

22:9
Gen 12:7
Heb 11:17
Jas 2:21

¹¹At that moment the Angel of God shouted to him from heaven, "Abraham! Abraham!"

"Yes, Lord!" he answered.

22:11
Gen 16:7; 21:17
Ex 3:2

¹²"Lay down the knife; don't hurt the lad in any way," the Angel said, "for I know that God is first in your life—you have not withheld even your beloved son from me."

22:12
Heb 11:17
22:13
Gen 8:20
22:15
Gen 22:11

¹³Then Abraham noticed a ram caught by its horns in a bush. So he took the ram and sacrificed it, instead of his son, as a burnt offering on the altar. ¹⁴Abraham named the place "Jehovah provides"—and it still goes by that name to this day.

22:16
49:13
Heb 6:13
Lk 1:73,74

¹⁵Then the Angel of God called again to Abraham from heaven. ¹⁶"I, the Lord, have sworn by myself that because you have obeyed me and have not withheld even your beloved son from me, ¹⁷I will bless you with incredible blessings and multiply

22:17
Gen 12:12
13:16; 15:15
17:5

ABRAHAM'S TRIP TO MOUNT MORIAH Abraham and Isaac traveled the 50 or 60 miles from Beer-sheba to Mount Moriah in about three days. This was a very difficult three days for Abraham who was on his way to sacrifice his beloved son, Isaac.

Mediterranean Sea

Sea of Galilee

Jordan River

Mount Moriah

Jerusalem (Salem)

Dead Sea

Beer-sheba

0   20 Mi.

0   20 Km.

We should not always expect our obedience to God to be easy or come naturally.

●**22:7, 8** Why did God ask Abraham to perform human sacrifice? Heathen nations practiced human sacrifice, but God himself condemned this as a terrible sin (Leviticus 20:1-5). God did not want the physical death of Isaac, but he wanted Abraham to "sacrifice" Isaac in his heart so Abraham would be convinced that he loved God more than he loved his promised and long-awaited son. God was really testing Abraham. The purpose of testing is to strengthen our character and deepen our commitment to God. Through this difficult experience, Abraham learned about his commitment to obey God. He also learned about God's ability to provide.

●**22:13** Notice the parallel between the ram offered on the altar as a substitute for Isaac and Christ himself offered on the cross as a substitute for us. Whereas God stopped Abraham from sacrificing his son, God did not spare his own Son, Jesus, from dying on the cross. If Jesus had lived, the rest of mankind would have died. God sent his only Son to die for us so that we can be spared from the eternal death we deserve, and instead receive eternal life.

●**22:17, 18** Abraham received incredible blessings because he obeyed God. But what is God's idea of an incredible blessing? First, God promised Abraham children and grandchildren who would grow up to honor and obey God. Second, God gave Abraham the ability to face his enemies and ultimately conquer them. Third, God gave Abraham the opportunity of being a positive influence upon others. Their lives would be changed as a result of knowing Abraham. Most often we think of blessings as gifts to be enjoyed. But God's ideas of a blessing also extend to others.

●**22:3** The next morning Abraham began one of the greatest acts of obedience known to man. Over the years he had learned many tough lessons about the importance of obeying God. This time his obedience was prompt and complete. Obeying God is often a struggle, because it may mean giving up something we truly want.

your descendants into countless thousands and millions, like the stars above you in the sky, and like the sands along the seashore. They will conquer their enemies, ¹⁸and your offspring will be a blessing to all the nations of the earth—all because you have obeyed me."

¹⁹So they returned to his young men, and traveled home again to Beer-sheba. ^{20–23}After this, a message arrived that Milcah, the wife of Abraham's brother Nahor, had borne him eight sons. Their names were: Uz, the oldest, Buz, the next oldest, Kemuel (father of Aram), Chesed, Hazo, Pildash, Jidlaph, Bethuel (father of Rebekah).

²⁴He also had four other children from his concubine, Reumah: Tebah, Gaham, Tahash, Maacah.

Abraham buries Sarah

23 When Sarah was 127 years old, she died in Hebron in the land of Canaan; there Abraham mourned and wept for her. ³Then, standing beside her body, he said to the men of Heth:

22:18 *your offspring,* or, "your seed."

22:18
Gen 18:18
Acts 3:25
Gal 3:8,16
22:19
Gen 21:31
22:20
Gen 11:29
31:53
22:23
Gen 24:15

23:2
Josh 14:15
23:3
Gen 10:15

HAGAR

Escape of some kind is usually the most tempting solution to our problems. In fact, it can become a habit. Hagar was a person who used that approach. When the going got tough, she usually got going—in the other direction.

However, it is worthwhile to note that the biggest challenges Hagar faced were brought on by *other* people's choices. Sarah chose her to be a substitute child-bearer— Hagar probably had little to say in the matter.

It isn't hard to understand how Hagar's pregnancy caused her to look down on Sarah. But that brought on hard feelings and Sarah consequently punished Hagar. This motivated her first escape. When she returned to the family and gave birth to Ishmael, Sarah's continued barrenness must have contributed to bitterness on both sides.

When Isaac was finally born, Sarah looked for any excuse to have Hagar and Ishmael sent away. She found it when she caught Ishmael teasing Isaac. In the desert, out of water and facing the death of her son, Hagar once again tried to escape. She walked away so she wouldn't have to watch her son die. Once again, God graciously intervened.

Have you noticed how patiently God operates to make our escape attempts fail? Have you begun to learn that escape is only a temporary solution? God's continual desire is for us to face our problems with his help. We experience his help most clearly in and through the conflicts and difficulties, not away from them. Are there problems in your life for which you've been using the "Hagar solution"? Choose one of those problems, ask for God's help, and begin to face it today.

Strength and accomplishment:
● Mother of Abraham's first child, Ishmael, who became founder of the Arab nations

Weaknesses and mistakes:
● When faced with problems, she tended to run away
● Her pregnancy brought out strong feelings of pride and arrogance

Lessons from her life:
● God is faithful to his plan and promises, even when humans complicate the process
● God shows himself as one who knows us and wants to be known by us
● The New Testament uses Hagar as a symbol of those who would pursue favor with God by their own efforts, rather than by trusting in his mercy and forgiveness

Vital statistics:
● Where: Canaan and Egypt
● Occupation: Slave/Maid/Single Parent
● Relatives: Son: Ishmael

Key verse:
"Return to your mistress and act as you should, for I will make you into a great nation" (Genesis 16:9).

Hagar's story is told in Genesis 16—21. She is also mentioned in Galatians 4:24, 25.

23:1–4 In Abraham's day, death and burial were steeped in rituals and traditions. Failing to honor a dead person demonstrated the greatest possible lack of respect. If someone didn't receive a proper burial, it was taken as a curse. Mourning was an essential part of the death ritual. Friends and relatives let out loud cries for the whole neighborhood to hear. Since there were no funeral homes or undertakers, these same friends and relatives helped prepare the body for burial, which usually took place on the same day because of the warm climate.

4"Here I am, a visitor in a foreign land, with no place to bury my wife. Please sell me a piece of ground for this purpose."

5, 6"Certainly," the men replied, "for you are an honored prince of God among us; it will be a privilege to have you choose the finest of our sepulchres, so that you can bury her there."

7Then Abraham bowed low before them and said, 8"Since this is your feeling in the matter, be so kind as to ask Ephron, Zohar's son, 9to sell me the cave of Mach-pelah, down at the end of his field. I will of course pay the full price for it, whatever is publicly agreed upon, and it will become a permanent cemetery for my family."

10Ephron was sitting there among the others, and now he spoke up, answering Abraham as the others listened, speaking publicly before all the citizens of the town: 11"Sir," he said to Abraham, "please listen to me. I will give you the cave and the field without any charge. Here in the presence of my people, I give it to you free. Go and bury your dead."

12Abraham bowed again to the men of Heth, 13and replied to Ephron, as all listened: "No, let me buy it from you. Let me pay the full price of the field, and then I will bury my dead."

14, 15"Well, the land is worth 400 pieces of silver," Ephron said, "but what is that between friends? Go ahead and bury your dead."

16So Abraham paid Ephron the price he had suggested—400 pieces of silver, as publicly agreed. 17, 18This is the land he bought: Ephron's field at Mach-pelah, near Mamre, and the cave at the end of the field, and all the trees in the field. They became his permanent possession, by agreement in the presence of the men of Heth at the city gate. 19, 20So Abraham buried Sarah there, in the field and cave deeded to him by the men of Heth as a burial plot.

23:4
Lev 25:23
1 Chron 29:15
Ps 39:12
Heb 11:9

23:6
Gen 13:2; 21:22
23:7
Gen 18:2; 19:1
23:9
Gen 25:9

23:10
Ruth 4:11

23:13
Gen 14:23
2 Sam 24:24

23:15
Ex 30:13
23:16
Ezra 8:25
Jer 32:9
23:17,18
Gen 25:9
49:29; 50:13

6. Isaac marries Rebekah

24 Abraham was now a very old man, and God blessed him in every way. 2One day Abraham said to his household administrator, who was his oldest servant,
3"Swear by Jehovah, the God of heaven and earth, that you will not let my son

24:1
Gen 12:2
18:11; 24:35
24:3
Gen 21:23
26:34; 28:1

23:4–6 Abraham was in a foreign land looking for a place to bury his wife. Strangers offered to help him, because he was "an honored prince of God," and they felt it would be a privilege to assist him. Abraham's reputation as a man of God had preceded him. Those who invest their time and money in obeying God will receive a good reputation as a pleasant return on that investment.

23:14, 15 The polite interchange between Abraham and Ephron was typical of bargaining at that time. Ephron graciously offered to give his land to Abraham at no charge; Abraham insisted on paying for it; Ephron politely mentioned the price but said, in effect, that it wasn't important; Abraham paid the 400 pieces of silver. Both men knew what was going on, but went through the bargaining process. If Abraham had accepted the land as a free gift when it was offered, he would have insulted Ephron, who then would have rescinded his offer.

Many shopkeepers in the Middle East still follow this ritual with their customers. But the customer would find himself in jail if he took the shopkeeper up on his initial offer.

23:16 Four hundred pieces of silver was a high price for the piece of property Abraham bought. The Hittites who lived in the land weren't thrilled about foreigners buying up lots of property, so Abraham had little bargaining leverage.

Ephron asked an outrageous price. The custom of the day was to ask double the fair market value of the land, fully expecting the buyer to offer half the stated price. The worth of a piece of silver was determined by its weight, but because the standards varied so often at this time, it is impossible to know exactly what Abraham

CAVE OF MACH-PELAH Sarah died in Hebron. Abraham bought the Cave of Mach-pelah, near Hebron, as her burial place. Abraham was also buried there, as were two of his descendants, Isaac and Jacob.

paid for the land by today's standards. Even though God had promised the land to Abraham, he did not just strip it away from Ephron.

24:4
Gen 12:1

24:5
Gen 24:58

24:7
Gen 12:7; 15:18
Gen 16:17; 22:11
Ex 23:20,23

24:10
Gen 11:22
22:20
Deut 23:4

24:11
Gen 24:43

24:12
Gen 24:27,48

24:14
a)Judg 6:17
1 Sam 14:9,10
Prov 19:14
b)Gen 15:8
Ex 4:1-9

24:15
Gen 22:20-24
25:20

24:16
Gen 12:11
26:7; 29:17

24:17
1 Kgs 17:10
Jn 4:7

24:19
Gen 24:14,45,
46

marry one of these local girls, these Canaanites. 4Go instead to my homeland, to my relatives, and find a wife for him there."

5"But suppose I can't find a girl who will come so far from home?" the servant asked. "Then shall I take Isaac there, to live among your relatives?"

6"No!" Abraham warned. "Be careful that you don't do that under any circumstance. 7For the Lord God of heaven told me to leave that land and my people, and promised to give me and my children this land. He will send his angel on ahead of you, and he will see to it that you find a girl from there to be my son's wife. 8But if you don't succeed, then you are free from this oath; but under no circumstances are you to take my son there."

9So the servant vowed to follow Abraham's instructions.

10He took with him ten of Abraham's camels loaded with samples of the best of everything his master owned, and journeyed to Iraq, to Nahor's village. 11There he made the camels kneel down outside the town, beside a spring. It was evening, and the women of the village were coming to draw water.

12"O Jehovah, the God of my master," he prayed, "show kindness to my master Abraham and help me to accomplish the purpose of my journey. 13See, here I am, standing beside this spring, and the girls of the village are coming out to draw water. 14This is my request: When I ask one of them for a drink and she says, 'Yes, certainly, and I will water your camels too!'—let her be the one you have appointed as Isaac's wife. That is how I will know."

15, 16As he was still speaking to the Lord about this, a beautiful young girl named Rebekah arrived with a water jug on her shoulder and filled it at the spring. (Her father was Bethuel the son of Nahor and his wife Milcah.) 17Running over to her, the servant asked her for a drink.

18"Certainly, sir," she said, and quickly lowered the jug for him to drink. 19Then she said, "I'll draw water for your camels, too, until they have enough!"

24:15, 16 *a beautiful young girl,* literally, "a virgin." *the son of Nahor,* Abraham's brother.

ELIEZER:	24:3, 9	Accepted the challenge
PROFILE OF A	24:5	Examined alternatives
TRUE SERVANT	24:9	Promised to follow instructions
Have you ever	24:12–14	Made a plan
approached a	24:12–14	Submitted the plan to God
responsibility with	24:12–14	Prayed for guidance
this kind of	24:12–14	Devised a strategy with room for God to operate
singlemindedness	24:21	Waited
and careful	24:21	Watched carefully
planning, while	24:26	Accepted the answer thankfully
ultimately	24:34–49	Explained the situation to concerned parties
depending on	24:56	Refused unnecessary delay
God?	24:66	Followed through with entire plan

24:4 Abraham wanted Isaac to marry within the family tribe. This was acceptable at this time to avoid intermarrying with heathen neighbors. A son's wife was usually chosen by the parents. It was common for a woman to be married at age 12 or 13, although Rebekah was probably older than this.

24:9 Literally, "put his hand under the thigh of Abraham his master and swore to him that. . . ." This was the cultural way of binding a promise—much like the handshake is today.

24:11 The well, people's chief source of water, was usually found outside town along the main road. Many people had to walk a mile or more for their water. They could use only what they could carry home. Rebekah would have visited the well twice daily to draw water for her family. Farmers and shepherds would come from nearby fields to draw water for their animals. It was the best place to meet new friends and chat with old ones.

24:14 Was it right for Abraham's servant to ask God for such a specific sign? The "sign" he requested was not out of the ordinary. The hospitality of the day required women at the well to offer water to weary travelers, but not to their animals. Eliezer was simply

asking God to show him a woman with an attitude of true service—someone who would go beyond the expected. An offer to water his camels would indicate that kind of servant attitude. Eliezer did not ask for a woman with looks or wealth—he knew the importance of having the right heart. And he knew the importance of asking God to help him with his task.

24:15, 16 Rebekah had physical beauty, but the servant was looking for a sign that revealed inner beauty. Appearance is important to us, and we spend time and money improving it. But how much effort do we put into developing our inner beauty? Patience, kindness, and joy are the beauty treatments that help us become truly lovely—on the inside.

24:18–20 Rebekah's "servant spirit" was clearly demonstrated as she willingly and quickly drew water for Eliezer and his camels. The pots used for carrying water were large and heavy. It took a lot of water to satisfy a thirsty camel (up to 25 gallons per camel after a week of travel). Eliezer was seeing a live demonstration of someone with a heart for doing far more than was expected.

²⁰So she emptied the jug into the watering trough and ran down to the spring again and kept carrying water to the camels until they had enough. ²¹The servant said no more, but watched her carefully to see if she would finish the job, so that he would know whether she was the one. ²²Then at last, when the camels had finished drinking, he produced a quarter-ounce gold earring and two five-ounce gold bracelets for her wrists.

²³"Whose daughter are you, miss?" he asked. "Would your father have any room to put us up for the night?"

²⁴"My father is Bethuel," she replied. "My grandparents are Milcah and Nahor. ²⁵Yes, we have plenty of straw and food for the camels, and a guest room."

²⁶The man stood there a moment with head bowed, worshiping Jehovah. ²⁷"Thank you, Lord God of my master Abraham," he prayed; "thank you for being so kind and true to him, and for leading me straight to the family of my master's relatives."

²⁸The girl ran home to tell her folks, ²⁹, ³⁰and when her brother Laban saw the ring, and the bracelets on his sister's wrists, and heard her story, he rushed out to the spring where the man was still standing beside his camels, and said to him, ³¹"Come and stay with us, friend; why stand here outside the city when we have a room all ready for you, and a place prepared for the camels!"

³²So the man went home with Laban, and Laban gave him straw to bed down the camels, and feed for them, and water for the camel drivers to wash their feet. ³³Then supper was served. But the old man said, "I don't want to eat until I have told you why I am here."

"All right," Laban said, "tell us your errand."

³⁴"I am Abraham's servant," he explained. ³⁵"And Jehovah has overwhelmed my master with blessings so that he is a great man among the people of his land. God has given him flocks of sheep and herds of cattle, and a fortune in silver and gold, and many slaves and camels and donkeys.

³⁶"Now when Sarah, my master's wife, was very old, she gave birth to my master's son, and my master has given him everything he owns. ³⁷And my master made me promise not to let Isaac marry one of the local girls, ³⁸but to come to his relatives here in this far-off land, to his brother's family, and to bring back a girl from here to marry his son. ³⁹'But suppose I can't find a girl who will come?' I asked him. ⁴⁰'She will,' he told me—'for my Lord, in whose presence I have walked, will send his angel with you and make your mission successful. Yes, find a girl from among my relatives, from my brother's family. ⁴¹You are under oath to go and ask. If they won't send anyone, then you are freed from your promise.'

⁴²"Well, this afternoon when I came to the spring I prayed this prayer: 'O Jehovah, the God of my master Abraham, if you are planning to make my mission a success, please guide me in this way: ⁴³Here I am, standing beside this spring. I will say to some girl who comes out to draw water, "Please give me a drink of water!" ⁴⁴And she will reply, "Certainly! And I'll water your camels too!" Let that girl be the one you have selected to be the wife of my master's son.'

⁴⁵"Well, while I was still speaking these words, Rebekah was coming along with her water jug upon her shoulder; and she went down to the spring and drew water and filled the jug. I said to her, 'Please give me a drink.' ⁴⁶She quickly lifted the jug down from her shoulder so that I could drink, and told me, 'Certainly, sir, and I will water your camels too!' So she did! ⁴⁷Then I asked her, 'Whose family are you from?' And she told me, 'Nahor's. My father is Bethuel, the son of Nahor and his wife Milcah.' So I gave her the ring and the bracelets. ⁴⁸Then I bowed my head and worshiped and blessed Jehovah, the God of my master Abraham, because he had led me along just the right path to find a girl from the family of my master's brother. ⁴⁹So tell me, yes or no. Will you or won't you be kind to my master and do what is right? When you tell me, then I'll know what my next step should be, whether to move this way or that."

24:21 2 Sam 7:18-20

24:22 Gen 24:47

24:24 Gen 24:15

24:26 Ex 4:31
24:27 Gen 14:20 24:12,48

24:28 Gen 29:12
24:29 Gen 24:50 25:20; 29:5
24:30 Gen 24:22,47
24:31 Gen 18:3-5 19:2

24:34 Gen 24:2
24:35 Gen 12:2; 13:2

24:36 Gen 21:1-7 25:5
24:37 Gen 24:3; 28:1

24:40 Gen 24:7

24:45 1 Sam 1:13

24:47 Gen 24:23,24

24:49 Gen 32:10 47:29

24:21 *to see if she would finish the job,* implied. **24:22** *gold earring,* literally, "nose-ring." **24:31** *friend,* literally, "blessed of Jehovah." **24:37** *local girls,* literally, "daughters of the Canaanites." **24:38** *to his brother's family,* literally, "go into my father's house." **24:48** *a girl from the family of my master's brother,* literally, "my master's brother's daughter."

24:50
Ps 118:23
Mt 21:42

24:51
Gen 20:15

24:52
Gen 24:26

24:54
Gen 28:6; 30:25

24:55
Judg 19:4

24:58
Ps 45:10

24:59
Gen 35:8

24:60
Gen 17:16
22:17
Dan 7:10

⁵⁰Then Laban and Bethuel replied, "The Lord has obviously brought you here, so what can we say? ⁵¹Take her and go! Yes, let her be the wife of your master's son, as Jehovah has directed."

⁵²At this reply, Abraham's servant fell to his knees before Jehovah. ⁵³Then he brought out jewels set in solid gold and silver for Rebekah, and lovely clothing; and he gave many valuable presents to her mother and brother. ⁵⁴Then they had supper, and the servant and the men with him stayed there overnight. But early the next morning he said, "Send me back to my master!"

⁵⁵"But we want Rebekah here at least another ten days or so!" her mother and brother exclaimed. "Then she can go."

⁵⁶But he pleaded, "Don't hinder my return; the Lord has made my mission successful, and I want to report back to my master."

⁵⁷"Well," they said, "we'll call the girl and ask her what she thinks."

⁵⁸So they called Rebekah. "Are you willing to go with this man?" they asked her. And she replied, "Yes, I will go."

⁵⁹So they told her good-bye, sending along the woman who had been her childhood nurse, ⁶⁰and blessed her with this blessing as they parted:

REBEKAH

Some people are initiators. They help get the ball rolling. Rebekah would easily stand out in this group. Her life was characterized by initiative. When she saw a need she took action—even though the action was not always right.

It was Rebekah's initiative that first caught the attention of Eliezer, the servant Abraham sent to find a wife for Isaac. It was common courtesy to give a drink to a stranger, but it took added character to also fetch water for ten thirsty camels. Later, after hearing the details of Eliezer's mission, Rebekah was immediately willing to be Isaac's bride.

Several later events help us see how initiative can be misdirected. Rebekah was aware that God's plan would be channeled through Jacob, not Esau (Genesis 25:23). So not only did Jacob become her favorite; she actually planned ways to ensure that he would overshadow his older twin. Meanwhile, Isaac had a preference for Esau. This created a conflict between the couple. She felt justified in deceiving her husband when the time came to bless the sons. Her ingenious plan was carried out to perfection.

Most of the time we try to justify the things we choose to do. Often we attempt to add God's approval to our actions. While it is true that our actions will not spoil God's plan, it is also true that we are responsible for our actions and must always be cautious about our motives. When thinking about a course of action, are you simply seeking God's stamp of approval on something you've already decided to do? Or are you willing to set the plan aside if the principles and commands of God's Word are against the action? Initiative and action are admirable and right when they are controlled by God's wisdom.

Strengths and accomplishments:
• When confronted with a need, she took immediate action
• She was accomplishment-oriented

Weaknesses and mistakes:
• Her initiative was not always balanced by wisdom
• She favored one of her sons
• She deceived her husband

Lessons from her life:
• Our actions must be guided by God's Word
• God even makes use of our mistakes in his plan
• Parental favoritism hurts a family

Vital statistics:
• Where: Haran, Canaan
• Occupation: Wife, mother, household manager
• Relatives: Parents: Bethuel and Milcah. Husband: Isaac. Brother: Laban. Twin sons: Esau and Jacob.

Key verses:
"And Isaac brought Rebekah into his mother's tent, and she became his wife. He loved her very much, and she was a special comfort to him after the loss of his mother" (Genesis 24:67).
". . . and Rebekah's favorite was Jacob" (Genesis 25:28).

Rebekah's story is told in Genesis 24—27. She is also mentioned in Romans 9:10.

"Our sister,
May you become
The mother of many millions!
May your descendants
Overcome all your enemies."

61So Rebekah and her servant girls mounted the camels and went with him.

62Meanwhile, Isaac, whose home was in the Negeb, had returned to Beer-lahai-roi. 63One evening as he was taking a walk out in the fields, meditating, he looked up and saw the camels coming. 64Rebekah noticed him and quickly dismounted.

24:62
Gen 16:14
25:11

24:63
Ps 119:15,27,
47,48

65"Who is that man walking through the fields to meet us?" she asked the servant.

And he replied, "It is my master's son!" So she covered her face with her veil.
66Then the servant told Isaac the whole story.

67And Isaac brought Rebekah into his mother's tent, and she became his wife. He loved her very much, and she was a special comfort to him after the loss of his mother.

24:66
Mk 6:30

24:67
Gen 23:2
25:20; 29:18

7. Abraham dies

25 Now Abraham married again. Keturah was his new wife, and she bore him several children: Zimran, Jokshan, Medan, Midian, Ishbak, Shuah. 3Jokshan's two sons were Sheba and Dedan. Dedan's sons were Asshurim, Letushim, and Leummim. 4Midian's sons were Ephah, Epher, Hanoch, Abida, and Eldaah.

25:1
1 Chron 1:32

5Abraham deeded everything he owned to Isaac; 6however, he gave gifts to the sons of his concubines and sent them off into the east, away from Isaac.

25:5
Gen 24:36

7, 8Then Abraham died, at the ripe old age of 175, 9, 10and his sons Isaac and Ishmael buried him in the cave of Mach-pelah near Mamre, in the field Abraham had purchased from Ephron the son of Zohar, the Hethite, where Sarah, Abraham's wife was buried.

25:7
Gen 12:4

25:8
Gen 25:17
35:29; 49:29,33

11After Abraham's death, God poured out rich blessings upon Isaac. (Isaac had now moved south to Beer-lahai-roi in the Negeb.)

25:9,10
Gen 23:17
49:29; 50:13

12-15Here is a list, in the order of their births, of the descendants of Ishmael, who was the son of Abraham and Hagar the Egyptian, Sarah's slave girl: Nebaioth, Kedar, Abdeel, Mibsam, Mishma, Dumah, Massa, Hadad, Tema, Jetur, Naphish, Kedemah. 16These twelve sons of his became the founders of twelve tribes that bore their names. 17Ishmael finally died at the age of 137, and joined his ancestors. 18These descendants of Ishmael were scattered across the country from Havilah to Shur (which is a little way to the northeast of the Egyptian border in the direction of Assyria). And they were constantly at war with one another.

25:11
Gen 24:62; 26:3

25:12
Gen 16:15
1 Chron 1:28-31

25:13
Gen 17:20

25:17
Gen 25:8

25:18
a)Gen 20:1
b)Gen 16:12

E. THE STORY OF ISAAC (25:19—28:9)
Isaac inherited everything from his father, including God's promise to make his descendants into a great nation. As a boy, Isaac did not resist as his father prepared to sacrifice him, and as a man, he gladly accepted the wife that others chose for him. Through Isaac, we learn how to let God guide our life and place his will ahead of our own.

1. Jacob and Esau, Isaac's twin sons

19This is the story of Isaac's children: 20Isaac was forty years old when he married Rebekah, the daughter of Bethuel the Aramean from Paddam-aram. Rebekah was the sister of Laban. 21Isaac pleaded with Jehovah to give Rebekah a child, for even after many years of marriage she had no children. Then at last she

25:19
Gen 21:3
1 Chron 1:34

25:21
Gen 21:2

24:65 *It is my master's son,* literally, "It is my master." **25:4** *and Eldaah.* The text adds, "all these were the children of Keturah." **25:17** *joined his ancestors,* literally, "and was gathered to his people." **25:21** *even after many years of marriage,* implied in vss 20 and 26.

25:21 As Isaac pleaded with God for something as precious as children, so we are encouraged throughout the Bible to ask, and even plead, for our most personal and important requests. God wants to give us good things, but he wants us to ask for them.

Even then, as Isaac learned, God may decide to withhold his answer for a while in order to (1) deepen our insight into what we really need, (2) broaden our appreciation for his answers, or (3) allow us to mature so we can use his gifts more wisely.

became pregnant. 22And it seemed as though children were fighting each other inside her!

"I can't endure this," she exclaimed. So she asked the Lord about it.

23And he told her, "The sons in your womb shall become two rival nations. One will be stronger than the other; and the older shall be a servant of the younger!"

24And sure enough, she had twins. 25The first was born so covered with reddish hair that one would think he was wearing a fur coat! So they called him "Esau." 26Then the other twin was born with his hand on Esau's heel! So they called him Jacob (meaning "Grabber"). Isaac was sixty years old when the twins were born.

Esau sells his birthright

27As the boys grew, Esau became a skillful hunter, while Jacob was a quiet sort who liked to stay at home. 28Isaac's favorite was Esau, because of the venison he brought home, and Rebekah's favorite was Jacob.

29One day Jacob was cooking stew when Esau arrived home exhausted from the hunt.

30*Esau:* "Boy, am I starved! Give me a bite of that red stuff there!" (From this came his nickname "Edom," which means "Red Stuff.")

25:25 which sounds a little like the Hebrew word for "hair."

25:23 Gen 17:2-4 27:29; 48:19 Num 20:14 Deut 2:4,8 Rom 9:12
25:25 Gen 27:11
25:26 Hos 12:3
25:30 Gen 36:1,9 Ex 15:15

Common sense isn't all that common. In fact, the common thread in many decisions is that they don't make sense. Esau's life was filled with choices he must have regretted bitterly. He appears to have been a person who found it hard to consider consequences. He reacted to the need of the moment without realizing what he was giving up to meet that need. Trading his birthright for a bowl of stew was the clearest example of this weakness. He also chose wives in direct opposition to his parents' wishes.

What are you willing to trade for the things you want? Do you find yourself, at times, willing to negotiate *anything* for what you feel you need *now*? Do your family, spouse, integrity, body, or soul get included in these deals? Do you sometimes feel that the important parts of life escaped while you were grabbing for something else?

If so, your initial response, like Esau's, may be deep anger. In itself that isn't wrong, as long as you direct the energy of that anger toward a solution and not toward yourself or others as the cause of the problem. Your greatest need is to find a focal point other than "what I need now." The only worthy focal point is God. A relationship with him will not only give an ultimate purpose to your life, but will also be a daily guideline for living.

Strengths and accomplishments:
- Ancestor of the Edomites
- Known for his archery skill
- Able to forgive after explosive anger

Weaknesses and mistakes:
- When faced with important decisions, tended to choose according to the immediate need rather than the long-range effect
- Angered his parents by poor marriage choices

Lessons from his life:
- God allows certain events in our lives to accomplish his overall purposes, but we are still responsible for our actions
- Consequences are important to consider
- It is possible to have great anger and yet not sin

Vital statistics:
- Where: Canaan
- Occupation: Skillful hunter
- Relatives: Parents: Isaac and Rebekah. Brother: Jacob. Wives: Judith, Basemath, and Mahalath.

Key verses:
"Watch out that no one becomes involved in sexual sin or becomes careless about God as Esau did: he traded his rights as the oldest son for a single meal. And afterwards, when he wanted those rights back again, it was too late, even though he wept bitter tears of repentance. So remember, and be careful" (Hebrews 12:16, 17).

Esau's story is told in Genesis 25—36. He is also mentioned in Malachi 1:2; Romans 9:13; Hebrews 12:16, 17.

³¹*Jacob:* "All right, trade me your birthright for it!

³²*Esau:* "When a man is dying of starvation, what good is his birthright?"

³³*Jacob:* "Well then, vow to God that it is mine!"

And Esau vowed, thereby selling all his eldest-son rights to his younger brother. ³⁴Then Jacob gave Esau bread, peas, and stew; so he ate and drank and went on about his business, indifferent to the loss of the rights he had thrown away.

25:31
Deut 21:15-17

25:33
Gen 27:36
Heb 12:16

2. Isaac and King Abimelech

26 Now a severe famine overshadowed the land, as had happened before, in Abraham's time, and so Isaac moved to the city of Gerar where Abimelech, king of the Philistines, lived.

26:1
Gen 12:10
20:1,2; 41:54

²Jehovah appeared to him there and told him, "Don't go to Egypt. ³Do as I say and stay here in this land. If you do, I will be with you and bless you, and I will give all this land to you and to your descendants, just as I promised Abraham your father. ⁴And I will cause your descendants to become as numerous as the stars! And I will give them all of these lands; and they shall be a blessing to all the nations of the earth. ⁵I will do this because Abraham obeyed my commandments and laws."

26:2
Gen 12:1,7

26:3
Gen 12:7; 15:8;

26:4
Gen 15:15
22:17
Ex 32:13
Gal 3:8

Isaac deceives the king

⁶So Isaac stayed in Gerar. ⁷And when the men there asked him about Rebekah, he said, "She is my sister!" For he feared for his life if he told them she was his wife; he was afraid they would kill him to get her, for she was very attractive. ⁸But sometime later, King Abimelech, king of the Philistines, looked out of a window and saw Isaac and Rebekah making love.

26:7
Gen 12:11,12
20:12

⁹Abimelech called for Isaac and exclaimed, "She is your wife! Why did you say she is your sister?"

26:8
Prov 5:18,19
Eccles 9:9

25:34 *indifferent to the loss of the rights he had thrown away,* literally, "thus did Esau consider his birthright to be of no value."

25:31 A birthright was a special honor given to the first-born son. It included a double portion of the family inheritance along with the honor of one day becoming the family leader. The oldest son could sell his birthright or give it away if he chose. But in so doing, he forfeited his position as family leader. Esau was within his rights to trade his birthright. But he showed complete disregard for the spiritual blessings that would have come his way if he had kept it.

●**25:32, 33** Esau traded the lasting benefits of his birthright for the immediate pleasure of food. He acted on impulse, satisfying his immediate desires without pausing to consider the long-range consequences of what he was about to do. We can fall into the same trap. When we see something we want, our first impulse is to get it. At first we feel intensely satisfied and sometimes even powerful because we have obtained what we set out to get. But immediate pleasure often loses sight of the future. We can avoid Esau's mistake by comparing the short-term satisfaction with its long-range consequences—before we act.

Esau exaggerated his hunger. "I'm dying of starvation," he said. This thinking made his choice much easier, for if he was starving, what good was an inheritance anyway? The pressure of the moment twisted his perspective and made his decision seem urgent. We often experience similar situations. For example, when we feel sexual pressure, a marriage license may not seem so important. We sometimes feel such great pressure in one area that nothing else seems to matter. The pressure of the moment makes us lose our perspective. Getting through that short, pressure-filled moment is often the hardest part of overcoming a temptation.

26:1 The Philistines were a tribe of people who were to become one of Israel's fiercest enemies. "Philistine" means "Sea People," for they originally were sailors from the Mediterranean Sea. These people, living along the southwest coast of Palestine, were few but ferocious in battle. Although friendly to Isaac, this small group was

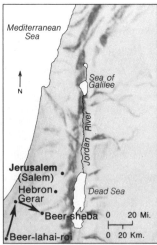

ISAAC'S MOVE TO GERAR
Isaac had settled in Beer-lahai-roi, where his sons, Jacob and Esau, were born. A famine drove him to Gerar. But when he became wealthy, his jealous neighbors asked him to leave. From Gerar he moved to Beersheba.

the forerunner of the nation that would plague Israel during the time of Joshua, the Judges, and King David.

26:7–11 Isaac was afraid that the men in Gerar would kill him to get his beautiful wife, Rebekah. So he lied, claiming that Rebekah was his sister. Where did he learn that trick? Evidently, Isaac knew about the actions of his father, Abraham (see Genesis 12:10–14 and 20:1–4). Parents help shape the future of their world by the way they shape the lifestyle and values of their children. The first step toward helping children live right is to have parents who live right. Your actions are often copied by those closest to you.

"Because I was afraid I would be murdered," Isaac replied. "I thought someone would kill me to get her from me."

26:10
Gen 20:7-10
26:11
Prov 6:29

10"How could you treat us this way?" Abimelech exclaimed. "Someone might carelessly have raped her, and we would be doomed." 11Then Abimelech made a public proclamation: "Anyone harming this man or his wife shall die."

JACOB

Abraham, Isaac, and Jacob are among the most significant people in the Old Testament. It is important to realize that this significance is not based upon their personal characters, but upon the character of God. They were all men who earned the grudging respect and even fear of their peers; they were wealthy and powerful, and each was capable of lying, deceit, and selfishness. They were not the perfect heroes we might have expected; instead, they were just like us, trying to please God, yet often falling short.

Jacob was the third link in God's plan to start a nation from Abraham. The success of that plan was more often in spite of than because of Jacob's life. Before Jacob was born, God promised that his plan would be worked out through Jacob and not his twin brother, Esau. Although Jacob's methods were not always respectable, his skill, determination, and patience have to be admired. As we follow him from birth to death, we are able to see God's work.

Jacob's life had four stages, each marked by a personal encounter with God. In the first stage, Jacob lived up to his name, "Grabber." He grabbed Esau's heel at birth and by the time he fled from home, he had also grabbed his brother's birthright and blessing. On his flight, God first appeared to him. Not only did God confirm to Jacob his blessing, but he awakened in Jacob a personal knowledge of himself. In the second stage, Jacob experienced life from the other side, being manipulated and deceived by Laban. But we note a curious fact: the Jacob of stage one would simply have left Laban; the Jacob of stage two decided to leave, but waited six years for God's permission. In the third stage, Jacob was in a new role as grabber. This time, by the Jordan River, he grabbed on to God and wouldn't let go. He realized his dependence on the God who had continued to bless him. His relationship to God became essential to his life, and his name was changed to Israel. Jacob's last stage of life was to *be* grabbed—God achieved a firm hold on him. In responding to Joseph's invitation to come to Egypt, Jacob was clearly unwilling to make a move without God's approval.

Can you think of times when God has made himself known to you? Do you allow yourself to meet him as you study his Word? What difference have these experiences made in your life? Are you more like the young Jacob, forcing God to track you down in the wilderness of your own plans and mistakes? Or are you more like the Jacob who placed his desires and plans before God for his approval before taking any action?

Strengths and accomplishments:
• Father of the twelve tribes of Israel
• Third in the Abrahamic line of God's plan
• Determined, willing to work long and hard for what he wanted
• Wealthy livestock owner

Weaknesses and mistakes:
• When faced with conflict, relied on his own resources rather than going to God for help
• Tended to accumulate wealth for its own sake

Lessons from his life:
• Security does not lie in the accumulation of goods
• All human intentions and actions—for good or for evil—are woven by God into his ongoing plan

Vital statistics:
• Where: Canaan
• Occupation: Shepherd/Livestock owner
• Relatives: Parents: Isaac and Rebekah. Brother: Esau. Father-in-law: Laban. Wives: Rachel and Leah. Twelve sons and one daughter are named in the Bible.

Key verse:
"What's more, I am with you, and will protect you wherever you go, and will bring you back safely to this land; I will be with you constantly until I have finished giving you all I am promising" (Genesis 28:15).

Jacob's story is told in Genesis 25—50. He is also mentioned in Hosea 12:3–5; Matthew 1:2; 22:32; Acts 3:13; 7:46; Romans 9:11–13; Hebrews 11:9, 20–21.

Isaac refuses to fight

¹²That year Isaac's crops were tremendous—100 times the grain he sowed. For Jehovah blessed him. ¹³He was soon a man of great wealth, and became richer and richer. ¹⁴He had large flocks of sheep and goats, great herds of cattle, and many servants. And the Philistines became jealous of him. ¹⁵So they filled up his wells with earth—all those dug by the servants of his father Abraham.

¹⁶And King Abimelech asked Isaac to leave the country. "Go somewhere else," he said, "for you have become too rich and powerful for us."

¹⁷So Isaac moved to Gerar Valley and lived there instead. ¹⁸And Isaac redug the wells of his father Abraham, the ones the Philistines had filled after his father's death, and gave them the same names they had had before, when his father had named them. ¹⁹His shepherds also dug a new well in Gerar Valley, and found a gushing underground spring.

²⁰Then the local shepherds came and claimed it. "This is our land and our well," they said, and argued over it with Isaac's herdsmen. So he named the well, "The Well of Argument!" ²¹Isaac's men then dug another well, but again there was a fight over it. So he called it, "The Well of Anger." ²²Abandoning that one, he dug again, and the local residents finally left him alone. So he called it, "The Well of Room Enough for Us at Last!" "For now at last," he said, "the Lord has made room for us and we shall thrive."

²³When he went to Beer-sheba, ²⁴Jehovah appeared to him on the night of his arrival. "I am the God of Abraham your father," he said. "Fear not, for I am with you and will bless you, and will give you so many descendants that they will become a great nation—because of my promise to Abraham, who obeyed me." ²⁵Then Isaac built an altar and worshiped Jehovah; and he settled there, and his servants dug a well.

²⁶One day Isaac had visitors from Gerar. King Abimelech arrived with his advisor, Ahuzzath, and also Phicol, his army commander. ²⁷"Why have you come?" Isaac asked them. "This is obviously no friendly visit, since you kicked me out in a most uncivil way."

²⁸"Well," they said, "we can plainly see that Jehovah is blessing you. We've decided to ask for a treaty between us. ²⁹Promise that you will not harm us, just as we have not harmed you, and in fact, have done only good to you and have sent you away in peace; we bless you in the name of the Lord."

³⁰So Isaac prepared a great feast for them, and they ate and drank in preparation for the treaty ceremonies. ³¹In the morning, as soon as they were up, they each took solemn oaths to seal a non-aggression pact. Then Isaac sent them happily home again.

³²That very same day Isaac's servants came to tell him, "We have found water"—in the well they had been digging. ³³So he named the well, "The Well of the Oath," and the city that grew up there was named "Oath," and is called that to this day.

26:12 Gen 26:3
26:13 Gen 24:35; 25:5
26:15 Gen 21:15
26:16 Ex 1:9
26:19 Jn 4:10,11
26:22 Ps 4:1; 18:19; 118:5 Isa 54:2
26:23 Gen 21:31; 46:1
26:24 Gen 12:1,2 17:1-7 Ex 3:6
26:25 Gen 12:7 13:3,4
26:26 Gen 21:22,23
26:27 Gen 26:14,16
26:28 Gen 26:3,12-16
26:29 Ps 115:15
26:30 Gen 21:8; 31:54
26:31 Gen 14:22 21:31; 31:55
26:33 Gen 21:31

26:20 *The Well of Argument*, i.e., Ezek. **26:21** *The Well of Anger*, i.e., Sitnah. **26:22** *The Well of Room Enough for Us at Last*, i.e., Rehoboth. **26:33** *The Well of the Oath*, i.e., Shibah. *Oath*, i.e., Beer-sheba.

26:12-16 God kept his promise to bless Isaac. The neighboring Philistines grew jealous because everything Isaac did seemed to go right. So they plugged his wells and tried to get rid of him. Jealousy is a dividing force strong enough to tear apart the mightiest of nations or the closest of friends. It forces you to separate yourself from what you were longing for in the first place. When you find yourself becoming jealous of others try thanking God for their good fortune.

●**26:17-22** Three times Isaac and his men dug new wells. When the first two disputes arose, Isaac moved on. Finally there was enough room for everyone. Rather than start a huge conflict, Isaac compromised for the sake of peace. Would you be willing to forsake an important position or valuable possession to keep peace? Ask God for the wisdom to know when to withdraw and when to stand and fight.

●**26:18** The area of Gerar was a desolate place on the edge of the wilderness. Water was as precious as gold. If someone dug a well, he was staking a claim to the land. Some wells had locks to keep thieves from stealing the water. To plug up someone's well was an act of war; it was one of the most serious crimes in the land. Isaac had every right to fight back when the Philistines ruined his wells. Yet he chose not to fight. In the end, the Philistines respected him for his patience and efforts for peace.

26:26-29 With his enemies wanting to make peace, Isaac was quick to respond, turning the occasion into a greater celebration. We should be just as receptive to those who want to patch things up with us. When the godliness in our lives begins to attract people—even enemies—we must let it be an opportunity to reach out to them with God's love.

3. Isaac blesses Jacob instead of Esau

26:34
Gen 28:6-8
26:35
Gen 27:46

· 34Esau, at the age of forty, married a girl named Judith, daughter of Be-eri the Hethite; and he also married Basemath, daughter of Elon the Hethite. 35But Isaac and Rebekah were bitter about his marrying them.

27:1
Gen 25:25
48:10

27 One day, in Isaac's old age when he was almost blind, he called for Esau his oldest son.

Isaac: "My son?"
Esau: "Yes, father?"

27:2
Gen 47:29
27:3
Gen 25:28
27:4
Gen 24:60
27:19; 48:9

2, 3, 4*Isaac:* "I am an old man now, and expect every day to be my last. Take your bow and arrows out into the fields and get me some venison, and prepare it just the way I like it—savory and good—and bring it here for me to eat, and I will give you the blessings that belong to you, my first-born son, before I die."

27:6
Gen 25:28
27:8
Gen 27:13,43

5But Rebekah overheard the conversation. So when Esau left for the field to hunt for the venison, 6, 7she called her son Jacob and told him what his father had said to his brother.

27:9
Judg 13:15

8, 9, 10*Rebekah:* "Now do exactly as I tell you. Go out to the flocks and bring me two young goats, and I'll prepare your father's favorite dish from them. Then take it to your father, and after he has enjoyed it he will bless *you* before his death, instead of Esau!"

27:11
Gen 25:25
27:12
Gen 9:25
27:21,22
27:13
Gen 27:8,43

11, 12*Jacob:* "But mother! He won't be fooled that easily. Think how hairy Esau is, and how smooth my skin is! What if my father feels me? He'll think I'm making a fool of him, and curse me instead of blessing me!"
13*Rebekah:* "Let his curses be on me, dear son. Just do what I tell you. Go out and get the goats."

27:15
Gen 27:27

14So Jacob followed his mother's instructions, bringing the dressed kids, which she prepared in his father's favorite way. 15Then she took Esau's best clothes—they were there in the house—and instructed Jacob to put them on. 16And she made him a pair of gloves from the hairy skin of the young goats, and fastened a strip of the hide around his neck; 17then she gave him the meat, with its rich aroma, and some fresh-baked bread.
18Jacob carried the platter of food into the room where his father was lying.

Jacob: "Father?"
Isaac: "Yes? Who is it, my son—Esau or Jacob?"

27:2-4 *that belong to you, my first-born son,* implied.   **27:8-10** *instead of Esau,* implied.   **27:11, 12** *He won't be fooled that easily,* implied.

26:34, 35 Esau married heathen women. This upset his parents greatly. Most parents have a lifetime of insight into the character of their children. They can be a storehouse of good advice. You may not agree with everything your parents say. But at least talk with them and listen carefully. This will help avoid the hard feelings Esau experienced.

27:5–10 When Rebekah learned that Isaac was preparing to bless Esau, she quickly devised a plan to trick him into blessing Jacob instead. Although God had already told her that Jacob would become the family leader (Genesis 25:23–26), Rebekah took matters into her own hands. She resorted to doing something wrong to try to bring about what God had already said would happen. For Rebekah, the end justified the means. No matter how good we think our goals may be, we should not attempt to achieve them unjustly.

27:11, 12 How we react to a dilemma often exposes our real motives. Frequently we are more worried about getting caught than about doing what is right. Jacob did not seem concerned about the deceitfulness of his mother's plan. Instead he was afraid of getting caught while carrying it out. If you are worried about getting caught, you may already be in a position that is less than honest.

Let your fear of getting caught be a warning to do right. Jacob paid a huge price for carrying out his dishonest plan.

27:11–13 Jacob hesitated when he heard Rebekah's deceitful plan. Although he questioned his mother's plan for the wrong reason (fear of getting caught), he protested and thus gave Rebekah one last chance to consider her actions. But Rebekah had become so wrapped up in her plan that she could no longer see clearly what she was doing. Sin had trapped her and was now degrading her character. Correcting yourself in the middle of doing wrong can bring hurt and disappointment, but it also brings freedom from the control of sin.

●**27:14** Although Jacob got the blessing he wanted, deceiving his father cost him dearly. These are some of the consequences of his actions: (1) he never saw his mother again; (2) his brother wanted to kill him; (3) he was deceived by his own uncle, Laban; (4) his family became torn by strife; (5) Esau became the founder of a nation of eternal enemies; (6) he was exiled from his family for years. Ironically, Jacob would have received the birthright and blessing anyway (Genesis 25:23). Imagine how different his life would have been had he and his mother allowed God to do things his way, in his time!

¹⁹*Jacob:* "It's Esau, your oldest son. I've done as you told me to. Here is the delicious venison you wanted. Sit up and eat it, so that you will bless me with all your heart!"

²⁰*Isaac:* "How were you able to find it so quickly, my son?"

Jacob: "Because Jehovah your God put it in my path!"

²¹*Isaac:* "Come over here. I want to feel you, and be sure it really is Esau!"

²²(Jacob goes over to his father. He feels him!)

Isaac: (to himself) "The voice is Jacob's, but the hands are Esau's!"

²³(The ruse convinces Isaac and he gives Jacob his blessings):

²⁴*Isaac:* "Are you really Esau?"

Jacob: "Yes, of course."

²⁵*Isaac:* "Then bring me the venison, and I will eat it and bless you with all my heart."

(Jacob takes it over to him and Isaac eats; he also drinks the wine Jacob brings him.)

²⁶*Isaac:* "Come here and kiss me, my son!"

(Jacob goes over and kisses him on the cheek. Isaac sniffs his clothes, and finally seems convinced.)

²⁷, ²⁸, ²⁹*Isaac:* "The smell of my son is the good smell of the earth and fields that Jehovah has blessed. May God always give you plenty of rain for your crops, and good harvests and grapes. May many nations be your slaves. Be the master of your brothers. May all your relatives bow low before you. Cursed are all who curse you, and blessed are all who bless you."

³⁰(As soon as Isaac has blessed Jacob, and almost before Jacob leaves the room, Esau arrives, coming in from his hunting. ³¹He also has prepared his father's favorite dish and brings it to him.)

Esau: "Here I am, father, with the venison. Sit up and eat it so that you can give me your finest blessings!"

³²*Isaac:* "Who is it?"

Esau: "Why, it's me, of course! Esau, your oldest son!"

³³(Isaac begins to tremble noticeably.)

Isaac: "Then who is it who was just here with venison, and I have already eaten it and blessed him with irrevocable blessing?"

³⁴(Esau begins to sob with deep and bitter sobs.)

Esau: "O my father, bless me, bless me too!"

³⁵*Isaac:* "Your brother was here and tricked me and has carried away your blessing."

³⁶*Esau:* (bitterly) "No wonder they call him 'The Cheater.' For he took my

27:36 *The Cheater.* "Jacob" means "Cheater."

27:19
Gen 27:21,24, 31

27:21
Gen 27:12

27:23
Gen 27:4,16

27:24
Prov 12:19,22

27:25
Gen 27:4

27:27
Ps 65:9,10
Heb 11:20

27:28
Gen 27:39
45:18
Deut 7:13; 33:13, 28
Zech 8:12

27:29
Gen 9:25; 12:3
22:17; 49:8
Num 24:9
Isa 45:14

27:31
Gen 27:4,19

27:32
Gen 27:18

27:33
Gen 27:35
Ps 55:5

27:34
Heb 12:17

27:35
Gen 27:12, 19-23

27:36
Gen 25:26
32:28

27:33-37 Before the father died, he performed a ceremony called "the blessing," in which he officially handed over the birthright to the rightful heir. Although the firstborn son was entitled to the birthright, it was not actually his until the blessing was pronounced. Before the blessing was given, the father could take the birthright away from the oldest son and give it to someone more deserving. But after the blessing was given, the birthright could no longer be taken away. This is why fathers usually waited until late in life to give away this irrevocable blessing. Although Jacob had been given the birthright by his older brother years ago, he still needed his father's blessing to make it binding.

birthright, and now he has stolen my blessing. Oh, haven't you saved even one blessing for me?"

27:37
Gen 27:27-29
2 Sam 8:14

37*Isaac:* "I have made him your master, and have given him yourself and all of his relatives as his servants. I have guaranteed him abundance of grain and wine—what is there left to give?"

27:38
Gen 27:34
Heb 12:17

38*Esau:* "Not one blessing left for me? O my father, bless me too."

(Isaac says nothing as Esau weeps.)

27:39
Heb 11:20
27:40
2 Kgs 8:20
2 Chron 21:8

39, 40*Isaac:* "Yours will be no life of ease and luxury, but you shall hew your way with your sword. For a time you will serve your brother, but you will finally shake loose from him and be free."

27:41
Gen 32:6
35:29; 37:4
Deut 34:8
27:43
Gen 11:31
12:4; 27:8,13
28:10
27:44
Gen 31:41
27:45
Prov 20:21
27:46
Gen 26:34,35

41So Esau hated Jacob because of what he had done to him. He said to himself, "My father will soon be gone, and then I will kill Jacob." 42But someone got wind of what he was planning, and reported it to Rebekah. She sent for Jacob and told him that his life was being threatened by Esau.

43"This is what to do," she said. "Flee to your Uncle Laban in Haran. 44Stay there with him awhile until your brother's fury is spent, 45and he forgets what you have done. Then I will send for you. For why should I be bereaved of both of you in one day?"

46Then Rebekah said to Isaac, "I'm sick and tired of these local girls. I'd rather die than see Jacob marry one of them."

28:1
Gen 24:3,4

28 So Isaac called for Jacob and blessed him and said to him, "Don't marry one of these Canaanite girls. 2Instead, go at once to Paddan-aram, to the house

27:38 *Isaac says nothing.* This appears in some versions, not in others.   **28:2** *your grandfather,* literally, "your mother's father." *your Uncle Laban,* literally, "your mother's brother."

JACOB'S FAMILY TREE
Marrying within the extended family was common and acceptable in this day. Had Jacob married outside his family, he would have married someone who didn't believe in God. So Jacob married his cousins, Rachel and Leah.

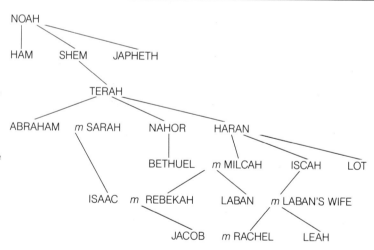

m: married

27:41 Esau was so angry at Jacob that he failed to see his own wrong in giving away the birthright in the first place. Jealous anger pollutes clear thinking by blinding us to the good things we have and making us dwell on what we don't have.

27:41 When Esau lost the valuable family blessing, his future suddenly changed. Reacting in anger, he decided to kill Jacob.

When you lose something of great value, or if others conspire against you and succeed, anger is the first and most natural reaction. But you can control your feelings by (1) recognizing your reaction for what it is, (2) praying for strength, and (3) asking God for help to see the opportunities that your bad situation may provide.

of your grandfather Bethuel, and marry one of your cousins—your Uncle Laban's daughters. ³God Almighty bless you and give you many children; may you become a great nation of many tribes! ⁴May God pass on to you and to your descendants the mighty blessings promised to Abraham. May you own this land where we now are foreigners, for God has given it to Abraham."

⁵So Isaac sent Jacob away, and he went to Paddan-aram to visit his Uncle Laban, his mother's brother—the son of Bethuel the Aramean. ⁶, ⁷, ⁸Esau realized that his father despised the local girls, and that his father and mother had sent Jacob to Paddan-aram, with his father's blessing, to get a wife from there, and that they had strictly warned him against marrying a Canaanite girl, and that Jacob had agreed and had left for Paddan-aram. ⁹So Esau went to his Uncle Ishmael's family and married another wife from there, besides the wives he already had. Her name was Mahalath, the sister of Nebaioth, and daughter of Ishmael, Abraham's son.

28:3
Gen 17:1-4
27:4,7
35:11

28:4
Gen 12:1-3
15:7; 35:11
48:3

28:7
Gen 27:8

28:8
Gen 26:34

28:9
Gen 36:3

F. THE STORY OF JACOB (28:10—36:43)

Jacob did everything, both right and wrong, with great zeal. He deceived his own brother Esau and his father Isaac. He wrestled with an angel and worked fourteen years to marry the woman he loved. Through Jacob we learn how a strong leader can also be a servant. We also see how wrong actions will always come back to haunt us.

1. Jacob starts a family

Jacob's dream

¹⁰So Jacob left Beer-sheba and journeyed toward Haran. ¹¹That night, when he stopped to camp at sundown, he found a rock for a headrest and lay down to sleep, ¹²and dreamed that a staircase reached from earth to heaven, and he saw the angels of God going up and down upon it.

¹³At the top of the stairs stood the Lord. "I am Jehovah," he said, "the God of Abraham, and of your father Isaac. The ground you are lying on is yours! I will give it to you and to your descendants. ¹⁴For you will have descendants as many as dust! They will cover the land from east to west and from north to south; and all the nations of the earth will be blessed through you and your descendants. ¹⁵What's more, I am with you, and will protect you wherever you go, and will bring you back safely to this land; I will be with you constantly until I have finished giving you all I am promising."

¹⁶, ¹⁷Then Jacob woke up. "God lives here!" he exclaimed in terror. "I've stumbled into his home! This is the awesome entrance to heaven!" ¹⁸The next morning he got up very early and set his stone headrest upright as a memorial pillar, and poured olive oil over it. ¹⁹He named the place Bethel ("House of God"), though the previous name of the nearest village was Luz.

28:10
Gen 12:4,5
26:23; 46:1

28:12
Gen 20:3
32:1,2; 37:5
Num 12:6
Jn 1:51

28:13
Gen 15:18

28:14
Gen 12:2
13:14,16; 22:18

28:15
Gen 26:3; 48:21
Deut 7:9; 31:6,8

28:16
Ex 3:5

28:17
2 Chron 5:14

28:18
Gen 35:14

28:19
Gen 12:8; 35:6

28:12 *a staircase*, literally, "ladder." **28:19** *of the nearest village*, literally, "of the city."

•28:9 Uncle Ishmael was Isaac's half brother. He was the son of Hagar, Abraham's servant girl (16:1–4, 15). After marrying two foreign girls, Esau hoped his marriage into Ishmael's family would please his parents, Isaac and Rebekah.

28:10–15 God's covenant promise to Abraham and Isaac was offered to Jacob as well. But it was not enough to be Abraham's grandson—Jacob had to establish his own personal relationship with God. God has no grandchildren, just children. Each of us must have a personal relationship with him. It is not enough to hear wonderful stories about Christians in your family. You need to become part of the story yourself (see Galatians 3:6, 7).

28:19 Bethel was about ten miles north of Jerusalem and 60 miles north of Beersheba, where Jacob left his family. This was where Abraham made one of his first sacrifices to God when he entered the land. Later Bethel became a center of idol worship, and the prophet Hosea condemned its evil practices.

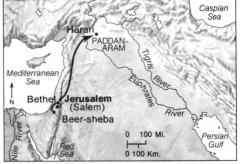

JACOB'S TRIP TO HARAN After Jacob deceived Esau, he literally ran for his life, traveling more than 400 miles to Haran where an uncle, Laban, lived. In Haran, Jacob married and started a family.

28:21
Gen 35:3
Ex 15:2
28:22
Gen 14:20; 35:7
Deut 14:22

20And Jacob vowed this vow to God: "If God will help and protect me on this journey and give me food and clothes, 21and will bring me back safely to my father, then I will choose Jehovah as my God! 22And this memorial pillar shall become a place for worship; and I will give you back a tenth of everything you give me!"

Jacob meets Rachel

29:1
Judg 6:3,33
29:2
Gen 24:11

29 Jacob traveled on, finally arriving in the land of the East. 2He saw in the distance three flocks of sheep lying beside a well in an open field, waiting to be watered. But a heavy stone covered the mouth of the well. 3(The custom was that the stone was not removed until all the flocks were there. After watering them, the stone was rolled back over the mouth of the well again.) 4Jacob went over to the shepherds and asked them where they lived.

29:4
Gen 11:31
28:10

"At Haran," they said.

29:5
Gen 24:29

5"Do you know a fellow there named Laban, the son of Nahor?"
"We sure do."

29:6
Gen 37:14
43:27

6"How is he?"
"He's well and prosperous. Look, there comes his daughter Rachel with the sheep."

7"Why don't you water the flocks so they can get back to grazing?" Jacob asked. "They'll be hungry if you stop so early in the day!"

8"We don't roll away the stone and begin the watering until all the flocks and shepherds are here," they replied.

29:10
Ex 2:16

9As this conversation was going on, Rachel arrived with her father's sheep, for she was a shepherdess. 10And because she was his cousin—the daughter of his mother's brother—and because the sheep were his uncle's, Jacob went over to the well and rolled away the stone and watered his uncle's flock. 11Then Jacob kissed Rachel and started crying! 12, 13He explained about being her cousin on her father's side, and that he was her Aunt Rebekah's son. She quickly ran and told her father, Laban, and as soon as he heard of Jacob's arrival, he rushed out to meet him and greeted him warmly and brought him home. Then Jacob told him his story.

29:11
Gen 27:26; 33:4
29:12
Gen 28:5

29:14
Judg 9:2
2 Sam 5:1

14"Just think, my very own flesh and blood," Laban exclaimed.

Jacob marries two sisters

29:15
Gen 30:28
31:7,41
29:16
Gen 29:25,26
29:17
Gen 12:11; 26:7
1 Sam 25:3
29:18
Gen 24:67
Hos 12:12

After Jacob had been there about a month, 15Laban said to him one day, "Just because we are relatives is no reason for you to work for me without pay. How much do you want?" 16Now Laban had two daughters, Leah, the older, and her younger sister, Rachel. 17Leah had lovely eyes, but Rachel was shapely, and in every way a beauty. 18Well, Jacob was in love with Rachel. So he told her father, "I'll work for you seven years if you'll give me Rachel as my wife."

19"Agreed!" Laban replied. "I'd rather give her to you than to someone outside the family."

29:20
Song 8:6,7
1 Cor 13:7

20So Jacob spent the next seven years working to pay for Rachel. But they seemed to him but a few days, he was so much in love. 21Finally the time came for him to marry her.

● **28:20–22** Was Jacob trying to bargain with God? It is possible that Jacob, in his ignorance of how to worship and serve God, treated God like a servant who would perform a service for a tip. Or it is possible that Jacob was not really bargaining, but pledging his future to God. In effect he was saying, "Since you have blessed me, even though I don't deserve it, I will promise to follow you." Whether Jacob was bargaining or pledging, God blessed him. But God also had some difficult lessons for him to learn.

29:18–27 It was the custom of the day for the man to pay a gift or "dowry" to the family of his future wife. This was done to compensate the family for the loss of the girl. Jacob's dowry was not a material possession—instead he agreed to work seven years for Laban. But there was another custom of the land that Laban did

not tell Jacob. The oldest daughter had to be married first. Thus, Laban deceived Jacob into giving him seven free years of hard work.

29:20–28 People often wonder if waiting a long time for something they truly desire is worth it. Jacob waited seven years to marry Rachel. After being tricked, he agreed to work seven more years for her! The most important goals and desires are worth waiting and paying for. Movies and television have created the illusion that people have to wait only an hour or two to solve their problems or get what they want. Don't be trapped into thinking the same is true in real life. Patience is hardest when we need it the most, but it is the key to achieving our goals.

"I have fulfilled my contract," Jacob said to Laban. "Now give me my wife, so that I can sleep with her."

22So Laban invited all the men of the settlement to celebrate with Jacob at a big party. 23Afterwards, that night, when it was dark, Laban took Leah to Jacob, and he slept with her. 24(And Laban gave to Leah a servant girl, Zilpah, to be her maid.) 25But in the morning—it was Leah!

"What sort of trick is this?" Jacob raged at Laban. "I worked for seven years for Rachel. What do you mean by this trickery?"

26"It's not our custom to marry off a younger daughter ahead of her sister," Laban replied smoothly. 27"Wait until the bridal week is over and you can have Rachel too—if you promise to work for me another seven years!"

28So Jacob agreed to work seven more years. Then Laban gave him Rachel, too. 29And Laban gave to Rachel a servant girl, Bilhah, to be her maid. 30So Jacob slept with Rachel, too, and he loved her more than Leah, and stayed and worked the additional seven years.

Jacob's many sons

31But because Jacob was slighting Leah, Jehovah let her have a child, while Rachel was barren. 32So Leah became pregnant and had a son, Reuben (meaning "God has noticed my trouble"), for she said, "Jehovah has noticed my trouble—now my husband will love me." 33She soon became pregnant again and had another son and named him Simeon (meaning "Jehovah heard"), for she said, "Jehovah heard that I was unloved, and so he has given me another son." 34Again she became pregnant and had a son, and named him Levi (meaning "Attachment") for she said, "Surely now my husband will feel affection for me, since I have given him three sons!" 35Once again she was pregnant and had a son and named him Judah (meaning "Praise"), for she said, "Now I will praise Jehovah!" And then she stopped having children.

30 Rachel, realizing she was barren, became envious of her sister. "Give me children or I'll die," she exclaimed to Jacob.

2Jacob flew into a rage. "Am I God?" he flared. "He is the one who is responsible for your barrenness."

3Then Rachel told him, "Sleep with my servant-girl Bilhah, and her children will be mine." 4So she gave him Bilhah to be his wife, and he slept with her, 5and she became pregnant and presented him with a son. 6Rachel named him Dan (meaning "Justice"), for she said, "God has given me justice, and heard my plea and given me a son." 7Then Bilhah, Rachel's servant-girl, became pregnant again and gave

29:22 Judg 14:10
29:23 Gen 24:65 38:14
29:24 Gen 30:9
29:25 Gen 12:18 27:35
29:27 Lev 18:18 Judg 14:10,12
29:29 Gen 30:3-8
29:30 Gen 29:17
29:31 Gen 20:18 Deut 21:15 Mal 1:2,3
29:32 Gen 35:23 37:21; 42:22 46:8,9
29:33 Gen 30:6
29:34 Gen 49:5
29:35 Gen 49:8
30:1 1 Sam 1:4-7 Eccles 4:4
30:2 Gen 25:21 31:36
30:3 Gen 16:2
30:4 Gen 22:24 35:22
30:6 Gen 29:32

29:26 *Laban replied smoothly*, implied from context. **30:6** *Dan* (meaning "Justice"). The meaning is not of the actual Hebrew name, but of a Hebrew word sounding like the name. The name given is a Hebrew pun. An example in English might be, "Because of the large hospital bill the child was named 'Bill.' "

●**29:23-25** Jacob flew into a rage when he learned that Laban had tricked him. The deceiver of Esau was now deceived himself. How natural it is for us to become enraged at an injustice done to us while closing our eyes to the injustices we do to others. Sin has a way of coming back to haunt us.

●**29:28-30** Although Jacob was tricked by Laban, he kept his part of the bargain. There was more at stake than just Jacob's hurt. There was Rachel to think about, as well as God's plan for his life. When we are tricked by others, keeping our part of the bargain may still be wise. "Nursing our wounds" or plotting revenge keeps us from seeing God's perspective.

29:32 Today parents usually give their children names that sound good or have sentimental appeal. But the Old Testament portrays a more dynamic use of names. Parents hoped their children would fulfill the meaning of the names given them. Later the parents could look back and see if their grown children had lived up to their names. Sometimes a person's name was changed because his or her character and name did not match. This happened to Jacob. His name (meaning "grabber") was changed to Israel

(meaning "one who has power with God"). Jacob's character had changed to the point that he was no longer seen as a deceiver, but rather as a godly man.

●**30:3** Each of the three great patriarchs (Abraham, Isaac, and Jacob) had wives who had difficulty conceiving children. It is interesting to note how each man reacted to his wife's predicament. Abraham had relations with Sarah's servant girl in order to have his own child. This relationship only caused bitterness and jealousy. Isaac, however, prayed to God when his wife was barren. God eventually answered his prayers and Rebekah had twin sons. But Jacob followed his grandfather's example. He too had relations with his wives' servant girls, leading to sad and sometimes bitter consequences.

30:4-12 Rachel and Leah were locked in a cruel contest. In their race to have more children, they both gave their servant girls to Jacob as concubines. Jacob would have been wise to refuse, even though this was an accepted custom of the day. The fact that a custom is socially acceptable does not mean it is wise. You will be spared much heartbreak if you look at the potential consequences, to you or to others, of your actions.

30:8
Gen 32:24
Mt 4:13

30:11
Gen 35:26
46:16; 49:19

30:14
Song 7:13

30:17
Gen 29:31; 30:6
Ex 3:7

Jacob a second son. [8]Rachel named him Naphtali (meaning "Wrestling"), for she said, "I am in a fierce contest with my sister and I am winning!"

[9]Meanwhile, when Leah realized that she wasn't getting pregnant anymore, she gave her servant-girl Zilpah to Jacob, to be his wife, [10]and soon Zilpah presented him with a son. [11]Leah named him Gad (meaning "My luck has turned!").

[12]Then Zilpah produced a second son, [13]and Leah named him Asher (meaning "Happy"), for she said, "What joy is mine! The other women will think me blessed indeed!"

[14]One day during the wheat harvest, Reuben found some mandrakes growing in a field and brought them to his mother Leah. Rachel begged Leah to give some of them to her.

[15]But Leah angrily replied, "Wasn't it enough to steal my husband? And now will you steal my son's mandrakes too?"

Rachel said sadly, "He will sleep with you tonight because of the mandrakes."

[16]That evening as Jacob was coming home from the fields, Leah went out to meet him. "You must sleep with me tonight!" she said; "for I am hiring you with some mandrakes my son has found!" So he did. [17]And God answered her prayers and she

30:14 Mandrakes were a leafy plant eaten by peasant women who supposed this would aid them in becoming pregnant.

RACHEL

History seems to repeat itself here. Twice a town well at Haran was the site of significant events in one family's story. It was here that Rebekah met Eliezer, Abraham's servant, who had come to find a wife for Isaac. Some 40 years later, Rebekah's son Jacob returned the favor by serving his cousin Rachel and her sheep from the same well. The relationship that developed between them not only reminds us that romance is not a modern invention, but also teaches us a few lessons about patience and love.

Jacob's love for Rachel was both patient and practical. Jacob had the patience to wait seven years for her, but he kept busy in the meantime. His commitment to Rachel kindled a strong loyalty within her. In fact, her loyalty to Jacob got out of hand and became self-destructive. She was frustrated by her barrenness and desperate to compete with her sister for Jacob's affection. She was trying to gain from Jacob what he had already given: devoted love.

Rachel's attempts to earn the unearnable are a picture of a much greater error we can make. Like her, we find ourselves trying somehow to earn love—God's love. But apart from his Word, we end up with one of two false ideas. Either we think we've been good enough to deserve his love, or we recognize we aren't able to earn his love and assume that it cannot be ours. If the Bible makes no other point, it shouts this one: God loves us! His love had no beginning and is incredibly patient. All we need to do is respond, not try to earn what is freely offered. God has said in many ways, "I love you. I have demonstrated that love to you by all I've done for you. I have even sacrificed my Son, Jesus, to pay the price for what is unacceptable about you (your sin). Now, live because of my love. Respond to me; love me with your whole being; give yourself to me in thanks, not as payment. Live life fully, in the freedom of knowing you are loved."

Strengths and accomplishments:
● She showed great loyalty to her family
● She mothered Joseph and Benjamin after being barren for many years

Weaknesses and mistakes:
● Her envy and competitiveness marred her relationship with her sister, Leah
● She was capable of dishonesty by taking her loyalty too far
● She failed to recognize that Jacob's devotion was not dependent on her ability to have children

Lessons from her life:
● Loyalty must be controlled by what is true and right
● Love is accepted, not earned

Vital statistics:
● Where: Haran
● Occupation: Shepherdess/Housewife
● Relatives: Father: Laban. Aunt: Rebekah. Sister: Leah. Husband: Jacob. Sons: Joseph and Benjamin.

Key verse:
"So Jacob spent the next seven years working to pay for Rachel. But they seemed to him but a few days, he was so much in love" (Genesis 29:20).

Rachel's story is told in Genesis 29—35:20. She is also mentioned in Ruth 4:11.

became pregnant again, and gave birth to her fifth son. ¹⁸She named him Issachar (meaning "Wages"), for she said, "God has repaid me for giving my slave-girl to my husband." ¹⁹Then once again she became pregnant, with a sixth son. ²⁰She named him Zebulun (meaning "Gifts"), for she said, "God has given me good gifts for my husband. Now he will honor me, for I have given him six sons." ²¹Afterwards she gave birth to a daughter and named her Dinah.

²²Then God remembered about Rachel's plight, and answered her prayers by giving her a child. ²³, ²⁴For she became pregnant and gave birth to a son. "God has removed the dark slur against my name," she said. And she named him Joseph (meaning "May I also have another!"), for she said, "May Jehovah give me another son."

30:18
Gen 35:23
49:14,15
30:20
Mt 4:13

30:22
1 Sam 1:19
30:23
Lk 1:25

30:24
Gen 35:17

Jacob becomes wealthy

²⁵Soon after the birth of Joseph to Rachel, Jacob said to Laban, "I want to go back home. ²⁶Let me take my wives and children—for I earned them from you—and be gone, for you know how fully I have paid for them with my service to you."

²⁷"Please don't leave me," Laban replied, "for a fortune-teller that I consulted told me that the many blessings I've been enjoying are all because of your being here. ²⁸How much of a raise do you need to get you to stay? Whatever it is, I'll pay it."

²⁹Jacob replied, "You know how faithfully I've served you through these many years, and how your flocks and herds have grown. ³⁰For it was little indeed you had before I came, and your wealth has increased enormously; Jehovah has blessed you from everything I do! But now, what about me? When should I provide for my own family?"

³¹, ³²"What wages do you want?" Laban asked again.

Jacob replied, "If you will do one thing, I'll go back to work for you. Let me go out among your flocks today and remove all the goats that are speckled or spotted, and all the black sheep. Give them to me as my wages. ³³Then if you ever find any white goats or sheep in my flock, you will know that I have stolen them from you!"

³⁴"All right!" Laban replied. "It shall be as you have said!"

³⁵, ³⁶So that very day Laban went out and formed a flock for Jacob of all the male goats that were ringed and spotted, and the females that were speckled and spotted with any white patches, and all of the black sheep. He gave them to Jacob's sons to take them three days' distance, and Jacob stayed and cared for Laban's flock. ³⁷Then Jacob took fresh shoots from poplar, almond, and sycamore trees, and peeled white streaks in them, ³⁸and placed these rods beside the watering troughs so that Laban's flocks would see them when they came to drink; for that is when they mated. ³⁹, ⁴⁰So the flocks mated before the white-streaked rods, and their offspring were streaked and spotted, and Jacob added them to his flock. Then he divided out the ewes from Laban's flock and segregated them from the rams, and let them mate only with Jacob's black rams. Thus he built his flocks from Laban's. ⁴¹Moreover, he watched for the stronger animals to mate, and placed the peeled branches before them, ⁴²but didn't with the feebler ones. So the less healthy lambs were Laban's and the stronger ones were Jacob's! ⁴³As a result, Jacob's flocks increased rapidly and he became very wealthy, with many servants, camels, and donkeys.

30:26
Gen 29:18,27
Hos 12:12

30:27
Gen 18:3
39:2-5
30:28
Gen 29:15; 31:7

30:30
Gen 30:43

30:32
Gen 31:8,10,12

30:37
Gen 31:9-13

30:43
Gen 13:2
24:35; 26:13
33:11

30:27 *a fortune-teller that I consulted*, literally, "I have learned by divination."

●**30:22–24** Eventually the Lord answered Rachel's prayers and gave her a child of her own. She caused herself many heartaches by taking matters into her own hands (giving Bilhah to Jacob). Trusting God when nothing seems to happen is difficult. But it is harder still to live with the consequences of taking matters into our own hands. Resist the temptation to feel that God has forgotten you. Have patience and courage to wait for God to act.

2. Jacob returns home

31:1
Prov 27:4

31:2
Gen 31:36
1 Sam 18:9

31:3
Gen 28:15; 32:9

31:5
Gen 31:42,53

31:6
Gen 30:29

31:7
Gen 29:15
30:28; 31:41

31:8
Gen 30:32

31 But Jacob learned that Laban's sons were grumbling, "He owes everything he owns to our father. All his wealth is at our father's expense." ²Soon Jacob noticed a considerable cooling in Laban's attitude towards him.

³Jehovah now spoke to Jacob and told him, "Return to the land of your fathers, and to your relatives there; and I will be with you."

⁴So one day Jacob sent for Rachel and Leah to come out to the field where he was with the flocks, ⁵to talk things over with them.

"Your father has turned against me," he told them, "and now the God of my fathers has come and spoken to me. ⁶You know how hard I've worked for your father, ⁷but he has been completely unscrupulous and has broken his wage contract with me again and again and again. But God has not permitted him to do me any harm! ⁸For if he said the speckled animals would be mine, then all the flock produced speckled; and when he changed and said I could have the streaked ones,

LABAN

We're all selfish, but some of us have a real corner on the weakness. Laban's whole life was stamped by self-centeredness. His chief goal was to look out for himself. The way he treated others was controlled by that goal. He made profitable arrangements for his sister Rebekah's marriage to Isaac, and used his daughters' lives as bargaining chips. Jacob eventually outmaneuvered Laban, but the older man was unwilling to admit defeat. His hold on Jacob was broken, but he still tried to maintain some kind of control by getting Jacob to promise to be gone for good. He realized that Jacob and Jacob's God were more than he could handle.

On the surface, we may find it difficult to identify with Laban. But his selfishness is one point we have in common. Like him, we often have a strong tendency to control people and events to our benefit. Our "good" reasons for treating others the way we do may simply be a thin cover over the motive of self-centeredness. We may not recognize our selfishness, however. One way to discover it is to examine our willingness to admit we're wrong. Laban could not bring himself to do this. If you find yourself amazed by what you sometimes say and do to avoid facing wrong actions, you are on the right road back to God.

Strengths and accomplishments:
• Controlled two generations of marriages in the Abrahamic family (Rebekah, Rachel, Leah)
• Possessed a quick wit

Weaknesses and mistakes:
• Manipulated and used others for his own benefit
• Unwilling to admit wrongdoing
• Benefited financially from using Jacob but never received the full benefit he could have gained by knowing and worshiping the God of Jacob

Lessons from his life:
• Those who set out to use people will eventually find themselves used
• God's plan cannot be stopped

Vital statistics:
• Where: Haran
• Occupation: Wealthy shepherd
• Relatives: Father: Bethuel. Sister: Rebekah. Brother-in-law: Isaac. Daughters: Rachel and Leah. Son-in-law: Jacob.

Key verse:
"In fact, except for the grace of God—The God of my grandfather Abraham, even the glorious God of Isaac, my father—you would have sent me off without a penny to my name. But God has seen your cruelty and my hard work, and that is why he appeared to you last night" (Genesis 31:42).

Laban's story is told in Genesis 27:43—31:55.

●**31:1–3** Jacob's wealth made Laban's sons jealous. It is sometimes difficult to be happy when others are doing well. To compare our success with that of others is a dangerous way to judge the quality of our life. By comparing ourselves to others, we may be giving jealousy a foothold. We can avoid jealousy by rejoicing in others' success (see Romans 12:15).

●**31:4–13** Although Laban treated Jacob unfairly, God still increased Jacob's prosperity. God's power is not limited by lack of fair play. He has the ability to meet our needs and make us thrive even though others treat us unfairly. To give in and play unfairly in return is to be no different from your enemies.

then all the lambs were streaked! ⁹In this way God has made me wealthy at your father's expense.

10"And at the mating season, I had a dream, and saw that the he-goats mating with the flock were streaked, speckled, and mottled. ¹¹Then, in my dream, the Angel of God called to me ¹²and told me that I should mate the white female goats with streaked, speckled, and mottled male goats. 'For I have seen all that Laban has done to you,' the Angel said. ¹³'I am the God you met at Bethel,' he continued, 'the place where you anointed the pillar and made a vow to serve me. Now leave this country and return to the land of your birth.' "

¹⁴Rachel and Leah replied, "That's fine with us! There's nothing for us here—none of our father's wealth will come to us anyway! ¹⁵He has reduced our rights to those of foreign women; he sold us, and what he received for us has disappeared. ¹⁶The riches God has given you from our father were legally ours and our children's to begin with! So go ahead and do whatever God has told you to."

Laban pursues Jacob

17-20So one day while Laban was out shearing sheep, Jacob set his wives and sons on camels, and fled without telling Laban his intentions. He drove the flocks before him—Jacob's flocks he had gotten there at Paddan-aram—and took everything he owned and started out to return to his father Isaac in the land of Canaan. ²¹So he fled with all of his possessions (and Rachel stole her father's household gods and took them with her) and crossed the Euphrates River and headed for the territory of Gilead.

²²Laban didn't learn of their flight for three days. ²³Then, taking several men with him, he set out in hot pursuit and caught up with them seven days later, at Mount Gilead. ²⁴That night God appeared to Laban in a dream.

"Watch out what you say to Jacob," he was told. "Don't give him your blessing

31:9
Gen 31:1,16

31:10
Gen 31:24

31:11
Gen 16:7-13
18:1; 22:1,11

31:12
Gen 30:37-43
Ex 3:7
Lev 19:13
Deut 24:14,15

31:13
Gen 28:13-19
35:7

31:15
Gen 29:20,27
30:26-28

31:18
Gen 24:29
25:20

31:20
Gen 31:27

31:21
Gen 15:18
Num 32:1
Deut 3:12
Judg 17:4,5
18:20

31:22
Gen 30:36

31:24
Gen 25:20
31:10

31:12 *and told me that I should mate the white female goats with streaked, speckled, and mottled male goats,* implied. Literally, "notice that all the mating males are speckled, streaked, and mottled."

```
JACOB   m   ZILPAH ─────────── GAD
            (Leah's         ─ ASHER
            servant girl)

        m   LEAH ═══════ REUBEN
                    ╲───── SIMEON
                     ╲──── LEVI
                      ╲─── JUDAH
                                    ───────── ISSACHAR
                                    ───────── ZEBULUN
                                    ───────── DINAH (only daughter)

        m   RACHEL ══════════════ JOSEPH
                              ───── BENJAMIN

        m   BILHAH ═══── DAN
            (Rachel's    ╲ NAPHTALI
            servant girl)                    m: married
```

JACOB'S CHILDREN
This chart shows from left to right Jacob's children in the order in which they were born.

Jacob's many wives (two wives and two "substitute" wives) led to sad and bitter consequences among the children. Anger, resentment, and jealousy were common among Jacob's sons. It is interesting to note that the worst fighting and rivalry occurred between Leah's children and Rachel's children, and among the tribes that descended from them.

31:14, 15 Leaving home was not difficult for Rachel and Leah because their father had treated them as poorly as he had Jacob. According to custom, they were supposed to receive the benefits of Jacob's dowry, which was fourteen years of hard work. When Laban did not give them what was rightfully theirs, they knew they would never inherit anything from their father.

31:21 Many people kept small wooden or metal idols in their homes. These idols were called teraphim, and they were thought to protect the home and offer advice in times of need. They had legal significance as well, for when they were passed on to an heir, the

31:25
Gen 33:18

and don't curse him." ²⁵Laban finally caught up with Jacob as he was camped at the top of a ridge; Laban, meanwhile, camped below him in the mountains.

²⁶"What do you mean by sneaking off like this?" Laban demanded. "Are my daughters prisoners, captured in a battle, that you have rushed them away like this? ²⁷Why didn't you give me a chance to have a farewell party, with singing and orchestra and harp? ²⁸Why didn't you let me kiss my grandchildren and tell them good-bye? This is a strange way to act. ²⁹I could crush you, but the God of your father appeared to me last night and told me, 'Be careful not to be too hard on Jacob!' ³⁰But see here—though you feel you must go, and long so intensely for your childhood home—why have you stolen my idols?"

31:28
Gen 29:13
31:55
Ex 4:27

31:29
Gen 31:24,42

31:30
Gen 31:21

31:31
Gen 20:11

31:32
Gen 44:9
1 Sam 12:3

³¹"I sneaked away because I was afraid," Jacob answered. "I said to myself, 'He'll take his daughters from me by force.' ³²But as for your household idols, a curse upon anyone who took them. Let him die! If you find a single thing we've stolen from you, I swear before all these men, I'll give it back without question." For Jacob didn't know that Rachel had taken them.

³³Laban went first into Jacob's tent to search there, then into Leah's, and then searched the two tents of the concubines, but didn't find them. Finally he went into Rachel's tent. ³⁴Rachel, remember, was the one who had stolen the idols; she had stuffed them into her camel saddle and now was sitting on them! So although Laban searched the tents thoroughly, he didn't find them.

31:35
Gen 18:11

31:36
Gen 30:2
Num 16:15

³⁵"Forgive my not getting up, father," Rachel explained, "but I'm having my monthly period." So Laban didn't find them.

³⁶, ³⁷Now Jacob got mad. "What did you find?" he demanded of Laban. "What is my crime? You have come rushing after me as though you were chasing a criminal and have searched through everything. Now put everything I stole out here in front of us, before your men and mine, for all to see and to decide whose it is! ³⁸Twenty years I've been with you, and all that time I cared for your ewes and goats so that they produced healthy offspring, and I never touched one ram of yours for food. ³⁹If any were attacked and killed by wild animals, did I show them to you and ask you to reduce the count of your flock? No, I took the loss. You made me pay for every animal stolen from the flocks, whether I could help it or not. ⁴⁰I worked for you through the scorching heat of the day, and through the cold and sleepless nights. ⁴¹Yes, twenty years—fourteen of them earning your two daughters, and six years to get the flock! And you have reduced my wages ten times! ⁴²In fact, except for the grace of God—the God of my grandfather Abraham, even the glorious God of Isaac, my father—you would have sent me off without a penny to my name. But

31:37
Gen 31:32
Josh 7:23

31:38
Gen 31:41

31:39
Ex 22:10-13

31:41
Gen 29:27
30:27-32

31:42
Gen 28:13-15,
20; 31:29

31:35 *but I'm having my monthly period*, implied. Literally, "The manner of women is upon me." She was pregnant with Benjamin, but was falsely claiming her menstrual period, which, under the later Mosaic law, caused ceremonial defilement of all that she sat upon. See Lev 15.   **31:39** *whether I could help it or not*, literally, "stolen by day or by night."

---

person who received them could rightfully claim the greatest amount of the family inheritance. No wonder Laban was concerned when he realized his idols were missing. Most likely Rachel stole her father's idols because she was afraid Laban would consult them and learn where she and Jacob had gone, or perhaps she wanted to claim the family inheritance.

●**31:32** Can you remember feeling absolutely sure about something? Jacob was so sure that no one had stolen Laban's idols that he vowed to kill the offender. Since Rachel took them, this statement put his wife's safety in serious jeopardy. Even when we are absolutely sure about a matter, it is safer to avoid rash statements. Someone may hold you to them.

●**31:38–42** Jacob worked hard even after several pay cuts. Jacob's diligence eventually paid off: his flocks began to multiply. Making a habit of doing more than expected can pay off by (1) pleasing God, (2) earning recognition and advancement, (3) enhancing your reputation, (4) building others' confidence in you, (5) giving you more experience and knowledge, and (6) developing your spiritual maturity.

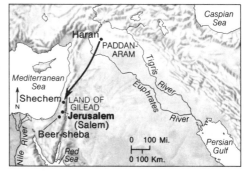

JACOB'S RETURN TO CANAAN   God told Jacob to leave Haran and return to his homeland. Jacob took his family, crossed the Euphrates River, and headed first for the land of Gilead. Laban caught up with him there.

God has seen your cruelty and my hard work, and that is why he appeared to you last night."

43Laban replied, "These women are my daughters, and these children are mine, and these flocks and all that you have—all are mine. So how could I harm my own daughters and grandchildren? 44Come now and we will sign a peace pact, you and I, and will live by its terms."

45So Jacob took a stone and set it up as a monument, 46and told his men to gather stones and make a heap, and Jacob and Laban ate together beside the pile of rocks. 47, 48They named it "The Witness Pile"—"Jegar-sahadutha," in Laban's language, and "Galeed" in Jacob's.

"This pile of stones will stand as a witness against us [if either of us trespasses across this line]," Laban said. 49So it was also called "The Watchtower" (Mizpah). For Laban said, "May the Lord see to it that we keep this bargain when we are out of each other's sight. 50And if you are harsh to my daughters, or take other wives, I won't know, but God will see it. 51, 52This heap," Laban continued, "stands between us as a witness of our vows that I will not cross this line to attack you and you will not cross it to attack me. 53I call upon the God of Abraham and Nahor, and of their father, to destroy either one of us who does."

So Jacob took oath before the mighty God of his father Isaac, to respect the boundary line. 54Then Jacob presented a sacrifice to God there at the top of the mountain, and invited his companions to a feast, and afterwards spent the night with them on the mountain. 55Laban was up early the next morning and kissed his daughters and grandchildren, and blessed them, and returned home.

Jacob takes gifts to Esau

32 So Jacob and his household started on again. And the angels of God came to meet him. When he saw them he exclaimed, "God lives here!" So he named the place "God's territory!"

3Jacob now sent messengers to his brother Esau in Edom, in the land of Seir, 4with this message: "Hello from Jacob! I have been living with Uncle Laban until recently, 5and now I own oxen, donkeys, sheep, goats, and many servants, both men and women. I have sent these messengers to inform you of my coming, hoping that you will be friendly to us."

6The messengers returned with the news that Esau was on the way to meet Jacob—with an army of 400 men! 7Jacob was frantic with fear. He divided his household, along with the flocks and herds and camels, into two groups; 8for he said, "If Esau attacks one group, perhaps the other can escape."

9Then Jacob prayed, "O God of Abraham my grandfather, and of my father Isaac—O Jehovah who told me to return to the land of my relatives, and said that you would do me good— 10I am not worthy of the least of all your lovingkindnesses shown me again and again just as you promised me. For when I left home I owned nothing except a walking stick! And now I am two armies! 11O Lord, please deliver me from destruction at the hand of my brother Esau, for I am frightened—terribly afraid that he is coming to kill me and these mothers and my children. 12But you

31:44
Gen 21:27
26:28-31
31:45
Gen 28:18
Josh 24:26,27
31:46
Gen 35:14
Josh 4:5
31:48
Gen 21:30
Deut 4:26
31:49
Judg 10:17
11:11,29
31:50
Judg 11:10
1 Sam 12:5
Jer 29:23; 42:5
31:52
Gen 31:29,42
31:53
Gen 28:13
31:29
31:54
Gen 26:30
Ex 18:12
31:55
Gen 31:28; 33:4

32:1
Gen 16:7
18:1,2; 19:1
22:11; 31:11
2 Kgs 6:16,17
Ps 34:7
32:2
Josh 13:26
21:38
2 Sam 2:8
32:3
Gen 14:5,6
25:30; 27:41
Mal 3:1
32:4
Gen 31:17,18
32:8
Gen 33:1-3
32:9
Gen 28:13-15
31:13
32:10
Gen 24:27
32:11
Gen 27:41; 33:4
32:12
Gen 28:14,15

31:47, 48 *if either of us trespasses across this line,* implied. **32:1, 2** *So Jacob and his household,* implied. *God's territory,* literally, "Two encampments." **32:10** *left home,* literally, "passed over this Jordan."

31:49 To be binding, an agreement had to be witnessed by a third party. In this case, both Jacob and Laban used God as their witness to make sure they kept their word.

32:1 Why did these angels of God meet Jacob? There are many places in the Bible where angels intervened in human situations. Although angels often came in human form, these angels must have looked different, for Jacob recognized them at once.

●**32:3** The last time Jacob had seen Esau, his brother was ready to kill him for stealing the family blessing (Genesis 25:29—27:42).

Esau was so angry he had vowed to kill Jacob as soon as their father, Isaac, died (27:41). Afraid of their reunion, Jacob sent a messenger ahead with gifts, hoping to buy Esau's favor.

●**32:9–12** How would you feel, knowing you were about to meet the person whom you had cheated out of his most precious possession? Jacob had taken Esau's birthright (25:33) and his blessing (27:27–29). Now he was about to meet his brother for the first time in twenty years, and he was frantic with fear. He collected his thoughts, however, and decided to pray. When we face a difficult or urgent conflict, we can run about frantically or we can pause to pray. Which approach will be more effective?

promised to do me good, and to multiply my descendants until they become as the sands along the shores—too many to count."

13, 14, 15Jacob stayed where he was for the night, and prepared a present for his brother Esau: 200 female goats, 20 male goats, 200 ewes, 20 rams, 30 milk camels, with their colts, 40 cows, 10 bulls, 20 female donkeys, 10 male donkeys. 16He instructed his servants to drive them on ahead, each group of animals by itself, separated by a distance between. 17He told the men driving the first group that when they met Esau and he asked, "Where are you going? Whose servants are you? Whose animals are these?"— 18they should reply: "These belong to your servant Jacob. They are a present for his master Esau! He is coming right behind us!"

19Jacob gave the same instructions to each driver, with the same message. 20Jacob's strategy was to appease Esau with the presents before meeting him face to face! "Perhaps," Jacob hoped, "he will be friendly to us." 21So the presents were sent on ahead, and Jacob spent that night in the camp.

Jacob wrestles with an angel

22, 23, 24But during the night he got up and wakened his two wives and his two concubines and eleven sons, and sent them across the Jordan River at the Jabbok ford with all his possessions, then returned again to the camp and was there alone; and a Man wrestled with him until dawn. 25And when the Man saw that he couldn't win the match, he struck Jacob's hip, and knocked it out of joint at the socket.

26Then the Man said, "Let me go, for it is dawn."

But Jacob panted, "I will not let you go until you bless me."

27"What is your name?" the Man asked.

"Jacob," was the reply.

28"It isn't anymore!" the Man told him. "It is Israel—one who has power with God. Because you have been strong with God, you shall prevail with men."

29"What is *your* name?" Jacob asked him.

"No, you mustn't ask," the Man told him. And he blessed him there.

30Jacob named the place "Peniel" ("The Face of God"), for he said, "I have seen God face to face, and yet my life is spared." 31The sun rose as he started on, and he was limping because of his hip. 32(That is why even today the people of Israel don't eat meat from near the hip, in memory of what happened that night.)

The brothers make peace

33 Then, far in the distance, Jacob saw Esau coming with his 400 men. 2Jacob now arranged his family into a column, with his two concubines and their children at the head, Leah and her children next, and Rachel and Joseph last. 3Then Jacob went on ahead. As he approached his brother he bowed low seven times before him. 4And then Esau ran to meet him and embraced him affectionately and kissed him; and both of them were in tears!

32:22, 23, 24 *and wakened,* implied.

32:18
Gen 32:4,5

32:20
Gen 43:11,12
1 Sam 25:18
Prov 21:14

32:22
Deut 3:16
Josh 12:2

32:24
Gen 18:3
Hos 12:3,4

32:26
Ex 32:10
1 Chron 4:10
Ps 67:1,6,7

32:28
Gen 35:10
1 Kgs 18:31

32:29
Ex 3:13
Judg 13:17

32:30
Gen 16:13
Ex 24:10; 33:20
Num 12:8
Deut 5:24; 34:10
Judg 6:22
Jn 1:18

32:31
Judg 8:8,9,17

33:1
Gen 32:6,16

33:3
Gen 18:2; 42:6
Prov 6:3

33:4
Gen 45:14
46:29

●**32:26** Jacob continued this wrestling match all night just to be blessed. He was persistent. God encourages persistence in all areas of our lives, including the spiritual. We should be aware of areas in our spiritual lives where we need to be more persistent. Strong character results from struggling under tough conditions.

●**32:27–29** God gave many Bible people new names (Abraham, Sarah, Jacob, Peter, Paul). Their new names were a symbol of how God had changed their lives. Here we see how Jacob's character had changed. Jacob, the ambitious deceiver, had now become Israel, the man who persistently clings to God.

●**33:1–11** It is refreshing to see Esau's change of heart when Jacob and Esau meet again. The bitterness over losing his birthright and blessing seems gone (Genesis 25:29–34). Instead we see Esau happy and content with what he has. Jacob even exclaims how great it is to see his brother's friendly smile (33:10).

Life can deal us some bad situations. We can feel cheated, as Esau did, but we don't have to remain bitter. We can remove the bitterness from our lives by honestly expressing our feelings to God, forgiving those who have wronged us, and being content with what we have.

●**33:3** Bowing low seven times was the sign of respect given to a king. Jacob was taking every precaution as he met Esau, hoping to dispel any thoughts of revenge.

●**33:4** Esau met his brother, Jacob, and greeted him with a great hug. Imagine how hard this was for Esau, who at one time had actually plotted his brother's death (27:41). But time away from each other allowed the bitter wounds to heal. With the passing of time each brother was able to see that their relationship was more important than their real estate.

⁵Then Esau looked at the women and children and asked, "Who are these people with you?"

"My children," Jacob replied. ⁶Then the concubines came forward with their children, and bowed low before him. ⁷Next came Leah with her children, and bowed, and finally Rachel and Joseph came and made their bows.

⁸"And what were all the flocks and herds I met as I came?" Esau asked. And Jacob replied, "They are my gifts, to curry your favor!"

⁹"Brother, I have plenty," Esau laughed. "Keep what you have."

¹⁰"No, but please accept them," Jacob said, "for what a relief it is to see your friendly smile! I was as frightened of you as though approaching God! ¹¹Please take my gifts. For God has been very generous to me and I have enough." So Jacob insisted, and finally Esau accepted them.

¹²"Well, let's be going," Esau said. "My men and I will stay with you and lead the way."

¹³But Jacob replied, "As you can see, some of the children are small, and the flocks and herds have their young, and if they are driven too hard, they will die. ¹⁴So you go on ahead of us and we'll follow at our own pace and meet you at Seir."

¹⁵"Well," Esau said, "at least let me leave you some of my men to assist you and be your guides."

"No," Jacob insisted, "we'll get along just fine. Please do as I suggest." ¹⁶So Esau started back to Seir that same day. ¹⁷Meanwhile Jacob and his household went as far as Succoth. There he built himself a camp, with pens for his flocks and herds. (That is why the place is called Succoth, meaning "huts.") ¹⁸Then they arrived safely at Shechem, in Canaan, and camped outside the city. ¹⁹(He bought the land he camped on from the family of Hamor, Shechem's father, for 100 pieces of silver. ²⁰And there he erected an altar and called it "El-Elohe-Israel," "The Altar to the God of Israel.")

Jacob's sons take revenge

34 One day Dinah, Leah's daughter, went out to visit some of the neighborhood girls, ²but when Shechem, son of King Hamor the Hivite, saw her, he took her and raped her. ³He fell deeply in love with her, and tried to win her affection.

⁴Then he spoke to his father about it. "Get this girl for me," he demanded. "I want to marry her."

⁵Word soon reached Jacob of what had happened, but his sons were out in the

33:5
Gen 48:8,9

33:8
Gen 32:5,13-16

33:9
Gen 27:39
33:10
Gen 19:19
47:29; 50:4
33:11
Gen 32:13-15

33:14
Gen 32:3
Deut 2:1

33:17
Josh 13:27
Judg 8:5
Ps 60:6
33:18
Gen 12:6
25:20; 28:6,7
33:19
Gen 23:17
33:20
Josh 24:32
Jn 4:5

34:1
Gen 30:21
34:2
Deut 21:14
22:29
2 Sam 11:2
34:4
Judg 14:2,6

33:10 *I was as frightened of you as though approaching God,* literally, "forasmuch as I have seen your face as one sees the face of God." **33:13** *as you can see,* implied.

●**33:11** Why did Jacob send gifts ahead for Esau? In Bible times, gifts were given for several reasons. (1) As a bribe. Even today, gifts are given to win someone over or buy his or her support. Esau may first have refused Jacob's gifts (33:9) because he didn't want or need to accept a bribe. He had already forgiven Jacob, and he had ample wealth of his own. (2) As an expression of affection. (3) Gifts were often exchanged before a meeting of two people. The gifts were often related to a person's occupation. This explains why Jacob sent Esau, who was a herdsman, sheep, goats, and cattle.

34:1-4 Shechem may have been a victim of "love at first sight," but he acted on it with an impulsive, evil act. Not only did he sin against Dinah, he sinned against her entire family (34:6, 7), which brought about severe consequences (34:25-31). Even Shechem's declared love for Dinah could not excuse the evil he did by forcefully raping her. Don't allow sexual passion to boil over into evil actions. Passion must be controlled.

JACOB'S JOURNEY TO SHECHEM
After a joyful re-union with his brother Esau (who journeyed from Edom), Jacob set up camp in Suc-coth. Later he moved on to Shechem where his daughter, Di-nah, was raped and two of his sons took revenge on the city.

34:7
2 Sam 13:12

fields herding cattle, so he did nothing until their return. 6, 7Meanwhile King Hamor, Shechem's father, went to talk with Jacob, arriving just as Jacob's sons came in from the fields, too shocked and angry to overlook the insult, for it was an outrage against all of them.

34:9
Gen 24:3; 28:1

8Hamor told Jacob, "My son Shechem is truly in love with your daughter, and longs for her to be his wife. Please let him marry her. 9, 10Moreover, we invite you folks to live here among us and to let your daughters marry our sons, and we will give our daughters as wives for your young men. And you shall live among us wherever you wish and carry on your business among us and become rich!"

34:11
Gen 33:10

11Then Shechem addressed Dinah's father and brothers. "Please be kind to me and let me have her as my wife," he begged. "I will give whatever you require.

34:12
Gen 24:53
29:18; 31:41
Ex 22:16

12No matter what dowry or gift you demand, I will pay it—only give me the girl as my wife."

34:13
Gen 27:35
31:7; 34:31

13Her brothers then lied to Shechem and Hamor, acting dishonorably because of what Shechem had done to their sister. 14They said, "We couldn't possibly. For you are not circumcised. It would be a disgrace for her to marry such a man. 15I'll tell you what we'll do—if every man of you will be circumcised, 16then we will intermarry with you and live here and unite with you to become one people. 17Otherwise we will take her and be on our way."

34:14
Gen 17:13,14
Josh 5:2

34:19
Gen 29:20

18, 19Hamor and Shechem gladly agreed, and lost no time in acting upon this request, for Shechem was very much in love with Dinah, and could, he felt sure, sell the idea to the other men of the city—for he was highly respected and very popular. 20So Hamor and Shechem appeared before the city council and presented their request.

34:20
Gen 23:10
Deut 17:5

21"Those men are our friends," they said. "Let's invite them to live here among us and ply their trade. For the land is large enough to hold them, and we can intermarry with them. 22But they will only consider staying here on one condition—that every one of us men be circumcised, the same as they are. 23But if we do this, then all they have will become ours and the land will be enriched. Come on, let's agree to this so that they will settle here among us."

34:22
Gen 34:15

34:24
Gen 17:23
Josh 5:2

24So all the men agreed, and all were circumcised. 25But three days later, when their wounds were sore and sensitive to every move they made, two of Dinah's brothers, Simeon and Levi, took their swords, entered the city without opposition, and slaughtered every man there, 26including Hamor and Shechem. They rescued Dinah from Shechem's house and returned to their camp again. 27Then all of Jacob's sons went over and plundered the city because their sister had been dishonored there. 28They confiscated all the flocks and herds and donkeys—everything they could lay their hands on, both inside the city and outside in the fields, 29and took all the women and children, and wealth of every kind.

34:25
Gen 49:5,6
Josh 5:8

34:28
Josh 7:21

34:30
Gen 13:7
Gen 49:5-7
Ex 5:21
1 Chron 16:19

30Then Jacob said to Levi and Simeon, "You have made me stink among all the people of this land—all the Canaanites and Perizzites. We are so few that they will come and crush us, and we will all be killed."

31"Should he treat our sister like a prostitute?" they retorted.

34:20 *appeared before the city council,* literally, "came into the gate of their city."

34:24–31 Why did Simeon and Levi take such harsh action against the city of Shechem? Jacob's family saw themselves as "set apart" from others. That is what God wanted. They were to remain separate from their heathen neighbors. But the brothers wrongly thought that being set apart also meant being better. This arrogant attitude led to the terrible slaughter of innocent people.

34:27–29 When Shechem raped Dinah, the consequences were far greater than he could have imagined. Dinah's brothers were outraged and took revenge. Pain, lying, deceit, and murder followed. Sexual sin is no more sinful than any other sin, but its consequences may be more devastating.

34:30, 31 In seeking revenge against Prince Shechem, Simeon and Levi lied, murdered, and stole. Their desire for justice was right. Their ways of achieving it were wrong. Because of their sin, their own father cursed them with his dying breath (49:5–7). Generations later, Simeon's descendants lost part of the Promised Land allotted to them. When tempted to return evil for evil, leave revenge to God and spare yourself the dreadful consequences of sin.

Rachel and Isaac die

35 "Move on to Bethel now, and settle there," God said to Jacob, "and build an altar to worship me—the God who appeared to you when you fled from your brother Esau."

²So Jacob instructed all those in his household to destroy the idols they had brought with them, and to wash themselves and to put on fresh clothing. ³"For we are going to Bethel," he told them, "and I will build an altar there to the God who answered my prayers in the day of my distress, and was with me on my journey."

⁴So they gave Jacob all their idols and their earrings, and he buried them beneath the oak tree near Shechem. ⁵Then they started on again. And the terror of God was upon all the cities they journeyed through, so that they were not attacked. ⁶Finally they arrived at Luz (also called Bethel), in Canaan. ⁷And Jacob erected an altar there and named it "The altar to the God who met me here at Bethel" because it was there at Bethel that God appeared to him when he was fleeing from Esau.

⁸Soon after this Rebekah's old nurse Deborah died and was buried beneath the oak tree in the valley below Bethel. And ever after it was called "The Oak of Weeping."

⁹Upon Jacob's arrival at Bethel, en route from Paddan-aram, God appeared to him once again and blessed him. ¹⁰And God said to him, "You shall no longer be called Jacob ('Grabber'), but Israel ('One who prevails with God'). ¹¹I am God Almighty," the Lord said to him, "and I will cause you to be fertile and to multiply and to become a great nation, yes, many nations; many kings shall be among your descendants. ¹²And I will pass on to you the land I gave to Abraham and Isaac. Yes, I will give it to you and to your descendants."

¹³, ¹⁴Afterwards Jacob built a stone pillar at the place where God had appeared to him; and he poured wine over it as an offering to God, and then anointed the pillar with olive oil. ¹⁵Jacob named the spot Bethel ("House of God"), because God had spoken to him there.

¹⁶Leaving Bethel, he and his household traveled on toward Ephrath (Bethlehem). But Rachel's pains of childbirth began while they were still a long way away. ¹⁷After a very hard delivery, the midwife finally exclaimed, "Wonder-

35:7 *the God who met me here at Bethel,* literally, "The God of Bethel." **35:8** *Soon after this,* implied.

35:1 Gen 12:1; 22:1 28:19; 31:3
35:2 Gen 31:19
35:3 Gen 28:15-22
35:4 Ex 32:2 Josh 24:23-26 Judg 8:24 Hos 2:13
35:5 Gen 34:30 Ex 15:16
35:6 Gen 12:8 28:19; 48:3
35:7 Gen 28:19
35:8 Gen 24:59
35:9 Gen 26:2 28:13; 48:3
35:10 Gen 17:5,15 32:28
35:11 Gen 12:1 17:1,5; 28:3
35:12 Gen 13:15 28:13
35:13 Judg 6:21; 13:20
35:14 Gen 28:18,19
35:16 Ruth 4:11
35:17 Gen 30:23,24 1 Sam 4:19,20

JACOB'S JOURNEY BACK TO HEBRON
After Jacob's sons Simeon and Levi destroyed Shechem, God told Jacob to move to Bethel, where Jacob's name was changed to *Israel.* He then traveled to Hebron, but along the way, his dear wife Rachel died in Ephrath (Bethlehem).

idols should have no place in his household. He wanted no good-luck charms to divert the spiritual focus of his family.

Jacob ordered his household to destroy all their idols. An idol is anything we put before God. Unless we remove idols from our lives, they can ruin our faith. Idols don't have to be physical objects. They can be thoughts or desires. Like Jacob, we should begin to remove the idols from our lives at once.

35:4 Why did the people give Jacob their earrings? Jewelry, in itself, was not evil. In Jacob's day, however, earrings were often worn by people in neighboring cultures as good-luck charms in order to ward off evil. The people had to cleanse away all heathen influences including reminders of foreign gods.

●**35:10** God reminded Jacob of his new name, Israel, which meant "one who has power with God" or "one who prevails with God." Jacob's life was littered with difficulties and trials. Yet his new name was a tribute to his desire to stay close to God despite life's disappointments.

Many people believe that Christianity should offer a problem-free life. Consequently, as life gets tough, they draw back disappointed. Instead, they should determine to prevail with God through the storms of life. Troubles and difficulties are painful but inevitable. Look at them as opportunities for growth. You can't prevail with God without troubles to prevail over.

35:2 Why did the people have these idols? Idols were sometimes seen more as good-luck charms than as gods. Some Israelites, even though they worshiped God, had idols in their homes, just as some Christians today own good-luck trinkets. Jacob believed that

35:13, 14 Anointing oil was olive oil of the finest grade of purity. It was expensive and very valuable. Anointing something with this precious oil showed the high value placed on the anointed object. Jacob was showing the greatest respect for the place where he met with God.

ful—another boy!" 18And with Rachel's last breath (for she died) she named him "Ben-oni" ("Son of my sorrow"); but his father called him "Benjamin" ("Son of my right hand").

19So Rachel died, and was buried near the road to Ephrath (also called Bethlehem). 20And Jacob set up a monument of stones upon her grave, and it is there to this day.

21Then Israel journeyed on and camped beyond the Tower of Eder. 22It was while he was there that Reuben slept with Bilhah, his father's concubine, and someone told Israel about it.

Here are the names of the twelve sons of Jacob:

23The sons of Leah: Reuben, Jacob's oldest child, Simeon, Levi, Judah, Issachar, Zebulun.

24The sons of Rachel: Joseph, Benjamin.

25The sons of Bilhah, Rachel's servant-girl: Dan, Naphtali.

26The sons of Zilpah, Leah's servant-girl: Gad, Asher.

All these were born to him at Paddan-aram.

27So Jacob came at last to Isaac his father at Mamre in Kiriath-arba (now called Hebron), where Abraham too had lived. 28, 29Isaac died soon afterwards, at the ripe old age of 180. And his sons Esau and Jacob buried him.

Esau's descendants

36 Here is a list of the descendants of Esau (also called Edom): 2, 3Esau married three local girls from Canaan:

Adah (daughter of Elon the Hethite),

Oholibamah (daughter of Anah and granddaughter of Zibeon the Hivite),

Basemath (his cousin—she was a daughter of Ishmael—the sister of Nebaioth). 4Esau and Adah had a son named Eliphaz. Esau and Basemath had a son named Reuel.

5Esau and Oholibamah had sons named Jeush, Jalam, and Korah. All these sons were born to Esau in the land of Canaan.

6, 7, 8Then Esau took his wives, children, household servants, cattle and flocks—all the wealth he had gained in the land of Canaan—and moved away from his brother Jacob to Mount Seir. (For there was not land enough to support them both because of all their cattle.)

9Here are the names of Esau's descendants, the Edomites, born to him in Mount Seir:

10, 11, 12Descended from his wife Adah, born to her son Eliphaz were:

Teman, Omar, Zepho, Gatam, Kenaz, Amalek (born to Timna, Eliphaz' concubine).

13, 14Esau also had grandchildren from his wife Basemath. Born to her son Reuel were:

Nahath, Zerah, Shammah, Mizzah.

36:2, 3 *Basemath (his cousin . . .),* implied. Literally, Basemath "the daughter of Ishmael." **36:13, 14** Verse 14 is a repetition of the names listed in verse 5.

35:22 Reuben's sin was costly, although not immediately. As the oldest son, he stood to receive a double portion of the family inheritance and a place of leadership among his people. Reuben may have thought he got away with his sin. No more was mentioned of it until Jacob, on his deathbed, assembled his family for the final blessing. Suddenly, Jacob took away Reuben's double portion and gave it to someone else. The reason? "You slept with one of my wives . . ." (Genesis 49:4).

Sin's consequences can plague us long after the sin is committed. When we do something wrong we may think we can escape unnoticed, only to discover later that the sin has been quietly breeding serious consequences.

36:9 The Edomites were descendants of Esau who lived south and east of the Dead Sea. The country featured rugged mountains and desolate wilderness. Several major roads led through Edom, for it was rich in natural resources. During the Exodus, God told Israel to leave the Edomites alone (Deuteronomy 2:5) because they were "brothers." But Edom refused to let them enter the land, and later they became bitter enemies of King David. The nations of Edom and Israel shared the same ancestor (Isaac) and the same border. Israel looked down on the Edomites because they intermarried with the Canaanites.

15, 16Esau's grandchildren became the heads of clans, as listed here: The clan of Teman, The clan of Omar, The clan of Zepho, The clan of Kenaz, The clan of Korah, The clan of Gatam, The clan of Amalek.

The above clans were the descendants of Eliphaz, the oldest son of Esau and Adah.

17The following clans were the descendants of Reuel, born to Esau and his wife Basemath while they lived in Canaan: The clan of Nahath, The clan of Zerah, The clan of Shammah, The clan of Mizzah.

18, 19And these are the clans named after the sons of Esau and his wife Oholibamah (daughter of Anah): The clan of Jeush, The clan of Jalam, The clan of Korah.

20, 21These are the names of the tribes that descended from Seir, the Horite—one of the native families of the land of Seir: The tribe of Lotan, The tribe of Shobal, The tribe of Zibeon, The tribe of Anah, The tribe of Dishon, The tribe of Ezer, The tribe of Dishan.

22The children of Lotan (the son of Seir) were Hori and Heman. (Lotan had a sister, Timna.)

23The children of Shobal: Alvan, Manahath, Ebal, Shepho, Onam.

24The children of Zibeon: Aiah, Anah. (This is the boy who discovered a hot springs in the wasteland while he was grazing his father's donkeys.)

25The children of Anah: Dishon, Oholibamah.

26The children of Dishon: Hemdan, Eshban, Ithran, Cheran.

27The children of Ezer: Bilhan, Zaavan, Akan.

28, 29, 30 The children of Dishan: Uz, Aran.

31-39These are the names of the kings of Edom (before Israel had her first king):

King Bela (son of Beor), from Dinhabah in Edom.

Succeeded by: King Jobab (son of Zerah), from the city of Bozrah.

Succeeded by: King Husham, from the land of the Temanites.

Succeeded by: King Hadad (son of Bedad), the leader of the forces that defeated the army of Midian when it invaded Moab. His city was Avith.

Succeeded by: King Samlah, from Masrekah.

Succeeded by: King Shaul, from Rehoboth-by-the-River.

Succeeded by: King Baal-hanan (son of Achbor).

Succeeded by: King Hadad, from the city of Paul.

King Hadad's wife was Mehetabel, daughter of Matred and granddaughter of Mezahab.

40-43Here are the names of the sub-tribes of Esau, living in the localities named after themselves: The clan of Timna, The clan of Alvah, The clan of Jetheth, The clan of Oholibamah, The clan of Elah, The clan of Pinon, The clan of Kenaz, The clan of Teman, The clan of Mibzar, The clan of Magdiel, The clan of Iram.

These, then, are the names of the subtribes of Edom, each giving its name to the area it occupied. (All were Edomites, descendants of Esau.)

G. THE STORY OF JOSEPH (37:1—50:26)

Joseph, one of Jacob's twelve sons, was obviously the favorite. Hated by his brothers for this, Joseph was sold to slave traders only to emerge as ruler of all Egypt. Through Joseph, we learn how suffering, no matter how unfair, develops strong character and deep wisdom.

1. Joseph is sold into slavery

37 So Jacob settled again in the land of Canaan, where his father had lived. 2Jacob's son Joseph was now seventeen years old. His job, along with his half-brothers, the sons of his father's wives Bilhah and Zilpah, was to shepherd his father's flocks. But Joseph reported to his father some of the bad things they were doing. 3Now as it happened, Israel loved Joseph more than any of his other children, because Joseph was born to him in his old age. So one day Jacob gave him

36:18 1 Chron 1:35
36:19 Gen 36:1,9
36:20 Gen 14:6 Deut 2:12,22 1 Chron 1:38-42
36:22 1 Chron 1:39
36:23 1 Chron 1:40
36:25 Gen 36:2,5,14, 18 1 Chron 1:41
36:27 1 Chron 1:38,42
36:29,30 Gen 36:20
36:31 Gen 17:6,16 20:14 1 Chron 1:43
36:35 1 Chron 1:46
36:37 1 Chron 1:48
36:40 1 Chron 1:51
37:1 Gen 17:8; 28:4
37:2 Gen 6:9 35:22-26; 41:46
37:3 Gen 37:23,32 44:20

36:15, 16 *grandchildren,* implied. **36:29, 30** These verses repeat the names listed in vss 20, 21. **36:31-39** *succeeded by,* more literally, "succeeded at his death by. . . ." *from the city,* implied. **37:3** *a brightly colored coat,* more literally, "an ornamented tunic," or "long-sleeved tunic."

a special gift—a brightly-colored coat. ⁴His brothers of course noticed their father's partiality, and consequently hated Joseph; they couldn't say a kind word to him. ⁵One night Joseph had a dream and promptly reported the details to his brothers, causing even deeper hatred.

⁶"Listen to this," he proudly announced. ⁷"We were out in the field binding sheaves, and my sheaf stood up, and your sheaves all gathered around it and bowed low before it!"

⁸"So you want to be our king, do you?" his brothers derided. And they hated him both for the dream and for his cocky attitude.

⁹Then he had another dream and told it to his brothers. "Listen to my latest

---

JOSEPH

As a youngster, Joseph was overconfident. His natural self-assurance, increased by being Jacob's favorite son and by knowing of God's designs on his life, was unbearable to his ten older brothers, who eventually conspired against him. But this self-assurance, molded by pain and combined with a personal knowledge of God, allowed him to survive and prosper where most would have failed. He added quiet wisdom to his confidence and won the hearts of everyone he met—Potiphar, the jailer, other prisoners, the king, and after many years, even those ten brothers.

Perhaps you can identify with one or more of these hardships Joseph experienced: he was betrayed and deserted by his family, was exposed to sexual temptation, was punished for doing the right thing, endured a long imprisonment, was forgotten by those he helped. As you read his story, note what Joseph did in each case. His positive response transformed each setback into a step forward. He didn't spend much time asking, "Why?" His approach was, "What shall I do now?" Those who saw his life were aware that wherever Joseph went and whatever he did, God was with him. When you're facing a setback, the beginning of a Joseph-like attitude is to acknowledge that God is with you. There is nothing like the reality of his presence to shed new light on a dark situation.

Strengths and accomplishments:
• Rose in power from slave to ruler of Egypt
• Was known for his personal integrity
• Was a man of spiritual sensitivity
• Prepared a nation to survive a famine

Weakness and mistake:
• His youthful pride caused friction with his brothers

Lessons from his life:
• What matters is not so much the events or circumstances of life, but our response to them
• With God's help any situation can be used for good, even when others intend it for evil

Vital statistics:
• Where: Canaan, Egypt
• Occupation: Shepherd, Slave, Convict, Ruler
• Relatives: Parents: Jacob and Rachel. Eleven brothers. Wife: Asenath. Sons: Manasseh and Ephraim.

Key verses:
"Joseph's suggestions were well received by Pharaoh and his assistants. As they discussed who should be appointed for the job, Pharaoh said, 'Who could do it better than Joseph? For he is a man who is obviously filled with the Spirit of God' " (Genesis 41:37, 38).

Joseph's story is told in Genesis 37—50. He is also mentioned in Hebrews 11:22.

37:3 In Joseph's day, everyone had a cloak. It was used to warm oneself, to bundle up belongings for a trip, to wrap babies, to sit on, or to serve as security for a loan. Most cloaks were plain, knee-length and short-sleeved. In contrast, Joseph's was probably the type of cloak royalty wore—long-sleeved, ankle-length, and colorful. This shows the favoritism Jacob showed Joseph.

It was obvious to the other boys that Joseph was Jacob's favorite son, especially when Joseph received the brightly-colored cloak. This gift aggravated the already strained relations between Joseph and his brothers. Favoritism in families may be unavoidable, but its divisive effects should be minimized. Parents may not be able to change their feelings toward a favorite child, but they can change their actions toward the others.

●**37:6–11** Joseph's brothers were already angry over the possibility of being ruled by their little brother. Joseph then fueled the fire with his immature attitude and boastful manner. No one enjoys a braggart. If you want to tell others about things you have done, share your successes in a way that gives the glory to God. Young Joseph learned his lesson the hard way. His angry brothers sold him into slavery to get rid of him. But later, in Genesis 41:16, Joseph does give God the credit for his successes.

dream," he boasted. "The sun, moon, and eleven stars bowed low before me!" 10This time he told his father as well as his brothers; but his father rebuked him. "What is this?" he asked. "Shall I indeed, and your mother and brothers come and bow before you?" 11His brothers were fit to be tied concerning this affair, but his father gave it quite a bit of thought and wondered what it all meant.

12One day Joseph's brothers took their father's flocks to Shechem to graze them there. 13, 14A few days later Israel called for Joseph, and told him, "Your brothers are over in Shechem grazing the flocks. Go and see how they are getting along, and how it is with the flocks, and bring me word."

"Very good," Joseph replied. So he traveled to Shechem from his home at Hebron Valley. 15A man noticed him wandering in the fields.

"Who are you looking for?" he asked.

16"For my brothers and their flocks," Joseph replied. "Have you seen them?"

17"Yes," the man told him, "they are no longer here. I heard your brothers say they were going to Dothan." So Joseph followed them to Dothan and found them there. 18But when they saw him coming, recognizing him in the distance, they decided to kill him!

19, 20"Here comes that master-dreamer," they exclaimed. "Come on, let's kill him and toss him into a well and tell father that a wild animal has eaten him. Then we'll see what will become of all his dreams!"

21, 22But Reuben hoped to spare Joseph's life. "Let's not kill him," he said; "we'll shed no blood—let's throw him alive into this well here; that way he'll die without our touching him!" (Reuben was planning to get him out later and return him to his father.) 23So when Joseph got there, they pulled off his brightly-colored robe, 24and threw him into an empty well—there was no water in it. 25Then they sat down for supper. Suddenly they noticed a string of camels coming towards them in the distance, probably Ishmaelite traders who were taking gum, spices, and herbs from Gilead to Egypt.

26, 27"Look there," Judah said to the others. "Here come some Ishmaelites. Let's sell Joseph to them! Why kill him and have a guilty conscience? Let's not be responsible for his death, for, after all, he is our brother!" And his brothers agreed. 28So when the traders came by, his brothers pulled Joseph out of the well and sold him to them for twenty pieces of silver, and they took him along to Egypt. 29Some time later, Reuben (who was away when the traders came by) returned to get

37:28 *traders,* literally, "Midianites." **37:29** *who was away when the traders came by,* implied.

37:10
Gen 27:29
Isa 60:14
Phil 2:10
37:11
Ps 106:16
Isa 11:13
Mt 27:18
Acts 7:9
37:12
Gen 33:18; 37:1
37:14
Gen 29:6; 35:27

37:17
2 Kgs 6:13

37:20
Gen 37:33
Prov 1:11
37:21
Gen 42:22
37:22
Gen 37:29
37:23
Gen 37:3
37:24
Jer 38:6
37:25
Gen 25:16-18
31:23; 37:28
Jer 8:22; 46:11
37:27
Ex 21:16
Neh 5:8
37:28
Gen 39:1; 45:4
Lev 27:5
Judg 8:22-24
Acts 7:9
37:29
Gen 37:34
44:13
Num 14:6

JOSEPH GOES TO MEET HIS BROTHERS
Jacob asked Joseph to go find his brothers, who were grazing their flocks near Shechem. When Joseph arrived, he learned that his brothers had gone on to Dothan, which lay along a major trade route to Egypt. There the jealous brothers sold Joseph as a slave to a group of Ishmaelite traders on their way to Egypt.

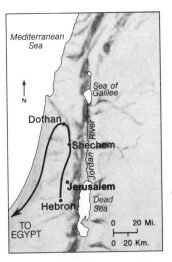

37:19, 20 Can your jealousy toward someone make you feel like killing him? Before you say, "Of course not," look at what happened in this story. Ten men were suddenly willing to kill their own brother over a colored coat. Their deep jealousy had grown into ugly rage, blinding them completely to what was right. Jealousy can be hard to recognize because our reasons for it seem to make sense. Left unchecked, jealousy can grow quickly and lead to more serious sins. The longer you let jealous feelings exist, the harder it is to correct them. The time to deal with jealousy is when you notice yourself keeping score of what others have.

37:26, 27 The brothers were worried about having the guilt of Joseph's death on them. Judah suggested an option that was not right, but would leave them guiltless of murder. Sometimes we jump at a solution because it is "the lesser of two evils," but it still is not the right action to take. When people propose a seemingly workable solution, first ask the question, "Is it right?"

●**37:28** Although Joseph's brothers didn't kill him outright, they thought he was as good as dead (or at least out of their lives) when they sold him to slave traders. They were quite willing to shift the blame to these cruel men. Joseph faced a 30-day journey through the desert, probably chained and on foot. He would be treated like baggage and, once in Egypt, would be sold as a piece of merchandise.

Joseph out of the well. When Joseph wasn't there, he ripped at his clothes in anguish and frustration.

37:30
Gen 5:24
42:13,32,36
37:32
Lk 15:30
37:33
Gen 37:20
44:28
37:34
Gen 37:29
44:13
37:35
Gen 31:43
44:29
2 Sam 12:17
Ps 77:2
37:36
Gen 39:1; 40:4

30"The child is gone; and I, where shall I go now?" he wept to his brothers. 31Then the brothers killed a goat and spattered its blood on Joseph's coat, 32and took the coat to their father and asked him to identify it.

"We found this in the field," they told him. "Is it Joseph's coat or not?" 33Their father recognized it at once.

"Yes," he sobbed, "it is my son's coat. A wild animal has eaten him. Joseph is without doubt torn in pieces."

34Then Israel tore his garments and put on sackcloth and mourned for his son in deepest mourning for many weeks. 35His family all tried to comfort him, but it was no use.

"I will die in mourning for my son," he would say, and then break down and cry.

36Meanwhile, in Egypt, the traders sold Joseph to Potiphar, an officer of the

---

Parents are usually the best judges of their children's character. Jacob summarized the personality of his son Reuben by comparing him to wild waves. Except when frozen, water has no stable shape of its own. It always shapes itself to its container or environment. Reuben usually had good intentions but seemed unable to stand against a crowd. His instability made him hard to trust. He had both private and public values, but these contradicted each other. He went along with his brothers in their action against Joseph while hoping to counteract the evil in private. The plan failed. Compromise has a way of destroying convictions. Without convictions, lack of direction will destroy life. It would seem that Reuben's action in sleeping with his father's concubine showed how little he had left of the integrity he had displayed earlier in life.

How consistent are your public and private lives? We may want to think they are separate, but we can't deny they affect each other. What convictions are present in your life at all times? How closely does Jacob's description of his son—"unstable as the wild waves"—describe your life?

Strengths and accomplishments:
● Saved Joseph's life by talking the other brothers out of murder
● Showed intense love for his father by offering his own sons as a guarantee that Benjamin's life would be safe

Weaknesses and mistakes:
● Gave in quickly to group pressure
● Did not directly protect Joseph from his brothers, although as eldest son he had the authority to do so
● Slept with his father's concubine

Lessons from his life:
● Public and private integrity must be the same, or one will destroy the other
● Punishment for sin may not be immediate, but it is certain

Vital statistics:
● Where: Canaan, Egypt
● Occupation: Shepherd
● Relatives: Parents: Jacob and Leah. Eleven brothers.

Key verse:
"But you are unruly as the wild waves of the sea, and you shall be first no longer. I am demoting you, for you slept with one of my wives and thus dishonored me" (Genesis 49:4).

Reuben's story is told in Genesis 29—50.

37:30 Reuben returned to the pit to find Joseph, but Joseph was gone. His first response was "What is going to happen to me?" rather than "What is going to happen to Joseph?" When you get into a tough situation, are you always concerned first about yourself? Consider the person who is most affected by the problem. This may clear up the problem for you as well.

37:33, 34 To cover their evil action, Jacob's sons deceived their father into thinking Joseph was dead. Jacob himself had deceived others many times (even *his* father, in 27:35). Now, though blessed by God, he still had to face the consequences of his sins. God may not have punished Jacob immediately for his sins of deceit, but the consequences came nevertheless and stayed with him for the rest of his life.

●**37:36** Imagine the culture shock Joseph experienced upon arriving in Egypt. Joseph had lived as a nomad, traveling the countryside with his family, caring for sheep. Suddenly he was thrust into the world's most advanced civilized society with great pyramids, beautiful homes, sophisticated people, and a new language. While Joseph saw Egypt's skill and intelligence at their best, he also saw the Egyptians' spiritual blindness: they worshiped countless gods pertaining to every facet of life.

Pharaoh—the king of Egypt. Potiphar was captain of the palace guard, the chief executioner.

2. Judah and Tamar

38 About this time, Judah left home and moved to Adullam and lived there with a man named Hirah. ²There he met and married a Canaanite girl—the daughter of Shua. ³, ⁴, ⁵They lived at Chezib and had three sons, Er, Onan, and Shelah. These names were given to them by their mother, except for Er, who was named by his father.

⁶When his oldest son Er grew up, Judah arranged for him to marry a girl named Tamar. ⁷But Er was a wicked man, and so the Lord killed him.

⁸Then Judah said to Er's brother, Onan, "You must marry Tamar, as our law requires of a dead man's brother; so that her sons from you will be your brother's heirs."

⁹But Onan was not willing to have a child who would not be counted as his own, and so, although he married her, whenever he went in to sleep with her, he spilled the sperm on the bed to prevent her from having a baby which would be his brother's. ¹⁰So far as the Lord was concerned, it was very wrong of him [to deny a child to his deceased brother], so he killed him, too. ¹¹Then Judah told Tamar, his daughter-in-law, not to marry again at that time, but to return to her childhood home and to her parents, and to remain a widow there until his youngest son Shelah was old enough to marry her. (But he didn't really intend for Shelah to do this, for fear God would kill him, too, just as he had his two brothers.) So Tamar went home to her parents.

¹²In the process of time Judah's wife died. After the time of mourning was over, Judah and his friend Hirah, the Adullamite, went to Timnah to supervise the shearing of his sheep. ¹³When someone told Tamar that her father-in-law had left for the sheep-shearing at Timnah, ¹⁴and realizing by now that she was not going to be permitted to marry Shelah, though he was fully grown, she laid aside her widow's clothing and covered herself with a veil to disguise herself, and sat beside the road at the entrance to the village of Enaim, which is on the way to Timnah.

¹⁵Judah noticed her as he went by and thought she was a prostitute, since her face was veiled. ¹⁶So he stopped and propositioned her to sleep with him, not realizing of course that she was his own daughter-in-law.

"How much will you pay me?" she asked.

¹⁷"I'll send you a young goat from my flock," he promised.

"What pledge will you give me, so that I can be sure you will send it?" she asked.

¹⁸"Well, what do you want?" he inquired.

"Your identification seal and your walking stick," she replied. So he gave them to her and she let him come and sleep with her; and she became pregnant as a result.

38:9 *although he married her,* implied. *he spilled the sperm on the bed,* literally, "spilled it on the ground."

38:1 Josh 12:15 15:35 1 Sam 22:1

38:2 Gen 24:3; 34:2 38:12

38:3 Gen 46:12 Num 26:19

38:6 Mt 1:3

38:7 Gen 6:5,13:13 19:13; 38:10 2 Chron 33:6

38:8 Lev 18:16 Num 36:8 Deut 25:5-10 Mt 22:24

38:10 2 Sam 11:27 1 Chron 21:7

38:11 Ruth 1:13

38:12 Gen 31:19 Josh 13:23-27 1 Sam 25:4 2 Sam 13:23-27

38:14 Gen 23:10 Josh 15:34

38:15 Gen 24:65

38:16 2 Sam 13:11 Deut 23:18 Ezek 16:33

38:17 Gen 38:20,25

38:18 Gen 41:42 Hos 4:11

●**38:1ff** This chapter vividly portrays the immoral character of Judah in contrast to the moral character of Joseph. Judah's character was tainted by jealousy and immorality. He was soon to learn some difficult lessons. In the following chapter, we see Joseph's godliness. His integrity and wise choices reflected his godly character. His faithfulness was rewarded with blessings greater than he could imagine.

38:8–10 This law about marrying a widow "in the family" is explained in Deuteronomy 25:5-10. The reason for the law was to ensure that a widow with no children would have an heir to whom she could pass on her inheritance. Because Judah's son (Tamar's husband) had no children, there was no family line through which the inheritance and the blessing of the covenant could continue. God killed Onan because he refused to fulfill his obligation to God's law and to Tamar.

38:11–26 When Tamar revealed she was pregnant, Judah (who unknowingly had gotten her pregnant) moved to have her killed. Judah had concealed his own sin, yet he came down harshly on Tamar. Often the sins we are trying to cover up in our lives are the ones that anger us most when we see them in others. If you find yourself feeling indignant at the sins of others, you may have a similar tendency to sin which you do not wish to face.

38:15–23 Why does this story seem to take a light view of prostitution? Prostitutes were common in heathen cultures such as Canaan. Public prostitutes served heathen goddesses and were common elements of the religious cults. They were more highly respected than private prostitutes who were sometimes punished when caught. Tamar was driven to prostitution because of her intense desire to have children; Judah was driven to prostitution because of lust. Neither case was justified.

38:18 A seal was a form of identification much like a fingerprint. It was usually a unique design carved in stone and worn on a ring or necklace that was inseparable from its owner. Persons of wealth or prestige used seals to make marks in clay or wax as a signature. Obviously, since Tamar had Judah's seal, she could prove he had been with her.

19Afterwards she resumed wearing her widow's clothing as usual. 20Judah asked his friend Hirah the Adullamite to take the young goat back to her, and to pick up the pledges he had given her, but Hirah couldn't find her!

21So he asked around of the men of the city, "Where does the prostitute live who was soliciting out beside the road at the entrance of the village?"

"But we've never had a public prostitute here," they replied. 22So he returned to Judah and told him he couldn't find her anywhere, and what the men of the place had told him.

23"Then let her keep them!" Judah exclaimed. "We tried our best. We'd be the laughingstock of the town to go back again."

24About three months later word reached Judah that Tamar, his daughter-in-law, was pregnant, obviously as a result of prostitution.

"Bring her out and burn her," Judah shouted.

25But as they were taking her out to kill her she sent this message to her father-in-law: "The man who owns this identification seal and walking stick is the father of my child. Do you recognize them?"

26Judah admitted that they were his and said, "She is more in the right than I am, because I refused to keep my promise to give her to my son Shelah." But he did not marry her.

27In due season the time of her delivery arrived and she had twin sons. 28As they were being born, the midwife tied a scarlet thread around the wrist of the child who appeared first, 29but he drew back his hand and the other baby was actually the first to be born. "Where did *you* come from!" she exclaimed. And ever after he was called Perez (meaning "Bursting Out"). 30Then, soon afterwards, the baby with the scarlet thread on his wrist was born, and he was named Zerah.

3. Joseph is thrown into jail

39 When Joseph arrived in Egypt as a captive of the Ishmaelite traders, he was purchased from them by Potiphar, a member of the personal staff of Pharaoh, the king of Egypt. Now this man Potiphar was the captain of the king's bodyguard and his chief executioner. 2The Lord greatly blessed Joseph there in the home of his master, so that everything he did succeeded. 3Potiphar noticed this and realized that the Lord was with Joseph in a very special way. 4So Joseph naturally became quite a favorite with him. Soon he was put in charge of the administration of Potiphar's household, and all of his business affairs. 5At once the Lord began

38:23
Prov 6:32,33

38:24
Gen 34:31
Lev 20:10; 21:9
Eccles 7:26

38:25
Gen 37:32

38:26
1 Sam 24:17
Ezek 16:52

38:27
Gen 25:24

38:29
Gen 46:12
Num 26:20
Ruth 4:12
1 Chron 2:4
Mt 1:3
Lk 3:33

39:1
Acts 7:9

39:2
Gen 21:22
26:24,28; 28:15

39:4
Gen 32:5; 41:40
Prov 14:35
17:2; 27:18

39:5
Deut 28:3-6

WOMEN IN JESUS' FAMILY TREE	Tamar	Canaanite	Genesis 38:1–30
	Rahab	Canaanite	Joshua 6:22–25
	Ruth	Moabite	Ruth 4:13–22
	Bath-sheba	Israelite	2 Samuel 12:24, 25

38:29, 30 Perez was born as a result of incest and prostitution, gross sins to the Israelites. Yet he became an ancestor of Christ, who would die for the sins of everyone (Matthew 1:3).

39:1 The exact date of Joseph's arrival in Egypt is highly debated. Many scholars believe he arrived during the period of the Hyksos rulers. The Hyksos were foreigners who came from the region of Canaan. They invaded Egypt and controlled the land for almost 150 years. Although the dates for the Hyksos rule are usually placed after the reign of Joseph as stated in the Genesis chronology, those dates are uncertain. If Joseph did arrive in the period of the Hyksos, they would have had no problems promoting a brilliant young foreigner up the royal ladder since they were foreigners themselves.

39:1 Ancient Egypt was a land of great contrasts. People were either rich beyond measure or poverty stricken. There wasn't much middle ground. Joseph found himself serving Potiphar, an extremely rich member of Pharaoh's cabinet. Rich families like

Potiphar's had elaborate homes two or three stories tall with beautiful gardens and balconies. They enjoyed live entertainment at home as they chose delicious fruit from expensive bowls. They were surrounded by alabaster vases of flowers, paintings, beautiful rugs, and hand-carved chairs. Dinner was served on golden tableware, and their rooms were lit with gold candlesticks. The servants, such as Joseph, worked on the first floor, while the family occupied the upper stories.

●**39:2ff** As a prisoner and slave, Joseph could have seen his situation as hopeless. Instead, he did his best with each small task given him. His diligence and positive attitude were soon noticed by the jail warden, who promoted him to prison administrator. Are you in the midst of a seemingly hopeless predicament? At work, at home, or at school, follow Joseph's example by taking each small task and doing your best. Remember how God turned Joseph's situation around. He will see your efforts and can reverse even overwhelming odds.

blessing Potiphar for Joseph's sake. All his household affairs began to run smoothly, his crops flourished and his flocks multiplied. 6So Potiphar gave Joseph the complete administrative responsibility over everything he owned. He hadn't a worry in the world with Joseph there, except to decide what he wanted to eat! Joseph, by the way, was a very handsome young man.

7One day at about this time Potiphar's wife began making eyes at Joseph, and suggested that he come and sleep with her.

8Joseph refused. "Look," he told her, "my master trusts me with everything in the entire household; 9he himself has no more authority here than I have! He has held back nothing from me except you yourself because you are his wife. How can I do such a wicked thing as this? It would be a great sin against God."

10But she kept on with her suggestions day after day, even though he refused to listen, and kept out of her way as much as possible. 11Then one day as he was in the house going about his work—as it happened, no one else was around at the time—12she came and grabbed him by the sleeve demanding, "Sleep with me." He tore himself away, but as he did, his jacket slipped off and she was left holding it as he fled from the house. 13When she saw that she had his jacket, and that he had fled, 14, 15she began screaming; and when the other men around the place came running in to see what had happened, she was crying hysterically. "My husband had to bring in this Hebrew slave to insult us!" she sobbed. "He tried to rape me, but when I screamed, he ran, and forgot to take his jacket."

16She kept the jacket, and when her husband came home that night, 17she told him her story.

"That Hebrew slave you've had around here tried to rape me, 18and I was only saved by my screams. He fled, leaving his jacket behind!"

19Well, when her husband heard his wife's story, he was furious. 20He threw Joseph into prison, where the king's prisoners were kept in chains. 21But the Lord was with Joseph there, too, and was kind to him by granting him favor with the chief jailer. 22In fact, the jailer soon handed over the entire prison administration to Joseph, so that all the other prisoners were responsible to him. 23The chief jailer had no more worries after that, for Joseph took care of everything, and the Lord was with him so that everything ran smoothly and well.

Joseph interprets two dreams

40 Some time later it so happened that the king of Egypt became angry with both his chief baker and his chief butler, so he jailed them both in the prison where Joseph was, in the castle of Potiphar, the captain of the guard, who was the chief executioner. 4They remained under arrest there for quite some time, and Potiphar assigned Joseph to wait on them. 5One night each of them had a dream. 6The next morning Joseph noticed that they looked dejected and sad.

7"What in the world is the matter?" he asked.

39:12 *sleeve.* The Hebrew word is not specific.

39:6 Gen 29:17; Ex 2:2; 1 Sam 16:12,18; Lk 16:10; Acts 7:20
39:7 Ps 119:37; Prov 2:16; 5:3; 7:13; Ezek 23:5
39:8 Gen 39:5; Prov 1:10; 6:23,24
39:9 2 Sam 12:13; Ps 51:4
39:10 1 Cor 6:18; 15:33; 1 Thess 5:22; 2 Tim 2:22
39:12 Prov 7:13; Eccles 7:26; Ezek 16:30
39:14 Isa 54:17
39:17 Ex 20:16; 23:1; Ps 37:14; 55:3
39:19 Prov 6:34; 18:17
39:20 Gen 40:1-3,15; 41:12,14; Ps 105:18
39:21 Gen 39:2,3; 49:25; Acts 7:9
39:22 Gen 39:4; 41:40
39:23 Gen 39:3; Ps 1:3
40:1 Neh 1:11
40:4 Gen 37:36; 39:1
40:5 Gen 20:3; 37:5-10; 40:8; 41:1-7,11

●**39:9** Potiphar's wife failed to seduce Joseph, who resisted this temptation by saying, "It would be a great sin against God." Joseph didn't say, "I'd be hurting you," or "I'd be sinning against Potiphar," or "I'd be sinning against myself." When under pressure, those kinds of excuses are easily rationalized away. Remember that sexual sin is not just between two consenting adults. It is an act of disobedience to God.

39:10-15 Joseph avoided Potiphar's advances and finally *ran* from her. He refused her advances and finally *ran* from her. Sometimes merely trying to avoid temptation is not enough; we must turn and run, especially when the temptations are too great for us. This is often the case in sexual temptations.

●**39:20** Prisons were grim places with vile conditions. They were used to house forced laborers or those accused and awaiting trial like Joseph. In ancient days, prisoners were guilty until proven innocent. Many prisoners never made it to court, for trials were held at the whim of the ruler. Joseph was in prison two years before appearing before Pharaoh, and then he was called out to interpret a dream, not to stand trial.

40:1 "Pharaoh" was the general name for all the kings of Egypt. It was a title like "Mr. President," used to address the country's leader. The Pharaohs in Genesis and Exodus were not the same man.

40:1-3 The baker and wine taster (cupbearer) were two of the most trusted men in Pharaoh's kingdom. The baker was in charge of making the king's food, and the wine-taster tasted all the king's food and drink *before* giving it to Pharaoh, in case any of it was contaminated or poisoned. These trusted men must have been suspected of a serious wrong to be thrown into prison. Perhaps Pharaoh suspected the men of conspiring against him. Later the wine taster was released and the baker executed.

40:8
Gen 41:15,16
Job 33:15,16
Dan 2:28

8And they replied, "We both had dreams last night, but there is no one here to tell us what they mean."

"Interpreting dreams is God's business," Joseph replied. "Tell me what you saw."

40:9
Gen 37:5
Judg 7:13

40:12
Gen 41:12
Judg 7:14
Dan 2:36

40:13
Gen 40:19,20

40:14
Josh 2:12
1 Sam 20:13,14

40:15
Gen 37:28
39:1,20

40:16
Gen 40:1,2

9, 10The butler told his dream first. "In my dream," he said, "I saw a vine with three branches that began to bud and blossom, and soon there were clusters of ripe grapes. 11I was holding Pharaoh's wine cup in my hand, so I took the grapes and squeezed the juice into it, and gave it to him to drink."

12"I know what the dream means," Joseph said. "The three branches mean three days! 13Within three days Pharaoh is going to take you out of prison and give you back your job again as his chief butler. 14And please have some pity on me when you are back in his favor, and mention me to Pharaoh, and ask him to let me out of here. 15For I was kidnapped from my homeland among the Hebrews, and now this—here I am in jail when I did nothing to deserve it."

16When the chief baker saw that the first dream had such a good meaning, he told his dream to Joseph, too.

"In my dream," he said, "there were three baskets of pastries on my head. 17In the top basket were all kinds of bakery goods for Pharaoh, but the birds came and ate them."

40:18
Gen 40:12
41:13

40:19
Gen 40:22
41:13
Deut 21:22

40:20
Gen 40:13,18
2 Kgs 25:27-30
Jer 52:31-34

40:22
Gen 40:19

40:23
Gen 40:14; 41:9

18, 19"The three baskets mean three days," Joseph told him. "Three days from now Pharaoh will take off your head and impale your body on a pole, and the birds will come and pick off your flesh!"

20Pharaoh's birthday came three days later, and he held a party for all of his officials and household staff. He sent for his chief butler and chief baker, and they were brought to him from the prison. 21Then he restored the chief butler to his former position; 22but he sentenced the chief baker to be impaled, just as Joseph had predicted. 23Pharaoh's wine taster, however, promptly forgot all about Joseph, never giving him a thought.

PARALLELS BETWEEN JOSEPH AND JESUS Genesis 37-50	*Joseph*	*Parallels*	*Jesus*
	37:3	His father loved him dearly	Matthew 3:17
	37:2	A shepherd of his father's sheep	John 10:11, 27–29
	37:13, 14	Sent by father to brothers	Hebrews 2:11
	37:4	Hated by brothers	John 7:4, 5
	37:20	Others plotted to harm them	John 11:53
	39:7	Tempted	Matthew 4:1
	37:26	Taken to Egypt	Matthew 2:14, 15
	37:23	Robes taken from them	John 19:23, 24
	37:28	Sold for the price of a slave	Matthew 26:15
	39:20	Bound in chains	Matthew 27:2
	39:16–18	Falsely accused	Matthew 26:59, 60
	40:2, 3	Placed with two other prisoners, one who was saved and the other lost	Luke 23:32
	41:46	Both 30 years old at the beginning of public recognition	Luke 3:23
	41:41	Exalted after suffering	Philippians 2:9–11
	45:1–15	Forgave those who wronged them	Luke 23:34
	45:7	Saved their nation	Matthew 1:21
	50:20	What men did to hurt them God turned to good	1 Corinthians 2:7, 8

40:8 When the subject of dreams came up, Joseph focused everyone's attention on God. Rather than use the situation to make himself look good, he turned it into a powerful witness for God. One of the secrets of effective witnessing is to recognize opportunities to relate God to the other person's experience. When the opportunity comes, we must have the courage to speak, as Joseph did.

●**40:23** When Pharaoh's wine taster was freed from prison, he forgot about Joseph, even though he had Joseph to thank for his freedom. It was two full years before Joseph had another opportunity to be freed (41:1). Yet Joseph's faith was deep and he would be ready when the next chance occurred. When we feel passed by, overlooked, or forgotten, we shouldn't be surprised that people are often ungrateful. In situations like this, work at trusting God as Joseph did. More opportunities may be waiting.

4. Joseph is placed in charge of Egypt
Pharaoh's strange dream

41 One night two years later, Pharaoh dreamed that he was standing on the bank of the Nile River, 2when suddenly, seven sleek, fat cows came up out of the river and began grazing in the grass. 3Then seven other cows came up from the river, but they were very skinny and all their ribs stood out. They went over and stood beside the fat cows. 4Then the skinny cows ate the fat ones! At which point, Pharaoh woke up!

5Soon he fell asleep again and had a second dream. This time he saw seven heads of grain on one stalk, with every kernel well formed and plump. 6Then, suddenly, seven more heads appeared on the stalk, but these were shriveled and withered by the east wind. 7And these thin heads swallowed up the seven plump, well-formed heads! Then Pharaoh woke up again and realized it was all a dream. 8Next morning, as he thought about it, he became very concerned as to what the dreams might mean; he called for all the magicians and sages of Egypt and told them about it, but not one of them could suggest what his dreams meant. 9Then the king's wine taster spoke up. "Today I remember my sin!" he said. 10"Some time ago when you were angry with a couple of us and put me and the chief baker in jail in the castle of the captain of the guard, 11the chief baker and I each had a dream one night. 12We told the dreams to a young Hebrew fellow there who was a slave of the captain of the guard, and he told us what our dreams meant. 13And everything happened just as he said: I was restored to my position of wine taster, and the chief baker was executed, and impaled on a pole."

14Pharaoh sent at once for Joseph. He was brought hastily from the dungeon, and after a quick shave and change of clothes, came in before Pharaoh.

15"I had a dream last night," Pharaoh told him, "and none of these men can tell me what it means. But I have heard that you can interpret dreams, and that is why I have called for you."

16"I can't do it by myself," Joseph replied, "but God will tell you what it means!"

17So Pharaoh told him the dream. "I was standing upon the bank of the Nile River," he said, 18"when suddenly, seven fat, healthy-looking cows came up out of the river and began grazing along the river bank. 19But then seven other cows came up from the river, very skinny and bony—in fact, I've never seen such poor-looking specimens in all the land of Egypt. 20And these skinny cattle ate up the seven fat ones that had come out first, 21and afterwards they were still as skinny as before! Then I woke up.

22"A little later I had another dream. This time there were seven heads of grain on one stalk, and all seven heads were plump and full. 23Then, out of the same stalk, came seven withered, thin heads. 24And the thin heads swallowed up the fat ones! I told all this to my magicians, but not one of them could tell me the meaning."

25"Both dreams mean the same thing," Joseph told Pharaoh. "God was telling you what he is going to do here in the land of Egypt. 26The seven fat cows (and also the seven fat, well-formed heads of grain) mean that there are seven years of prosperity ahead. 27The seven skinny cows (and also the seven thin and withered heads of grain) indicate that there will be seven years of famine following the seven years of prosperity.

28"So God has showed you what he is about to do: 29The next seven years will be

41:2
Job 8:11
Isa 19:7

41:3
Gen 41:20,21

41:4
1 Kgs 3:15

41:6
Ezek 17:10
19:12

41:8
Ex 7:11
Dan 2:1-3; 4:5
Mt 2:1

41:9
Gen 40:14,23

41:10
Gen 40:2

41:11
Gen 40:5-8

41:12
Gen 40:12-19

41:13
Gen 40:22

41:14
Ex 10:16
Ps 105:16-22

41:15
Gen 41:8
Dan 2:25

41:16
Gen 40:8
Num 12:6
Dan 2:28-30
Acts 3:12

41:17
Gen 41:1-7,
26,27

41:18
Gen 41:28,32

41:26
Gen 40:12,18

41:27
Gen 41:30,54
2 Sam 24:13
2 Kgs 8:1

41:29
Gen 41:47

41:8 Magicians and sages were common in the palaces of ancient rulers. Their job description included studying sacred arts and sciences, reading the stars, interpreting dreams, predicting the future, and performing magic. These men had power (see Exodus 7:11, 12), but their power was satanic. They were unable to interpret Pharaoh's dream, but God had revealed it to Joseph in prison.

●**41:14** Our most important opportunities may come when we least expect them. Joseph was brought hastily from the dungeon and

pushed before Pharaoh. Did he have time to prepare? Yes and no. He had no warning that he would be suddenly pulled from prison and questioned by the king. Yet Joseph was ready for almost anything because of his right relationship with God. It was not Joseph's knowledge of dreams that helped him interpret their meaning. It was his knowledge of God. Be ready for opportunities by getting to know more about God. Then you will be ready to take on almost anything that comes your way.

41:28–36 After interpreting Pharaoh's dream, Joseph gave the

41:30
Gen 47:13

41:32
Gen 37:9
Job 33:14
Isa 14:24; 46:10

41:33
Gen 41:39
Dan 4:27

41:34
Ex 18:19
Deut 1:13
2 Chron 34:12

41:36
Gen 47:13

41:37
Prov 25:11
Acts 7:10

41:38
Job 32:8
Dan 4:8,18
Dan 5:11,14

41:39
Gen 41:28,33

41:40
Gen 39:4,22
42:6; 45:8
Ps 105:21
Prov 22:29
Acts 7:10

41:41
Esth 10:3
Prov 17:2
Dan 6:3

41:42
Esth 3:10
Esth 6:8

41:44
Gen 45:8
Ps 105:21,22

41:45
Ezek 30:17

41:46
Gen 37:2; 50:22

41:47
Gen 26:12

41:48
Gen 47:21

41:49
Judg 6:5; 7:12
1 Sam 13:5

41:50
Gen 46:20

41:51
Gen 48:5
Deut 33:17
Prov 31:7

a period of great prosperity throughout all the land of Egypt; 30but afterwards there will be seven years of famine so great that all the prosperity will be forgotten and wiped out; famine will consume the land. 31The famine will be so terrible that even the memory of the good years will be erased. 32The double dream gives double impact, showing that what I have told you is certainly going to happen, for God has decreed it, and it is going to happen soon. 33My suggestion is that you find the wisest man in Egypt and put him in charge of administering a nation-wide farm program. 34, 35Let Pharaoh divide Egypt into five administrative districts, and let the officials of these districts gather into the royal storehouses all the excess crops of the next seven years, 36so that there will be enough to eat when the seven years of famine come. Otherwise, disaster will surely strike."

Joseph becomes a ruler

37Joseph's suggestions were well received by Pharaoh and his assistants. 38As they discussed who should be appointed for the job, Pharaoh said, "Who could do it better than Joseph? For he is a man who is obviously filled with the Spirit of God." 39Turning to Joseph, Pharaoh said to him, "Since God has revealed the meaning of the dreams to you, you are the wisest man in the country! 40I am hereby appointing you to be in charge of this entire project. What you say goes, throughout all the land of Egypt. I alone will outrank you."

41, 42Then Pharaoh placed his own signet ring on Joseph's finger as a token of his authority, and dressed him in beautiful clothing and placed the royal gold chain about his neck and declared, "See, I have placed you in charge of all the land of Egypt."

43Pharaoh also gave Joseph the chariot of his second-in-command, and wherever he went the shout arose, "Kneel down!" 44And Pharaoh declared to Joseph, "I, the king of Egypt, swear that you shall have complete charge over all the land of Egypt."

45Pharaoh gave him a name meaning "He has the god-like power of life and death!" And he gave him a wife, a girl named Asenath, daughter of Potiphera, priest of Heliopolis. So Joseph became famous throughout the land of Egypt. 46He was thirty years old as he entered the service of the king. Joseph went out from the presence of Pharaoh, and began traveling all across the land.

47And sure enough, for the next seven years there were bumper crops everywhere. 48During those years, Joseph requisitioned for the government a portion of all the crops grown throughout Egypt, storing them in nearby cities. 49After seven years of this, the granaries were full to overflowing, and there was so much that no one kept track of the amount.

50During this time before the arrival of the first of the famine years, two sons were born to Joseph by Asenath, the daughter of Potiphera, priest of the sun god Re of Heliopolis. 51Joseph named his oldest son Manasseh (meaning "Made to Forget"—what he meant was that God had made up to him for all the anguish of his youth, and for the loss of his father's home). 52The second boy was named Ephraim

41:34, 35 *Let Pharaoh divide Egypt into five administrative districts,* or, "Let Pharaoh appoint officials to collect a fifth of all the crops . . ."

---

king a survival plan for the next 14 years. The only way to prevent starvation was through careful planning; without a "famine plan" Egypt would have turned from might to ruin. Many find detailed planning boring or unnecessary. But believers must recognize that planning is a responsibility, not an option. Joseph was able to save a nation by translating God's plan for Egypt into practical actions (implementation). We must take time to translate God's plan for us into practical actions too.

●**41:38–40** Joseph rose quickly to the top, from prison walls to Pharaoh's palace. His training for this important position involved being a slave first and then a prisoner. In each situation he learned the importance of serving God and others. Whatever your situation, no matter how undesirable, consider it part of your training program for future service to God.

●**41:45** Pharaoh may have been trying to acculturate Joseph by giving him an Egyptian name and wife. He probably wanted to (1) play down the fact that Joseph was a nomadic shepherd, an occupation disliked by the Egyptians, (2) make Joseph's name easier for Egyptians to pronounce and remember, and (3) demonstrate how highly he was honored by giving him the daughter of a prominent Egyptian official.

●**41:46** Joseph was 30 years old when he became governor of Egypt. He was 17 when he was sold into slavery by his brothers. Therefore, he had spent 11 years as an Egyptian slave and two years in prison.

(meaning "Fruitful"—"For God has made me fruitful in this land of my slavery," he said). 53So at last the seven years of plenty came to an end. 54Then the seven years of famine began, just as Joseph had predicted. There were crop failures in all the surrounding countries too, but in Egypt there was plenty of grain in the storehouses. 55The people began to starve. They pleaded with Pharaoh for food, and he sent them to Joseph. "Do whatever he tells you to," he instructed them.

56, 57So now, with severe famine all over the world, Joseph opened up the storehouses and sold grain to the Egyptians and to those from other lands who came to Egypt to buy grain from Joseph.

41:54
Gen 41:27
45:11
Acts 7:11

41:55
Gen 41:40,41,
49
Jer 14:1

41:57
Gen 42:5; 50:20
Ps 105:16

5. Joseph and his brothers meet in Egypt

42 When Jacob heard that there was grain available in Egypt he said to his sons, "Why are you standing around looking at one another? 2I have heard that there is grain available in Egypt. Go down and buy some for us before we all starve to death."

3So Joseph's ten older brothers went down to Egypt to buy grain. 4However, Jacob wouldn't let Joseph's younger brother Benjamin go with them, for fear some harm might happen to him [as it had to his brother Joseph]. 5So it was that Israel's sons arrived in Egypt along with many others from many lands to buy food, for the famine was as severe in Canaan as it was everywhere else.

6Since Joseph was governor of all Egypt, and in charge of the sale of the grain, it was to him that his brothers came, and bowed low before him, with their faces to the earth. 7Joseph recognized them instantly, but pretended he didn't.

"Where are you from?" he demanded roughly.

"From the land of Canaan," they replied. "We have come to buy grain." 8, 9Then Joseph remembered the dreams of long ago! But he said to them, "You are spies. You have come to see how destitute the famine has made our land."

10"No, no," they exclaimed. "We have come to buy food. 11We are all brothers and honest men, sir! We are not spies!"

12"Yes, you are," he insisted. "You have come to see how weak we are."

13"Sir," they said, "there are twelve of us brothers, and our father is in the land of Canaan. Our youngest brother is there with our father, and one of our brothers is dead."

14"So?" Joseph asked. "What does that prove? You are spies. 15This is the way I will test your story: I swear by the life of Pharaoh that you are not going to leave Egypt until this youngest brother comes here. 16One of you go and get your brother! I'll keep the rest of you here, bound in prison. Then we'll find out whether your story is true or not. If it turns out that you don't have a younger brother, then I'll know you are spies."

17So he threw them all into jail for three days.

42:1
Acts 7:12

42:2
Gen 43:2; 45:9

42:3
Gen 42:13

42:4
Gen 43:8

42:5
Gen 41:57
Acts 7:11

42:6
Ps 105:16-21

42:7
Gen 42:14-17

42:8
Gen 37:2,6-9

42:9
Gen 42:16,
30-34

42:10
Gen 27:29
37:8; 42:2

42:11
Gen 42:19,
31-34

42:13
Gen 37:30
42:4; 43:7
44:20; 46:8-26

42:14
Gen 42:9

42:15
Gen 42:34

42:17
Gen 40:4

42:3 *ten older,* implied.   **42:4** *[as it had to his brother Joseph],* implied.   **42:14** *What does that prove?* Literally, "It is as I said: you are spies."

41:54 Famine was a catastrophe in ancient times. Almost perfect conditions were needed to produce good crops, because there were no chemical fertilizers or pesticides. Any variances in the delicate balance of rain or insects could cause crop failure and great hunger, for the people relied almost exclusively on their own crops for food. Lack of storage, refrigeration, or transportation turned an average famine into a desperate situation. The famine Joseph prepared for was described as "terrible." Without God's intervention, the Egyptian nation would have crumbled.

42:1 Why was grain so valuable in those days? As a food source it was universal and used in nearly everything eaten. It could be dried and stored much longer than any vegetables, milk products, or meat. It was so important that it was even used as money.

42:4 Jacob was especially fond of Benjamin because (1) he was the only true brother of Joseph, and (2) he was the only other son of his beloved wife, Rachel. Benjamin was Jacob's youngest son and a child of his old age.

●**42:7** Joseph could have revealed his identity to his brothers at once. But Joseph's last memory of them was of staring in horror at their faces as Ishmaelite slave traders carried him away. Were his brothers still evil and treacherous, or had they changed over the years? Joseph decided to put them through a few tests to find out.

●**42:8, 9** Joseph remembered the dreams he had had as a boy about his brothers bowing down to him (37: 9). Those dreams were coming true! As a young boy, Joseph was boastful about his dreams. As a man, he no longer flaunted his superior status. He did not feel the need to say "I told you so." It was not yet time to reveal his identity, so he kept quiet. Sometimes it is best for us to remain quiet, even when we would like to have the last word.

●**42:15** Joseph was testing his brothers to make sure they had not been as cruel to Benjamin as they had been to him. Benjamin was his only full brother and he wanted to see him face to face.

42:18
Gen 20:11
Lev 25:43

42:20
Gen 42:34
43:15

42:21
Gen 37:23-28
41:9
Num 32:23

42:22
Gen 9:6
37:21,22
Lk 23:41

42:24
Gen 43:14,23,
30; 45:14

42:25
Gen 44:1

42:27
Gen 43:21
Ex 4:24

42:28
Gen 27:33
Isa 45:7
Lam 3:37

42:30
Gen 42:7

42:31
Gen 42:11

42:32
Gen 42:13

42:33
Gen 42:19

42:34
Gen 42:20

42:35
Gen 42:27
43:12,21

42:36
Gen 43:14
44:20-22

42:37
Gen 43:9; 44:32

42:38
Gen 37:35
44:20-22,29
1 Kgs 2:6

43:1
Gen 41:5,6,7
42:5

43:2
Gen 43:15

43:3
Gen 42:15
44:23

¹⁸The third day Joseph said to them, "I am a God-fearing man and I'm going to give you an opportunity to prove yourselves. ¹⁹I'm going to take a chance that you are honorable; only one of you shall remain in chains in jail, and the rest of you may go on home with grain for your families; ²⁰but bring your youngest brother back to me. In this way I will know whether you are telling me the truth; and if you are, I will spare you." To this they agreed.

²¹Speaking among themselves, they said, "This has all happened because of what we did to Joseph long ago. We saw his terror and anguish and heard his pleadings, but we wouldn't listen."

²²"Didn't I tell you not to do it?" Reuben asked. "But you wouldn't listen. And now we are going to die because we murdered him."

²³Of course they didn't know that Joseph understood them as he was standing there, for he had been speaking to them through an interpreter. ²⁴Now he left the room and found a place where he could weep. Returning, he selected Simeon from among them and had him bound before their eyes. ²⁵Joseph then ordered his servants to fill the men's sacks with grain, but also gave secret instructions to put each brother's payment at the top of his sack! He also gave them provisions for their journey. ²⁶So they loaded up their donkeys with the grain and started for home. ²⁷But when they stopped for the night and one of them opened his sack to get some grain to feed the donkeys, there was his money in the mouth of the sack!

²⁸"Look," he exclaimed to his brothers, "my money is here in my sack." They were filled with terror. Trembling, they exclaimed to each other. "What is this that God has done to us?" ²⁹So they came to their father Jacob in the land of Canaan and told him all that had happened.

³⁰"The king's chief assistant spoke very roughly to us," they told him, "and took us for spies. ³¹'No, no,' we said, 'we are honest men, not spies. ³²We are twelve brothers, sons of one father; one is dead, and the youngest is with our father in the land of Canaan.' ³³Then the man told us, 'This is the way I will find out if you are what you claim to be. Leave one of your brothers here with me and take grain for your families and go on home, ³⁴but bring your youngest brother back to me. Then I shall know whether you are spies or honest men; if you prove to be what you say, then I will give you back your brother and you can come as often as you like to purchase grain.' "

³⁵As they emptied out the sacks, there at the top of each was the money paid for the grain! Terror gripped them, as it did their father.

³⁶Then Jacob exclaimed, "You have bereaved me of my children—Joseph didn't come back, Simeon is gone, and now you want to take Benjamin too! Everything has been against me."

³⁷Then Reuben said to his father, "Kill my two sons if I don't bring Benjamin back to you. I'll be responsible for him."

³⁸But Jacob replied, "My son shall not go down with you, for his brother Joseph is dead and he alone is left of his mother's children. If anything should happen to him, I would die."

Jacob lets Benjamin go

43 But there was no relief from the terrible famine throughout the land. ²When the grain they had brought from Egypt was almost gone, their father said to them, "Go again and buy us a little food."

³, ⁴, ⁵But Judah told him, "The man wasn't fooling one bit when he said, 'Don't ever come back again unless your brother is with you.' We cannot go unless you let Benjamin go with us."

42:19 *I'm going to take a chance that you are honorable,* literally, "If you are forthright men."

● **43:1** Jacob and his sons had no relief from the famine. They could not see God's overall plan of sending them to Egypt to be reunited with Joseph and fed from Egypt's storehouses. If you are praying for relief from suffering or pressure and God is not bringing it as quickly as you would like, remember that God may be leading you to special treasures.

6"Why did you ever tell him you had another brother?" Israel moaned. "Why did you have to treat me like that?"

7"But the man specifically asked us about our family," they told him. "He wanted to know whether our father was still living and he asked us if we had another brother, so we told him. How could we know that he was going to say, 'Bring me your brother'?"

43:7
Gen 42:13
43:27

8Judah said to his father, "Send the lad with me and we will be on our way; otherwise we will all die of starvation—and not only we, but you and all our little ones. 9I guarantee his safety. If I don't bring him back to you, then let me bear the blame forever. 10For we could have gone and returned by this time if you had let him come."

43:8
Gen 42:2
44:26; 45:18,19
43:9
Gen 42:37
44:32
Heb 7:22

11So their father Israel finally said to them, "If it can't be avoided, then at least do this. Load your donkeys with the best products of the land. Take them to the man as gifts—balm, honey, spices, myrrh, pistachio nuts, and almonds. 12Take double money so that you can pay back what was in the mouths of your sacks, as it was probably someone's mistake, 13and take your brother and go. 14May God Almighty give you mercy before the man, so that he will release Simeon and return Benjamin. And if I must bear the anguish of their deaths, then so be it."

43:11
Gen 32:13
37:25; 43:25
43:12
Gen 42:35
43:13
Gen 42:38; 43:4
43:14
Gen 39:21
42:36
Ps 106:46

15So they took the gifts and double money and went to Egypt, and stood before Joseph. 16When Joseph saw that Benjamin was with them he said to the manager of his household, "These men will eat with me this noon. Take them home and prepare a big feast." 17So the man did as he was told and took them to Joseph's palace. 18They were badly frightened when they saw where they were being taken.

43:16
Gen 31:54; 44:1

43:18
Gen 42:28,35

"It's because of the money returned to us in our sacks," they said. "He wants to pretend we stole it and seize us as slaves, with our donkeys."

19As they arrived at the entrance to the palace, they went over to Joseph's household manager, 20and said to him, "O sir, after our first trip to Egypt to buy food, 21as we were returning home, we stopped for the night and opened our sacks, and the money was there that we had paid for the grain. Here it is; we have brought it back again, 22along with additional money to buy more grain. We have no idea how the money got into our sacks."

43:21
Gen 42:27,35
43:12
43:22
Gen 42:25

23"Don't worry about it," the household manager told them; "your God, even the God of your fathers, must have put it there, for we collected your money all right."

43:23
Gen 42:24

Then he released Simeon and brought him out to them. 24They were then conducted into the palace and given water to refresh their feet; and their donkeys were fed. 25Then they got their presents ready for Joseph's arrival at noon, for they were told that they would be eating there. 26When Joseph came home they gave him their presents, bowing low before him.

43:24
Gen 18:4; 24:32
Lk 7:44

43:26
Gen 42:6

27He asked how they had been getting along. "And how is your father—the old man you spoke about? Is he still alive?"

43:27
Gen 43:7; 45:3
Ex 18:7

28"Yes," they replied. "He is alive and well." Then again they bowed before him.

43:28
Ex 18:7

29Looking at his brother Benjamin, he asked, "Is this your youngest brother, the one you told me about? How are you, my son? God be gracious to you." 30Then Joseph made a hasty exit, for he was overcome with love for his brother and had to

43:29
Num 6:25
Ps 67:1
43:30
Gen 42:24
45:2,14,15
46:29

43:29 *Looking at his brother Benjamin,* literally, "his brother Benjamin, his mother's son."

•**43:9** Judah accepted full responsibility for Benjamin's safety. He did not know what that might mean for him, but he was determined to carry it out. In the end it was Judah's stirring words that caused Joseph to break down and reveal himself to his brothers (44:18–34). Accepting and fulfilling responsibilities is difficult, but it builds character and confidence, earns others' respect, and motivates us to complete our work. When you have been given an assignment to complete or a responsibility to fulfill, commmit yourself to seeing it through.

43:11 These gifts of balm, honey, spices, myrrh, pistachio nuts, and almonds were highly valuable. They were specialty items not common in Egypt. Because of the famine, they were even more rare.

43:12 Joseph's brothers arrived home from Egypt only to find in their grain sacks the money they had used to pay for the grain. Some months later, when it was time to return to Egypt for more food, Jacob paid back double the cost of the grain to maintain his integrity. We should follow Jacob's example and guard our integrity. A reputation for honesty and integrity is worth far more than whatever we may spend earning and keeping it.

43:31
Gen 43:25; 45:1
Isa 42:14

43:32
Gen 46:34
Ex 8:26

43:33
Gen 44:12

go out and cry. Going into his bedroom, he wept there. 31Then he washed his face and came out, keeping himself under control. "Let's eat," he said.

32Joseph ate by himself, his brothers were served at a separate table, and the Egyptians at still another; for Egyptians despise Hebrews and never eat with them. 33He told each of them where to sit, and seated them in the order of their ages, from the oldest to the youngest, much to their amazement! 34Their food was served to them from his own table. He gave the largest serving to Benjamin—five times as much as to any of the others! They had a wonderful time bantering back and forth, and the wine flowed freely!

44:1
Gen 42:25
43:16

44:4
Prov 17:13

44:5
Gen 30:27
Lev 19:26
Deut. 18:10-14

44:8
Gen 43:21
Ex 20:15

44:9
Gen 31:32
44:16
Ps 7:3-5

44:12
Gen 44:2

44:13
Gen 37:29,34
Num 14:6

44:14
Gen 43:26

44:15
Gen 41:38; 44:5

44:16
Gen 42:21
43:8,9
Num 32:23
Ezra 9:10

44:18
Gen 37:7,8
41:40

44 When his brothers were ready to leave, Joseph ordered his household manager to fill each of their sacks with as much grain as they could carry—and to put into the mouth of each man's sack the money he had paid! 2He was also told to put Joseph's own silver cup at the top of Benjamin's sack, along with the grain money. So the household manager did as he was told. 3The brothers were up at dawn and on their way with their loaded donkeys.

4But when they were barely out of the city, Joseph said to his household manager, "Chase after them and stop them and ask them why they are acting like this when their benefactor has been so kind to them? 5Ask them, 'What do you mean by stealing my lord's personal silver drinking cup, which he uses for fortune telling? What a wicked thing you have done!' " 6So he caught up with them and spoke to them along the lines he had been instructed.

7"What in the world are you talking about?" they demanded. "What kind of people do you think we are, that you accuse us of such a terrible thing as that? 8Didn't we bring back the money we found in the mouth of our sacks? Why would we steal silver or gold from your master's house? 9If you find his cup with any one of us, let that one die. And all the rest of us will be slaves forever to your master."

10"Fair enough," the man replied, "except that only the one who stole it will be a slave, and the rest of you can go free."

11They quickly took down their sacks from the backs of their donkeys and opened them. 12He began searching the oldest brother's sack, going on down the line to the youngest. And the cup was found in Benjamin's! 13They ripped their clothing in despair, loaded the donkeys again, and returned to the city. 14Joseph was still home when Judah and his brothers arrived, and they fell to the ground before him.

15"What were you trying to do?" Joseph demanded. "Didn't you know such a man as I would know who stole it?"

16And Judah said, "Oh, what shall we say to my lord? How can we plead? How can we prove our innocence? God is punishing us for our sins. Sir, we have all returned to be your slaves, both we and he in whose sack the cup was found."

17"No," Joseph said. "Only the man who stole the cup, he shall be my slave. The rest of you can go on home to your father."

18Then Judah stepped forward and said, "O sir, let me say just this one word to you. Be patient with me for a moment, for I know you can doom me in an instant, as though you were Pharaoh himself.

44:1 *When his brothers were ready to leave,* implied.

43:32 Why did Joseph eat by himself? Eating alone followed the law of the ancient caste system. Egyptians considered themselves highly intelligent and sophisticated. They looked upon shepherds and nomads as uncultured and even vulgar. As foreigners and shepherds, Joseph's brothers were lower in rank than any Egyptian citizens. And Joseph could not even eat with fellow Egyptians who were lower than he in rank.

44:2 Joseph's silver cup was a symbol of his authority. It was thought to have supernatural powers, and to steal it was a serious crime. Such goblets were used for predicting the future. A person poured water into the cup and interpreted the reflections, ripples, and bubbles. Joseph wouldn't have needed his cup—God told

him everything he needed to know about the future.

44:13 The ripping of clothing was an expression of deep sorrow and a customary manner of showing grief. The brothers were deeply upset that Benjamin might be harmed.

44:16–34 When Judah was younger, he showed no regard for his brother Joseph or his father, Jacob. First he convinced his brothers to sell Joseph as a slave (37:26); then he lied to his father about Joseph's fate (37:32). But what a change took place in Judah! Now the man was so concerned for his father and younger brother, Benjamin, that he was willing to die for them. When you are ready to give up hope on yourself or others, remember that God can work a complete change in even the most selfish personality.

¹⁹"Sir, you asked us if we had a father or a brother, ²⁰and we said, 'Yes, we have a father, an old man, and a child of his old age, a little one. And his brother is dead, and he alone is left of his mother's children, and his father loves him very much.' ²¹And you said to us, 'Bring him here so that I can see him.' ²²But we said to you, 'Sir, the lad cannot leave his father, for his father would die.' ²³But you told us, 'Don't come back here unless your youngest brother is with you.' ²⁴So we returned to our father and told him what you had said. ²⁵And when he said, 'Go back again and buy us a little food,' ²⁶we replied, 'We can't, unless you let our youngest brother go with us. Only then may we come.' ²⁷"Then my father said to us, 'You know that my wife had two sons, ²⁸and that one of them went away and never returned—doubtless torn to pieces by some wild animal; I have never seen him since. ²⁹And if you take away his brother from me also, and any harm befalls him, I shall die with sorrow.' ³⁰And now, sir, if I go back to my father and the lad is not with us—seeing that our father's life is bound up in the lad's life— ³¹when he sees that the boy is not with us, our father will die; and we will be responsible for bringing down his gray hairs with sorrow to the grave. ³²Sir, I pledged my father that I would take care of the lad. I told him, 'If I don't bring him back to you, I shall bear the blame forever.' ³³Please sir, let me stay here as a slave instead of the lad, and let the lad return with his brothers. ³⁴For how shall I return to my father if the lad is not with me? I cannot bear to see what this would do to him."

44:19
Gen 42:13-16
43:7

44:21
Gen 42:20,34
43:7

44:22
Gen 42:38

44:23
Gen 42:20

44:24
Gen 42:29-34

44:25
Gen 43:2

44:26
Gen 43:4,5

44:27
Gen 46:19

44:28
Gen 37:33

44:29
Gen 42:38

44:30
1 Sam 18:1

44:32
Gen 43:9

Joseph sends for Jacob

45 Joseph could stand it no longer. "Out, all of you," he cried out to his attendants, and he was left alone with his brothers. ²Then he wept aloud. His sobs could be heard throughout the palace, and the news was quickly carried to Pharaoh's palace.

³"I am Joseph!" he said to his brothers. "Is my father still alive?" But his brothers couldn't say a word, they were so stunned with surprise.

⁴"Come over here," he said. So they came closer. And he said again, "I am Joseph, your brother whom you sold into Egypt! ⁵But don't be angry with yourselves that you did this to me, for God did it! He sent me here ahead of you to preserve your lives. ⁶These two years of famine will grow to seven, during which there will be neither plowing nor harvest. ⁷God has sent me here to keep you and your families alive, so that you will become a great nation. ⁸Yes, it was God who sent me here, not you! And he has made me a counselor to Pharaoh, and manager of this entire nation, ruler of all the land of Egypt.

⁹"Hurry, return to my father and tell him, 'Your son Joseph says, "God has made me chief of all the land of Egypt. Come down to me right away! ¹⁰You shall live in the land of Goshen so that you can be near me with all your children, your grandchildren, your flocks and herds, and all that you have. ¹¹, ¹²I will take care of you there" ' (you men are witnesses of my promise, and my brother Benjamin has heard me say it) ' "for there are still five years of famine ahead of us. Otherwise you will come to utter poverty along with all your household." ' ¹³Tell our father about all my power here in Egypt, and how everyone obeys me. And bring him to me quickly."

¹⁴Then, weeping with joy, he embraced Benjamin and Benjamin began weeping

45:1
Gen 42:24
43:30

45:3
Gen 50:17-19
Mt 14:27
Acts 7:13

45:4
Gen 37:28

45:5
Gen 50:20

45:6
Gen 41:29,30
47:18,23

45:8
Gen 41:39
Judg 17:10
Ps 105:21
Jn 15:16; 19:11

45:9
Acts 7:14

45:10
Gen 46:28,34
47:6
Ex 8:22

45:11
Gen 45:8; 47:12

45:13
Acts 7:14

45:14
Gen 43:30
46:29

44:32 In Genesis 43:9, Judah promised Jacob that he would guarantee the safety of young Benjamin. Now Judah had a chance to keep that promise. Though becoming a slave was a terrible fate, Judah was determined to keep his word to his father. He showed great courage in carrying out his promise. Accepting a responsibility means carrying it out with determination and courage, regardless of the personal sacrifice.

●**44:33** Joseph wanted to see if his brothers' attitudes had changed for the better, so he tested the way they treated each other. Judah had stepped forward with the plan to sell Joseph (37:26). In this situation, Judah stepped forward to take Benjamin's

punishment so Benjamin could return to their father. This courageous act convinced Joseph that his brothers had changed for the better—in a dramatic way.

●**45:4-8** Although Joseph's brothers had wanted to get rid of him (Genesis 37:26-36), God's ultimate plan was being fulfilled through their evil actions. He sent Joseph ahead to preserve their lives, save Egypt, and prepare the way for the beginning of the nation of Israel. God is sovereign. His plans are not dictated by human actions. When others intend evil for your life, remember that they are only God's tools. In Genesis 50:20 Joseph said, "As far as I am concerned, God turned into good what you meant for evil."

too. 15And he did the same with each of his brothers, who finally found their tongues! 16The news soon reached Pharaoh—"Joseph's brothers have come"; and Pharaoh was very happy to hear it, as were his officials.

17Then Pharaoh said to Joseph, "Tell your brothers to load their pack animals and return quickly to their homes in Canaan, 18and to bring your father and all of your families and come here to Egypt to live. Tell them, 'Pharaoh will assign to you the very best territory in the land of Egypt. You shall live off the fat of the land!' 19And tell your brothers to take wagons from Egypt to carry their wives and little ones, and to bring your father here. 20Don't worry about your property, for the best of all the land of Egypt is yours."

21So Joseph gave them wagons, as Pharaoh had commanded, and provisions for the journey, 22and he gave each of them new clothes—but to Benjamin he gave five changes of clothes and three hundred pieces of silver! 23He sent his father ten donkey-loads of the good things of Egypt, and ten donkeys loaded with grain and all kinds of other food, to eat on his journey. 24So he sent his brothers off.

"Don't quarrel along the way!" was his parting shot! 25And leaving, they returned to the land of Canaan, to Jacob their father.

45:16
Acts 7:13

45:17
Gen 42:25; 44:1

45:18
Gen 27:28; 47:6

45:19
Gen 45:27; 46:5

45:20
Gen 20:15

45:22
Gen 43:34
Judg 14:12
2 Kgs 5:5

45:23
Gen 43:11

45:24
Gen 37:22
42:21
Ps 133:1-3

JUDAH

People who are leaders stand out. They don't necessarily act or look a certain way until the need for their action is apparent. Among their skills are outspokenness, decisiveness, action, and control. These skills can be used for great good or great evil. Jacob's fourth son, Judah, was a natural leader. The events of his life provided many opportunities to exercise those skills.Unfortunately Judah's decisions were often shaped more by the pressures of the moment than by a conscious desire to cooperate with God's plan. But when he did recognize his mistakes, he was willing to admit them. His experience with Tamar and the final confrontation with Joseph are both examples of Judah's willingness to bear the blame when confronted. It was one of the qualities he passed on to his descendant David.

Whether or not we have Judah's natural leadership qualities, we do share with him a tendency to be blind toward our own sin. But too often we don't share his willingness to admit our mistakes. From Judah we can learn that it is not wise to wait until our errors force us to admit to wrongdoing. It is far better to openly admit our mistakes, shoulder the blame, and seek forgiveness.

Strengths and accomplishments:
● Was a natural leader—outspoken and decisive
● Thought clearly and took action in pressure situations
● Was willing to stand by his word and put himself on the line when necessary
● Was the fourth son of 12, through whom God would eventually bring King David and Jesus, the Messiah

Weaknesses and mistakes:
● Suggested to his brothers they sell Joseph into slavery
● Failed to keep his promise to his daughter-in-law, Tamar

Lessons from his life:
● God is in control far beyond the immediate situation
● Procrastination often brings about a worse result
● Judah's offer to substitute his life for Benjamin's is a picture of what his descendant Jesus would do for all men

Vital statistics:
● Where: Canaan and Egypt
● Occupation: Shepherd
● Relatives: Parents: Jacob and Leah. Wife: Bathshua. Daughter-in-law: Tamar. Eleven brothers and at least five sons (Genesis 29:31—30:24).

Key verses:
"Judah, your brothers shall praise you. You shall destroy your enemies. Your father's sons shall bow before you. Judah is a young lion that has finished eating its prey. He has settled down as a lion—who will dare to rouse him?" (Genesis 49:8, 9).

Judah's story is told in Genesis 29:35—50:26. He is also mentioned in 1 Chronicles 2—4.

●**45:17-20** Joseph was rejected, kidnaped, enslaved, and imprisoned. Although his brothers had been unfaithful to him, he graciously forgave them and shared his prosperity. Joseph demonstrated how God forgives us and showers us with goodness even though we have sinned against him. This same forgiveness and blessing are ours if only we ask for them.

26"Joseph is alive," they shouted to him. "And he is ruler over all the land of Egypt!" But Jacob's heart was like a stone; he couldn't take it in. 27But when they had given him Joseph's messages, and when he saw the wagons filled with food that Joseph had sent him, his spirit revived.

28And he said, "It must be true! Joseph my son is alive! I will go and see him before I die."

6. Jacob's family moves to Egypt

46 So Israel set out with all his possessions, and came to Beer-Sheba, and offered sacrifices there to the God of his father Isaac. 2During the night God spoke to him in a vision.

"Jacob! Jacob!" he called.

"Yes?" Jacob answered.

3, 4"I am God," the voice replied, "the God of your father. Don't be afraid to go down to Egypt, for I will see to it that you become a great nation there. And I will go down with you into Egypt and I will bring your descendants back again; but you shall die in Egypt with Joseph at your side."

5So Jacob left Beer-sheba, and his sons brought him to Egypt, along with their little ones and their wives, in the wagons Pharaoh had provided for them. 6They brought their livestock too, and all their belongings accumulated in the land of Canaan, and came to Egypt—Jacob and all his children, 7sons and daughters, grandsons and granddaughters—all his loved ones.

8-14Here are the names of his sons and grandchildren who went with him into Egypt:

Reuben, his oldest son;
Reuben's sons: Hanoch, Pallu, Hezron, and Carmi.
Simeon and his sons: Jemuel, Jamin, Ohad, Jachin, Zohar, and Shaul (Shaul's mother was a girl from Canaan).
Levi and his sons: Gershon, Kohath, Merari.
Judah and his sons: Er, Onan, Shelah, Perez, Zerah (however, Er and Onan died while still in Canaan, before Israel went to Egypt).
The sons of Perez were Hezron and Hamul.
Issachar and his sons: Tola, Puvah, Iob, Shimron.
Zebulun and his sons: Sered, Elon, Jahleel.
15So these descendants of Jacob and Leah, not including their daughter Dinah, born to Jacob in Paddan-aram, were thirty-three in all.

45:26
Gen 37:31-35
45:27
Gen 45:19,21
Judg 15:19
1 Sam 30:12
45:28
Gen 46:30
Lk 2:28-30

46:1
Gen 21:14
26:22
28:10,13
31:42; 33:20
35:7
46:2
Gen 22:11
31:11
Num 12:6
46:3
Gen 15:1; 17:1
26:2
Isa 41:10
46:4
Gen 28:15
48:21; 50:5
Ex 3:8
46:5
Gen 45:19
46:6
Num 20:15
Deut 10:22; 26:5
Acts 7:14,15
46:8
Gen 29:32
35:23; 49:3
46:9
1 Chron 5:3
46:10
1 Chron 4:24
46:11
1 Chron 6:1
46:12
1 Chron 2:3
46:13
1 Chron 7:1
46:14
Gen 30:20
49:13
46:15
Gen 30:21

45:26, 27 Jacob needed some evidence before he could believe the incredible news that Joseph was alive. Similarly, Thomas refused to believe that Jesus had risen from the dead until he could see and touch him (John 20:25). It is hard to change what you believe without all the facts—or sometimes even with the facts. Good news can be hard to believe. Don't ever give up hope that God has wonderful news in store for you.

●**46:3, 4** God told Jacob to leave his home and travel to a strange and faraway land. But God reassured him by promising to go with him and take care of him. When new situations or surroundings frighten or worry you, recognize that experiencing fear is normal. To be paralyzed by fear, however, is an indication that you question God's ability to take care of you.

46:32–34 Jacob moved his whole family to Egypt, but they wanted to live apart from the Egyptians. To ensure this, Joseph told them to let Pharaoh know they were shepherds. Although Pharaoh may have been sympathetic to shepherds (for he was probably a nomadic king from the Hyksos line), the Egyptian culture looked down on shepherds and was not yet ready to accept them. The strategy worked and Jacob's family was able to benefit from Pharaoh's generosity *and* from the prejudice of the Egyptians.

JACOB MOVES TO EGYPT
After hearing the joyful news that Joseph was alive, Jacob packed up and moved his family to Egypt. Stopping first in Beer-sheba, Jacob offered sacrifices and received assurance from God that Egypt was where he should go. Jacob and his family settled in the land of Goshen, in the northeastern part of Egypt.

46:16
Gen 30:11
35:26; 49:19
Num 26:15
1 Chron 5:11

46:17
Gen 30:13
49:20
Num 26:44
1 Chron 7:30

16, 17Also accompanying him were:

Gad and his sons: Ziphion, Haggi, Shuni,
Ezbon, Eri, Arodi, and Areli.
Asher and his sons: Imnah, Ishvah, Ishvi,
Beriah, and a sister, Serah.
Beriah's sons were Heber and Malchiel.

18These sixteen persons were the sons of Jacob and Zilpah, the slave-girl given to
Leah by her father, Laban.

46:19
Gen 30:24
35:18

46:20
Gen 41:45,
50-52

46:21
Num 26:38
1 Chron 7:6

46:22
Gen 35:24

46:23
Gen 30:6
35:25; 49:16
Num 26:42

46:24
Gen 30:8; 49:21
Num 26:48
1 Chron 7:13

46:25
Gen 35:25

19-22Also in the total of Jacob's household were these fourteen sons and descendants of Jacob and Rachel:

Joseph and Benjamin;
Joseph's sons, born in the land of Egypt, were Manasseh and Ephraim (their
mother was Asenath, the daughter of Potiphera, priest of Heliopolis);
Benjamin's sons: Bela, Becher, Ashbel, Gera, Naaman, Ehi, Rosh, Muppim,
Huppim, and Ard.

23, 24, 25Also in the group were these seven sons and descendants of Jacob and
Bilhah, the slave-girl given to Rachel by her father, Laban:

Dan and his son: Hushim.
Naphtali and his sons: Jahzeel, Guni, Jezer, and Shillem.

46:27
Ex 1:5; 24:1
Deut 10:22
Acts 7:14

46:28
Gen 43:8
45:10; 47:1

46:29
Gen 33:4
45:10,14
Lk 15:20

46:30
Gen 45:28
Lk 2:29

46:31
Gen 45:16; 47:1

46:32
Gen 37:2,14
47:3

46:33
Gen 47:2

46:34
Gen 13:7
43:32; 47:4

26So the total number of those going to Egypt, of his own descendants, not
counting the wives of Jacob's sons, was sixty-six. 27With Joseph and his two sons
included, this total of Jacob's household there in Egypt totaled seventy.

28Jacob sent Judah on ahead to tell Joseph that they were on the way, and would
soon arrive in Goshen—which they did. 29Joseph jumped into his chariot and
journeyed to Goshen to meet his father and they fell into each other's arms and wept
a long while.

30Then Israel said to Joseph, "Now let me die, for I have seen you again and
know you are alive."

31And Joseph said to his brothers and to all their households, "I'll go and tell
Pharaoh that you are here, and that you have come from the land of Canaan to join
me. 32And I will tell him, 'These men are shepherds. They have brought with them
their flocks and herds and everything they own.' 33So when Pharaoh calls for you
and asks you about your occupation, 34tell him, 'We have been shepherds from our
youth, as our fathers have been for many generations.' When you tell him this, he
will let you live here in the land of Goshen." For shepherds were despised and hated
in other parts of Egypt.

47:1
Gen 46:31

47:2
Acts 7:13

47:3
Gen 46:33
Amos 7:14

47:4
Gen 15:13
43:1; 46:34
Deut 26:5

47

Upon their arrival, Joseph went in to see Pharaoh.
"My father and my brothers are here from Canaan," he reported, "with all
their flocks and herds and possessions. They wish to settle in the land of Goshen."
2He took five of his brothers with him, and presented them to Pharaoh.
3Pharaoh asked them, "What is your occupation?"
And they replied, "We are shepherds like our ancestors. 4We have come to live
here in Egypt, for there is no pasture for our flocks in Canaan—the famine is very
bitter there. We request permission to live in the land of Goshen."
5, 6And Pharaoh said to Joseph, "Choose anywhere you like for them to live.

46:34 The Israelites did become a great nation, and Jacob's
descendants did eventually return to Canaan. The book of Exodus
recounts the story of Israel's slavery in Egypt for 400 years
(fulfilling God's words to Abram in 15:13-16), and the book of
Joshua tells the exciting account of the Israelites entering and
conquering Canaan, the "Promised Land."

Give them the best land of Egypt. The land of Goshen will be fine. And if any of them are capable, put them in charge of my flocks, too."

7Then Joseph brought his father Jacob to Pharaoh. And Jacob blessed Pharaoh. 8"How old are you?" Pharaoh asked him.

9Jacob replied, "I have lived 130 long, hard years, and I am not nearly as old as many of my ancestors." 10Then Jacob blessed Pharaoh again before he left.

11So Joseph assigned the best land of Egypt—the land of Rameses—to his father and brothers, just as Pharaoh had commanded. 12And Joseph furnished food to them in accordance with the number of their dependents.

13The famine became worse and worse, so that all the land of Egypt and Canaan were starving. 14Joseph collected all the money in Egypt and Canaan in exchange for grain, and he brought the money to Pharaoh's treasure-houses. 15When the people were out of money, they came to Joseph crying again for food.

"Our money is gone," they said, "but give us bread; for why should we die?" 16"Well then," Joseph replied, "give me your livestock. I will trade you food in exchange."

17So they brought their cattle to Joseph in exchange for food. Soon all the horses, flocks, herds, and donkeys of Egypt were in Pharaoh's possession.

18The next year they came again and said, "Our money is gone, and our cattle are yours, and there is nothing left but our bodies and land. 19Why should we die? Buy us and our land and we will be serfs to Pharaoh. We will trade ourselves for food, then we will live, and the land won't be abandoned."

20So Joseph bought all the land of Egypt for Pharaoh; all the Egyptians sold him their fields because the famine was so severe. And the land became Pharaoh's. 21Thus all the people of Egypt became Pharaoh's serfs. 22The only land he didn't buy was that belonging to the priests, for they were assigned food from Pharaoh and didn't need to sell.

23Then Joseph said to the people, "See, I have bought you and your land for Pharaoh. Here is grain. Go and sow the land. 24And when you harvest it, a fifth of everything you get belongs to Pharaoh. Keep four parts for yourselves to be used for next year's seed, and as food for yourselves and for your households and little ones."

25"You have saved our lives," they said. "We will gladly be the serfs of Pharaoh."

26So Joseph made it a law throughout the land of Egypt—and it is still the law—that Pharaoh should have as his tax twenty percent of all the crops except those produced on the land owned by the temples.

7. Jacob and Joseph die in Egypt
Jacob blesses Joseph

27So Israel lived in the land of Goshen in Egypt, and soon the people of Israel began to prosper, and there was a veritable population explosion among them. 28Jacob lived seventeen years after his arrival, so that he was 147 years old at the time of his death. 29As the time drew near for him to die, he called for his son Joseph and said to him, "Swear to me most solemnly that you will honor this, my last request: do not bury me in Egypt. 30But when I am dead, take me out of Egypt and bury me beside my ancestors." And Joseph promised. 31"Swear that you will do it," Jacob insisted. And Joseph did. Soon afterwards Jacob took to his bed.

48 One day not long after this, word came to Joseph that his father was failing rapidly. So, taking with him his two sons, Manasseh and Ephraim, he went to visit him. 2When Jacob heard that Joseph had arrived, he gathered his strength and sat up in the bed to greet him, 3and said to him, "God Almighty appeared to me at Luz in the land of Canaan and blessed me, 4and said to me, 'I will make you a

47:6
Gen 45:18
46:34; 47:11
Ex 18:21

47:7
Gen 47:10
Ex 12:32
Num 6:23

47:9
Gen 35:28
1 Chron 29:15

47:10
Gen 14:19

47:11
Ex 1:11; 12:37

47:12
Gen 45:11
47:24

47:13
Gen 41:30
Jer 14:1-6
Acts 7:11

47:14
Gen 41:56
1 Cor 4:2

47:15
Gen 47:18,
19,24

47:17
Ex 9:3
1 Kgs 10:28

47:19
Neh 5:2
Job 2:4
Lam 1:11
Mt 16:26

47:22
Gen 41:45
Deut 12:19

47:23
Gen 45:6
Prov 11:26

47:24
Gen 41:34
Lev 27:32

47:25
Gen 33:15
45:7; 50:20
Ruth 2:13

47:26
Gen 47:22

47:27
Gen 13:16; 46:3
Ex 1:7

47:29
Gen 24:2,49
50:24,25
Acts 7:15,16
Heb 11:21

47:30
Gen 15:15
23:19; 25:9
49:29

48:1
Gen 41:50-52
46:20
Heb 11:21

48:3
Gen 28:3,
12-19; 35:9-15

47:29–31 Jacob had Joseph promise to bury him in his homeland. Few things were written in this culture, so a person's word carried as much force as a written contract. People today seem to find it easy to say, "I didn't mean that." God's people, however, are to speak the truth and live the truth. Let your words be as binding as a written contract.

great nation and I will give this land of Canaan to you and to your children's children, for an everlasting possession.' ⁵And now, as to these two sons of yours, Ephraim and Manasseh, born here in the land of Egypt before I arrived, I am adopting them as my own, and they will inherit from me just as Reuben and Simeon will. ⁶But any other children born to you shall be your own, and shall inherit Ephraim's and Manasseh's portion from you. ⁷For your mother Rachel died after only two children when I came from Paddan-aram, as we were just a short distance from Ephrath, and I buried her beside the road to Bethlehem." ⁸Then Israel looked over at the two boys. "Are these the ones?" he asked.

⁹"Yes," Joseph told him, "these are my sons whom God has given me here in Egypt."

And Israel said, "Bring them over to me and I will bless them."

¹⁰Israel was half blind with age, so that he could hardly see. So Joseph brought the boys close to him and he kissed and embraced them.

¹¹And Israel said to Joseph, "I never thought that I would see you again, but now God has let me see your children too."

¹², ¹³Joseph took the boys by the hand, bowed deeply to him, and led the boys to their grandfather's knees—Ephraim at Israel's left hand and Manasseh at his right. ¹⁴But Israel crossed his arms as he stretched them out to lay his hands upon the boys' heads, so that his right hand was upon the head of Ephraim, the younger boy, and his left hand was upon the head of Manasseh, the older. He did this purposely.

¹⁵Then he blessed Joseph with this blessing: "May God, the God of my fathers Abraham and Isaac, the God who has shepherded me all my life, wonderfully bless these boys. ¹⁶He is the Angel who has kept me from all harm. May these boys be an honor to my name and to the names of my fathers Abraham and Isaac; and may they become a mighty nation."

¹⁷But Joseph was upset and displeased when he saw that his father had laid his right hand on Ephraim's head; so he lifted it to place it on Manasseh's head instead. ¹⁸"No, father," he said. "You've got your right hand on the wrong head! This one over here is the older. Put your right hand on him!"

¹⁹But his father refused. "I know what I'm doing, my son," he said. "Manasseh too shall become a great nation, but his younger brother shall become even greater."

²⁰So Jacob blessed the boys that day with this blessing: "May the people of Israel bless each other by saying, 'God make you as prosperous as Ephraim and Manasseh.' " (Note that he put Ephraim before Manasseh.)

²¹Then Israel said to Joseph, "I am about to die, but God will be with you and will bring you again to Canaan, the land of your fathers. ²²And I have given the choice land of Shekem to you instead of to your brothers, as your portion of that land which I took from the Amorites with my sword and with my bow."

48:7 *after only two children,* implied.

48:5
Gen 46:20,27

48:6
Josh 14:4

48:7
Gen 35:19
1 Sam 10:2
Mt 2:18

48:9
Gen 27:4; 33:5
49:28

48:10
Gen 27:1

48:11
Gen 37:33,34
42:36

48:12
Gen 33:3; 42:6

48:14
Gen 41:51,52
Ex 15:6
Ps 110:1

48:15
Gen 17:1; 27:4
28:20,21
49:24,28

48:16
Gen 22:11
28:13; 31:11
32:28
Deut 28:11

48:19
Gen 28:14; 46:3
Deut 1:10

48:20
Gen 28:3
Ruth 4:11

48:21
Gen 28:15
46:4; 50:24

48:22
Gen 15:16
Josh 17:17,18
24:32; Jn 4:5

●**48:9–20** Jacob gave Ephraim, instead of his older brother Manasseh, the greater blessing. When Joseph objected, Jacob scolded him, for God had told him that Ephraim would become greater. God often works in unexpected ways. When he chooses people to fulfill his plans, he always goes deeper than appearance, tradition, or position. He sometimes surprises us by choosing the less obvious person—at least by human reasoning. God can use you to carry out his plans, even if you don't think you have all the qualifications.

48:11 When Joseph became a slave (37:30), Jacob thought he was dead and wept in despair. But eventually God's plan allowed Jacob to regain not only his son, but grandchildren as well. Circumstances are never so bad that they are beyond God's help. Jacob regained his son. In like manner, Job regained a new family (Job 42:10–17), and Mary regained her brother Lazarus (John

11:1–44). We need not despair, because we belong to a loving God. We never know what good he will bring out of a seemingly hopeless situation.

48:15 Jacob spoke of God as one who had "shepherded" him all his life. He pictured himself as a sheep who needed a shepherd's wisdom and guidance to lead him along the best path. This marks a total attitude change from his scheming and dishonest youth. To develop an attitude like Jacob's, you must begin by recognizing that God's advice for living is what you need most. Follow the voice of the Good Shepherd, and he will lead you.

48:20–22 Jacob was giving these young boys land occupied by the Philistines and Canaanites. But Jacob's gift became reality when the tribe of Ephraim and the half-tribe of Manasseh occupied the east and west sides of the Jordan River (Joshua 16).

Jacob's prophecies

49 Then Jacob called together all his sons and said, "Gather around me and I will tell you what is going to happen to you in the days to come. ²Listen to me, O sons of Jacob; listen to Israel your father.

³"Reuben, you are my oldest son, the child of my vigorous youth. You are the head of the list in rank and in honor. ⁴But you are unruly as the wild waves of the sea, and you shall be first no longer. I am demoting you, for you slept with one of my wives and thus dishonored me.

⁵"Simeon and Levi are two of a kind. They are men of violence and injustice. ⁶O my soul, stay away from them. May I never be a party to their wicked plans. For in their anger they murdered a man, and maimed oxen just for fun. ⁷Cursed be their anger, for it is fierce and cruel. Therefore, I will scatter their descendants throughout Israel.

⁸"Judah, your brothers shall praise you. You shall destroy your enemies. Your father's sons shall bow before you. ⁹Judah is a young lion that has finished eating its prey. He has settled down as a lion—who will dare to rouse him? ¹⁰The scepter shall not depart from Judah until Shiloh comes, whom all people shall obey. ¹¹He has chained his steed to the choicest vine, and washed his clothes in wine. ¹²His eyes are darker than wine and his teeth are whiter than milk.

¹³"Zebulun shall dwell on the shores of the sea and shall be a harbor for ships, with his borders extending to Sidon.

¹⁴"Issachar is a strong beast of burden resting among the saddle bags. ¹⁵When he saw how good the countryside was, how pleasant the land, he willingly bent his shoulder to the task and served his masters with vigor.

¹⁶"Dan shall govern his people like any other tribe in Israel. ¹⁷He shall be a serpent in the path that bites the horses' heels, so that the rider falls off. ¹⁸I trust in your salvation, Lord.

¹⁹"A marauding band shall stamp upon Gad, but he shall rob and pursue them! ²⁰"Asher shall produce rich foods, fit for kings!

²¹"Naphtali is a deer let loose, producing lovely fawns.

²²"Joseph is a fruitful tree beside a fountain. His branches shade the wall. ²³He has been severely injured by those who shot at him and persecuted him, ²⁴but their weapons were shattered by the Mighty One of Jacob, the Shepherd, the Rock of Israel. ²⁵May the God of your fathers, the Almighty, bless you with blessings of

49:3
Num 26:5
Deut 21:17
1 Chron 2:1; 5:1
49:4
Gen 35:22
Deut 27:20
49:5
Gen 29:33,34
34:25
49:6
Gen 34:30
49:7
Josh 1:9
21:1-42
49:8
Deut 33:7
Judg 1:1,2
20:18; Heb 7:14
49:9
Num 24:9
Mic 5:8
49:10
Num 24:17
Ps 2:6-9; 60:7
49:13
Deut 33:19
Josh 19:10
49:14
Josh 19:17
Judg 5:16
49:16
Deut 33:22
Judg 13:2; 15:20
Judg 18:26
49:19
Deut 33:20
49:20
Deut 33:24
49:21
Deut 33:23
49:22
Deut 33:13-17
49:23
Gen 37:4,18
49:24
Isa 28:16; 49:26

49:7 *I will scatter their descendants throughout Israel.* That is, the tribes of Simeon and Levi were not given land holdings, as were their brother-tribes. **49:11** *washed his clothes in wine.* Showing wealth and extravagance.

●**49:3–28** Jacob blessed each of his sons, then gave a prediction about their future. The way they had lived their past played an important part in the way Jacob predicted their future. The same is true for us. By sunrise tomorrow, our actions of today will have become part of our past. Yet at the same time they begin shaping our future. What actions can you choose or avoid today that will positively shape your future?

49:4 The oldest child was supposed to receive twice the inheritance. But Reuben lost his special honor. Wild and uncontrollable, especially in his younger days, he had gone so far as to sleep with one of his father's wives. Jacob could not give an honored blessing to such a dishonorable son.

●**49:8–12** Why was Judah, one of Jacob's most wicked sons, so greatly blessed? God had chosen Judah to be the ancestor of Israel's royal line of kings (referred to as the "scepter" in these verses). This may have been due to Judah's dramatic change of character (44:33, 34). Judah's line would also produce the promised Messiah, Jesus Christ.

49:10 What does Shiloh mean? This is a difficult passage to understand and the meaning is disputed. Shiloh may be used as another name for the Messiah, for translated literally it means, "until he to whom it belongs comes, whom all people shall obey." Shiloh might also refer to the Tabernacle set up at the city of Shiloh in Joshua 18:1.

49:18 In the middle of his prophecy to Dan, Jacob exclaimed, "I trust in your salvation, Lord." He was emphasizing to Dan that he would be a strong leader, but only if his trust was in God, not in his natural strength or ability. Those who are strong, attractive, or talented often find it easier to trust in themselves than in God, who gave them these gifts. Remember to thank God for what you are and have so your trust does not become misplaced.

●**49:22** Joseph was indeed a "fruitful tree" with some heroic descendants. Among them Joshua (who will lead the Israelites into the Promised Land, Joshua 1:10, 11); Deborah (a judge of Israel, Judges 4:4); Gideon (a judge of Israel, Judges 6:11,12); and Samuel (a great prophet of Israel, 1 Samuel 3:19).

●**49:24** Jacob summarized God's work in Joseph's life with the phrase, "their weapons were shattered by the Mighty One." This was his way of expressing how God had come to the rescue when Joseph was attacked by those who hated him. So often we struggle and strain without thinking that God is able to help us fight our battles, whether they are against men with weapons or against spiritual forces. Joseph was able to draw closer to God as adversity mounted. To trust God to rescue you shows great faith. Can you trust him to shatter the weapons of injury or persecution directed at you? Such spiritual battles require teamwork between courageous, faithful people and a mighty God.

heaven above and of the earth beneath—blessings of the breasts and of the womb, 26blessings of the grain and flowers, blessings reaching to the utmost bounds of the everlasting hills. These shall be the blessings upon the head of Joseph who was exiled from his brothers.

27"Benjamin is a wolf that prowls. He devours his enemies in the morning, and in the evening divides the loot."

28So these are the blessings that Israel their father blessed his twelve sons with.

29, 30Then he told them, "Soon I will die. You must bury me with my fathers in the land of Canaan, in the cave in the field of Mach-pelah, facing Mamre—the field Abraham bought from Ephron the Hethite for a burial ground. 31There they buried Abraham and Sarah his wife; there they buried Isaac and Rebekah his wife; and there I buried Leah. 32It is the cave which my grandfather Abraham purchased from the sons of Heth." 33Then, when Jacob had finished his prophecies to his sons, he lay back in the bed, breathed his last, and died.

Jacob is buried in Canaan

50 Joseph threw himself upon his father's body and wept over him and kissed him. 2Afterwards he commanded his morticians to embalm the body. 3The embalming process required forty days, with a period of national mourning of seventy days. 4Then, when at last the mourning was over, Joseph approached Pharaoh's staff and requested them to speak to Pharaoh on his behalf.

5"Tell his majesty," he requested them, "that Joseph's father made Joseph swear to take his body back to the land of Canaan, to bury him there. Ask his majesty to permit me to go and bury my father; assure him that I will return promptly."

6Pharaoh agreed. "Go and bury your father, as you promised," he said.

7So Joseph went, and a great number of Pharaoh's counselors and assistants—all the senior officers of the land, 8as well as all of Joseph's people—his brothers and their families. But they left their little children and flocks and herds in the land of Goshen. 9So a very great number of chariots, cavalry, and people accompanied Joseph.

10When they arrived at Atad (meaning "Threshing Place of Brambles"), beyond the Jordan River, they held a very great and solemn funeral service, with a seven-day period of lamentation for Joseph's father. 11The local residents, the Canaanites, renamed the place Abel-mizraim (meaning "Egyptian Mourners") for

50:10 *Atad.* Located just west of the Jordan River, near Jericho.

Margin references:
49:26 Num 6:2; Deut 33:15,16
49:27 Deut 33:12; Judg 3:15
49:29 Gen 23:16; 25:8,9; 35:29; 47:29; 50:5
49:31 Gen 23:19; 25:9; 35:29
49:33 Gen 25:8,17; 35:29; Acts 7:15; Heb 11:21
50:1 Gen 23:2; 46:4,29
50:2 Gen 50:26
50:3 Num 20:29; Deut 34:8
50:5 Gen 47:29; 48:21
50:8 Ex 10:9; Num 32:24
50:9 Gen 41:43; 46:29; Ex 14:7

JACOB'S SONS AND THEIR NOTABLE DESCENDANTS		
Jacob's 12 sons were the ancestors of the 12 tribes of Israel. The entire nation of Israel came from these men.	REUBEN	none
	SIMEON	none
	LEVI	Aaron, Moses, Eli, John the Baptist
	JUDAH	David, Jesus
	DAN	Samson
	NAPHTALI	Barak, Elijah (?)
	GAD	Jephthah (?)
	ASHER	none
	ISSACHAR	none
	ZEBULUN	none
	JOSEPH	Joshua, Gideon, Samuel
	BENJAMIN	Saul, Esther, Paul

50:1–11 When Jacob died at the age of 147, Joseph wept and mourned for months. When someone close to us dies, we need a long period of time to work through our grief. Crying and sharing our feelings with others helps us recover and go on with life. Allow yourself and others the freedom to grieve over the loss of a loved one and a long enough time to bring grieving to completion.

50:2, 3 Embalming was typical for Egyptians but unusual for these nomadic shepherds. Believing that the dead went to the next world in their physical bodies, the Egyptians embalmed a body to preserve it so it could function in the world to come. Jacob's family allowed him to be embalmed as a sign of courtesy and respect to the Egyptians.

50:5 Joseph had proven himself trustworthy as Pharaoh's advisor. Because of Joseph's record, Pharaoh had little doubt that he would return to Egypt as promised after burying his father in Canaan. Privileges and freedom often result when we have demonstrated our trustworthiness. Since trust must be built gradually over time, take every opportunity to prove your reliability no matter how unimportant the occasion may seem.

they said, "It is a place of very deep mourning by these Egyptians." 12, 13So his sons did as Israel commanded them, and carried his body into the land of Canaan and buried it there in the cave of Mach-pelah—the cave Abraham had bought in the field of Ephron the Hethite, close to Mamre.

Joseph treats his brothers kindly

14Then Joseph returned to Egypt with his brothers and all who had accompanied him to the funeral of his father. 15But now that their father was dead, Joseph's brothers were frightened.

"Now Joseph will pay us back for all the evil we did to him," they said. 16, 17So they sent him this message: "Before he died, your father instructed us to tell you to forgive us for the great evil we did to you. We servants of the God of your father beg you to forgive us." When Joseph read the message, he broke down and cried.

18Then his brothers came and fell down before him and said, "We are your slaves."

19But Joseph told them, "Don't be afraid of me. Am I God, to judge and punish you? 20As far as I am concerned, God turned into good what you meant for evil, for he brought me to this high position I have today so that I could save the lives of many people. 21No, don't be afraid. Indeed, I myself will take care of you and your families." And he spoke very kindly to them, reassuring them.

Joseph dies

22So Joseph and his brothers and their families continued to live in Egypt. Joseph was 110 years old when he died. 23He lived to see the birth of his son Ephraim's children, and the children of Machir, Manasseh's son, who played at his feet.

24"Soon I will die," Joseph told his brothers, "but God will surely come and get you, and bring you out of this land of Egypt and take you back to the land he promised to the descendants of Abraham, Isaac and Jacob." 25Then Joseph made his brothers promise with an oath that they would take his body back with them when they returned to Canaan. 26So Joseph died at the age of 110, and they embalmed him, and his body was placed in a coffin in Egypt.

50:12
Ex 20:12
Acts 7:16
50:13
Gen 23:16-18

50:15
Gen 42:17,22
50:16
Prov 29:25
50:17
Gen 45:5
Deut 32:35
Mt 6:12
Lk 6:27
Rom 12:19
50:18
Gen 37:7-11
42:6; 44:14
50:19
Gen 30:2
50:20
Gen 37:26
Ps 76:10
105:17-19
50:21
Gen 45:11

50:23
Gen 16:3; 30:3

50:24
Gen 13:15
28:13; 35:12
48:21; 49:29
50:25
Gen 47:29
Ex 13:19
Josh 24:32
Heb 11:22

50:12, 13 Abraham had purchased the Cave of Mach-pelah as a burial place for his wife, Sarah (23:1–9). It was to be a burial place for his entire family. Jacob was Abraham's grandson, and Jacob's sons returned to Canaan to bury him in this cave along with Abraham and Isaac. Their desire to be buried in this cave expressed their faith in God's promise to give their descendants the land of Canaan.

50:15–21 Now that Jacob was dead, the brothers expected revenge from Joseph. Could he really forgive them for selling him into slavery (Genesis 37)? But to their surprise, Joseph not only forgave them but offered to care for them and their families. Joseph's forgiveness was complete. Joseph demonstrates how God graciously accepts us even though we don't deserve it. Realizing that God forgives us, even when we have ignored or rejected him, will motivate us to forgive others.

50:20 Even when powerful people plotted to cause him harm, Joseph saw God bring good from it. The experiences in Joseph's life taught him that God brings good from evil for those who trust him. Do you trust God enough to wait patiently for him to bring good from the bad that happens to you? You can trust him because, as Joseph learned, God can transform evil into good.

50:24 Joseph was ready to die. But he had no doubts that God would keep his promise and one day bring the Israelites back to their homeland. What a tremendous example! The secret of that kind of faith is a lifetime of trusting God. Our faith is like a muscle—it grows with exercise, gaining strength over time. After a lifetime of exercising trust, our faith can be as strong as Joseph's. Then at our death, we can be confident that God will fulfill all his promises to us and to those who come after.

●**50:24** This verse is a vivid statement of what will begin to happen in Exodus and come to completion in Joshua. God was going to make Jacob's family into a great nation, lead them out of Egypt, and bring them into the land he had promised them. The nation would rely heavily on this promise, and Joseph emphasized his belief that God would do what he promised.

●**50:26** The book of Genesis gives us rich descriptions of the lives of many great men and women who walked with God. They sometimes succeeded and often failed. Yet we learn much by reading the biographies of these famous people and key historical figures. But where did they get their inspiration? They got it by realizing that God was with them despite their inadequacies. Knowing this should inspire us to maintain our walk with God and reach for the potential he has given us.

REFLECT
on your life

1 Name a few comic strip or cartoon super heros from your childhood. Who are your real heros?

_____

_____

_____

_____

_____

2 What are the qualities in a person's life that make him or her a hero to you?

_____

_____

_____

_____

READ
the passage

Read the introductory material to Genesis, pages 1–3. Note how biographies make up the Blueprint of the book. The following questions are based on your reading.

3 Why is Genesis a good name for this Bible book?

_____

_____

_____

4 Of all the key people in Genesis, describe the one you know the most about.

_____

_____

_____

_____

5 Which Megatheme is least familiar to you (see page 3)?

_____

_____

6 If God uses all kinds of people to accomplish his purposes, what could you expect to see God do through your group study and your life as you study Genesis?

_____

_____

_____

_____

7 Using the following chart, try to list one strength and one flaw for each person.

Person	Strengths	Flaws
Adam	_____	_____
	_____	_____
Eve	_____	_____
	_____	_____
Noah	_____	_____
	_____	_____
Abraham	_____	_____
	_____	_____
Sarah	_____	_____
	_____	_____
Isaac	_____	_____
	_____	_____

Rebekah   _____   _____

          _____   _____

Jacob   _____   _____

          _____   _____

Rachel   _____   _____

          _____   _____

Joseph   _____   _____

          _____   _____

REALIZE
the principle

8 Of the key people in Genesis, who would best fit your definition of a hero? Which person do you think you can learn the most from at this point in your life?

_____

_____

_____

RESPOND
to the message

It's easy to assume that the Bible only tells us about spiritual giants. But the book of Genesis tells about real people facing real-life dilemmas like we do. Each person had strengths and flaws, just as we do; and yet these are the very people whom God used and loved. By studying their lives, what God told them, and how God dealt with them, we can see how we should live. The Bible is not a comic book—it is real life.

9 What does it mean to be used by God? Give an example or two from your life, or someone you know.

_____

_____

_____

_____

10 What does it mean to be loved by God?

_____

_____

_____

11 What are some of the strengths and flaws in your character?

_____

_____

_____

12 What one strength or character quality would you most like to develop as a result of this study?

_____

_____

_____

13 Begin praying now and throughout this week that God will give you insight and teach you lessons as you study the lives of these real people in Genesis.

RESOLVE
to take action

A Leaf through Genesis and read some of the profiles of real people. Choose one to introduce to someone else. When you make this introduction, begin by saying, "I met someone very interesting recently . . ."

MORE
for studying
other themes
in this section

B List everything you can remember that began in Genesis. What do you want God to begin in you?

REFLECT
on your life

1 Think of a time when you consulted an owner's manual recently. How was it helpful?

_____

_____

_____

_____

READ
the passage

As you read Genesis 1:1—2:3, compare it to the first pages in an owner's manual. Read the two charts entitled "Beginnings" and "Days of Creation" and the following notes:

❏1:1 ❏1:25 ❏1:26 ❏1:28 ❏1:31

2 If you could have had a front row seat to watch any of the days of Creation, which one would you have chosen? Why?

_____

_____

_____

_____

3 What can you learn about God from the Creation story?

_____

_____

_____

_____

_____

4 What responsibilities did God give Adam that are still ours today?

_____

_____

_____

_____

_____

_____

_____

The Bible begins by telling us of our personal Creator. Among the qualities God passed on to his human creations was dignity. God himself said we were well-made and worth making. Like any quality appliance or advanced computer, we come with an owner's manual, the Bible. Only a fool would ignore the mainte-nance schedule and repair procedures outlined in the manual that comes with a piece of expensive equipment. How much worse it is to ignore the Bible.

REALIZE
the principle

5 The Bible can be seen as an owner's manual for the world. Describe its uses.

_____

_____

_____

_____

_____

_____

_____

Owner's manual uses	How the Bible does this for us
Names the designer of the tool	_____
Describes the purpose of the machine	_____
Tells how the item was built	_____
Gives maintenance schedules	_____
Provides rules and guidelines for use	_____
Tells how to solve problems	_____

6 How can you show that you recognize the dignity and worth given to you by God?

RESPOND
to the message

_____

_____

_____

_____

7 What specific part of Creation most awakens a feeling of wonder in you? Have you ever thanked God for that part of his work?

_____

_____

_____

8 In what ways can you put to use your "owner's manual"?

_____

_____

_____

_____

_____

9 Set up a spiritual maintenance schedule for your life.

RESOLVE
to take action

_____

_____

_____

_____

_____

_____

MORE
for studying
other themes
in this section

A What work was done each day of Creation?

B Why do you think God chose to create the universe? What does Creation tell you about God? Why did God say Creation was good?

C Why is human life special? How are we like God? What should this mean for our self-worth?

D How would you explain human dignity without having a personal Creator? Compare your answers with footnote 1:26.

E Read again the chart entitled "Beginnings." Your group may well represent a variety of opinions about how God brought the world into existence. Rather than sharing those opinions, spend some time talking about how your opinion shapes what you think about God.

F What can we learn from the account of what God did on the seventh day? How important is rest for human beings?

REFLECT
on your life

1 What sins does our society tend to rationalize, minimize, or ignore?

_____

_____

_____

_____

_____

2 In what area of life are you most tempted to do wrong? What makes it so tempting?

_____

_____

_____

_____

READ
the passage

Read Genesis 2:4—5:32. Read the profiles of Adam and Eve and the following notes:

❏ 2:9,16,17 ❏ 2:15-17 ❏ 3:1 ❏ 3:1-6 ❏ 3:2-6 ❏ 3:5b ❏ 3:6 ❏ 3:6,7 ❏ 3:7

❏ 3:8 ❏ 3:12,13 ❏ 3:14-19 ❏ 4:6,7 ❏ 4:8-10 ❏ 4:19-26

3 What can we learn from the way God created Adam and Eve?

_____

_____

_____

_____

4 Why was it so terrible for Adam and Eve to eat from the Tree of Conscience (Knowledge of Good and Evil)?

_____

_____

_____

_____

5 What was the serpent's strategy to make Adam and Eve disobey God? How could they have resisted temptation?

_____

_____

_____

_____

_____

_____

_____

6 How did Adam and Eve respond to God's presence after they disobeyed?

_____

_____

_____

_____

7 How does disobedience affect our attitude toward God?

_____

_____

_____

_____

_____

_____

_____

8 Describe the before-sin and after-sin experiences of Adam and Eve.

REALIZE
the principle

Before sin they were . . .   *After sin they became . . .*

_____   _____

_____   _____

_____   _____

_____   _____

_____   _____

9 What were some of the consequences of Cain's sin?

_____

_____

_____

_____

_____

RESPOND
to the message

The world may make us insensitive to sin. While concerned at one point, we can learn to disregard or ignore it over time. This section shows us just how deep the sin problem runs and how far back it goes. We dare not take sin in our lives lightly.

10 After several thousand years of human existence on earth, how much progress have we made in controlling our tendency to sin?

_____

_____

_____

11 What sins and mistakes in your life make you feel like hiding when you sense God's closeness?

_____

_____

_____

_____

_____

12 What situations in your life came to mind as you read about Adam blaming Eve, then Eve blaming the serpent for their own sins?

_____

_____

_____

_____

13 What can we do to avoid taking sin lightly?

_____

_____

_____

_____

14 Ask God to help you take sin as seriously as He does. Confess your sins and ask for God's forgiveness.

RESOLVE
to take action

A How did God create Adam and Eve? Why did God create Eve? What does this teach us about what the relationship should be between husband and wife?

MORE
for studying
other themes
in this section

B What parts of God's plan for marriage need the most attention today?

C What do you learn about the character of Satan in this section?

D How can a couple include God in the day-to-day experience of marriage?

E How did work fit into Adam and Eve's lives? How should work fit into our lives?

F How did Adam and Eve react to being caught by God? What does this show us about God's desire for fellowship with us? What can we do to improve our fellowship with God?

G What were the consequences of Adam's sin? How does sin affect us today? What can we do to reverse or correct the effects of sin in our lives?

H What work did Cain and Abel do? Why was Cain angry? How did Cain's anger affect him? In what ways can sin destroy us?

I How did God punish Cain? Why was this a fitting punishment? What does this story tell us about God's judgment and mercy?

REFLECT
on your life

1 Describe a time when you felt alone, isolated, and very much in the minority.

_____

_____

_____

_____

READ
the passage

Read this lesson's passages in three parts, pausing after each part to answer the clarifying questions for that section of Scripture.

Read Genesis 6:1—8:22 and the following notes:

❑6:1-4 ❑6:3 ❑6:6-8 ❑6:18 ❑7:17-21 ❑8:21-22

2 How would you compare Noah's sense of aloneness with the one you just described from your own life?

_____

_____

_____

3 Why was God so angry with civilization?

_____

_____

_____

4 Compare the world situation today to the one in Noah's day.

_____

_____

_____

5 How did Noah respond to God's announcement of judgment on the earth?

_____

_____

_____

6 What examples of God's patience do you find in these chapters?

_____

_____

_____

_____

Read Genesis 9:1—10:32 and the following notes: ❑9:8-13 ❑10:8-12

7 After the flood, what responsibilities and directions did God give Noah?

_____

_____

_____

_____

8 In what ways does a rainbow remind you of God's faithfulness?

_____

_____

_____

Read Genesis 11:1-32 and the following notes: ❑11:3,4 ❑11:4

9 What was the purpose of the tower?

_____

_____

_____

10 What were the causes and results of God's anger?

_____

_____

_____

11 Describe some modern towers of Babel. Why are these efforts and attitudes anti-God?

_____

_____

_____

_____

REALIZE
the principle

After the entrance of sin, the world continued to become worse and worse until it was almost completely evil. In the middle of this depravity, however, stood a godly man and his family. God destroyed the wicked world with a flood, but saved the human race through Noah. God told him to carry out a plan that took 120 years to accomplish. When the floods came, the boat was ready. May we be as faithful and consistent over the course of our lives.

12 Which do you think is a better measure of obedience—how quickly someone obeys God, or how long they obey God? Why?

_____

_____

_____

13 As you look back over the challenges Noah had to face, which one would have been most difficult for you to overcome?

_____

_____

14 What is God's attitude toward sin in these chapters?

_____

_____

_____

15 What is God's attitude toward those who obey Him?

_____

_____

RESPOND
to the message

16 What specific encouragement can you find in these stories for the next time you feel outnumbered and under pressure?

_____

_____

17 Knowing how God responds to sin, how should you change your life?

_____

_____

_____

_____

18 How has God carried you through some situations in life?

_____

_____

_____

_____

19 What areas of your life will take a lifetime to change? Recommit yourself to obeying God in those areas.

_____

_____

_____

RESOLVE
to take action

20 Ask God to show you areas where you can increase your obedience to Him.

_____

_____

A What broke God's heart in Noah's day? What breaks his heart today?

MORE
for studying
other themes
in this section

B Why was Noah called righteous? How can you live in a way that is pleasing to God?

C What does the judgement of Noah's day tell us about God's announced judgment to come?

D What did Noah do when he left the ark? How can you express your thanks to God?

E What was Ham's sin? In what ways might we be in danger of committing similar sins?

F Compare the flood and the confusion of languages as different ways of God starting over.

G What facts about God's consistent character do you find helpful remembering in today's world situation?

REFLECT
on your life

1 What is something that someone has promised you lately that you will soon receive? What is something you have promised to someone else?

_____

_____

_____

_____

READ
the passage

Read Genesis 12:1—17:27 and mark or highlight every passage that has to do with a promise (or covenant). Also read the following notes:

❐12:1-3 ❐12:2 ❐12:7 ❐15:1 ❐15:5 ❐15:6 ❐15:17 ❐16:1-3 ❐16:3 ❐17:2-4 ❐17:5 ❐17:5-8 ❐17:9,10 ❐17:17-27

2 What was the promise God made to Abram?

_____

_____

_____

_____

_____

3 What was Abram required to do as his part of the promise or covenant?

_____

_____

_____

_____

4 Which examples of Abram's faith are most impressive to you?

_____

_____

_____

_____

_____

5 Which of Abram's and Sarai's mistakes remind you of yourself?

_____

_____

_____

_____

_____

6 God promised to bless the world through Abram and his children. This was difficult to accept and believe because Abram and Sarai were very old. Sometimes we also find God's promises difficult to comprehend. Although they wavered and erred from time to time, Abram and Sarai are themselves examples of faith in God who keeps his promises. We must believe, not only for our own sakes, but also for those who follow after us.

REALIZE
the principle

7 What happened when Abram and Sarai tried to hurry God's promise?

_____

_____

_____

_____

RESPOND
to the message

8 How do you try to take matters into your own hands and hurry his promises?

_____

_____

_____

_____

9 In what ways are the people in your life affected by your relationship with God? Who is most likely to be hurt or helped by your obedience to God?

_____

_____

_____

_____

_____

_____

10 List three or four promises that God has given us. Share one of these promises with another person to help strengthen his or her faith.

_____

_____

_____

RESOLVE
to take action

_____

_____

_____

MORE
for studying
other themes
in this section

A Why did Abram travel such a long distance?

B Why did Abram lie about Sarai? How is it possible for a man of faith like Abram to give in to pressure? In what ways do believers give in to pressure today?

C What obstacles to obedience did Abram have to overcome? What obstacles stand between you and obeying God? What kept Abram on track?

D Why did Abram and Lot separate? Which land did Lot choose? What does Lot's choice tell us about his character?

E When you had first choice recently, what was your primary consideration? How do our choices reflect our values?

F What did Abram do when Lot was taken captive? What did Abram do after his victory? What do Abram's actions tell us about his character?

G What can we do to instill Abram's character qualities in our lives?

H Later on in the Old Testament (Isaiah 41:8), God calls Abraham his friend. Based on what you've learned so far about Abraham, what would it take for you to be called a friend of God?

I What objection did Abram raise with God? How did God answer?

J What do we learn about God from his response to Hagar? What does this mean for you when you feel left out and alone?

K What would it be like to have Abraham for a friend? How did his relationship with God affect the people around him?

L How is your record of keeping the promises you make? Would your children, spouse, friends, and God say that you are a keeper of promises?

M Review other promises you have made and determine which ones need to be kept. You may well have to ask forgiveness to some who have given up waiting for you to keep promises. Ask God to help you be more faithful.

LESSON 6
THOUSE COMPLICATING COMPROMISES
GENESIS 18:1—20:18

REFLECT
on your life

1 When is compromise good? When is compromise bad?

_____

_____

_____

_____

_____

READ
the passage

Read Genesis 18:1—20:18. Read the profiles of Lot and Abraham and the following notes:

❐18:15 ❐18:25 ❐19:1 ❐19:8 ❐19:14 ❐19:16 ❐19:26 ❐19:30-38

2 What are the most striking differences between Lot and Abraham?

_____

_____

_____

_____

_____

3 Why was it right and fair for God to destroy Sodom?

_____

_____

_____

_____

Compromises have both short and long term effects. Although both need to be carefully considered, the temptation is to look no further than the short term effects. It is a simple matter to compromise ourselves into long term misery. It's not bad to find compromise solutions to difficult problems, but we must never compromise our faith or Biblical values.

4 Beginning with his choice of where to live (chapter 13), trace the pattern of Lot's dangerous compromises. Use the following chart to note some of the consequences:

REALIZE
the principle

Lot's compromising choices	Short term results	Long term results
Chose to live near Sodom	Easy life	Deadly morality

5 From what you have learned of Lot's life, what are some warning signs that might keep people from making dangerous compromises?

_____

_____

_____

_____

_____

_____

6 What habits, possessions and positions might be hard to give up today? How do these measure our level of compromise?

RESPOND
to the message

_____

_____

_____

_____

_____

_____

7 If you had to convince someone not to hold on to something God wanted him or her to let go of, what kinds of things might you say?

_____

_____

_____

_____

_____

8 To what degree have you allowed God to determine these areas of your life?

	low	. . . .			high
Who you are	1	2	3	4	5
Where you are	1	2	3	4	5
What you are	1	2	3	4	5

Are you satisfied with your answers? What could be done to change them?

_____

_____

_____

_____

RESOLVE
to take action

9 Have a serious conversation with God. Ask him to show you specific places where you may be making dangerous compromises.

10 If a dangerous compromising situation comes to mind, what can or should you do about it?

_____

_____

_____

A What purposes brought the visitors to Abraham's tent at the beginning of chapter 18? How do you feel about entertaining strangers?

MORE
for studying
other themes
in this section

B What message did the visitors have for Abraham? For Lot?

C Why did Sarah laugh? Why did she lie? How did God respond to Sarah's skepticism?

D What might God say about some situation in your life that would have you chuckling along with Sarah?

E Why was Sodom under God's judgement? Why was it just for God to destroy the whole city? What does this tell us about the way God looks at sin?

F Why was it wrong for Lot's wife to look back? When is it tempting to look back with longing at your old life?

G After lying to Abimelech, how do you think Abraham would respond to this definition: "Experience is a wonderful thing—it enables you to recognize a mistake when you make it again"? What repeated sins in your life need special attention?

H Discuss the sin of Lot's daughters. Note how compromise may complicate the lives of children. How aware are you of the people who are watching your life?

REFLECT
on your life

1 Describe the most unforgettable test you ever had to take. Was it a fair test? Would you say the test measured what you knew, or what you didn't know?

_____

_____

_____

_____

_____

_____

READ
the passage

Read Genesis 21:1—25:18, the profiles of Isaac and Ishmael, and the following notes:

❒ 22:1 ❒ 22:3 ❒ 22:7,8 ❒ 22:13 ❒ 22:17,18

2 How did Abraham and Sarah respond to the birth of Isaac? How do you think they felt at the birth of their son?

_____

_____

_____

_____

3 What did God's test do for Abraham's faith? What have been the most challenging tests of your faith?

_____

_____

_____

_____

Most tests quickly and painfully show us what we don't know. But a good teacher gives tests to help us discover what we know. We don't really have a good measure of what we know until that knowledge is tested in some way. Tests are for us, not against us. They become our enemy if we haven't done what we were supposed to do to prepare for them. Was Abraham ready for his test? You cannot cram for a test of faith. What should you be doing now to prepare?

REALIZE
the principle

4 How did faith and obedience affect each other in Abraham's test? How do you respond to a difficult choice where the outcome seems uncertain or painful?

_____

_____

_____

_____

_____

5 If God did not hesitate to ask Abraham to sacrifice his son, what might he ask us to sacrifice in those most important areas of our lives?

_____

_____

_____

_____

6 What might have happened if Abraham had considered God's request too much to ask?

_____

_____

_____

_____

_____

7 Describe the events of the test from Isaac's point of view. What lessons do you think he learned that could help you?

_____

RESPOND
to the message

_____

_____

_____

8 What people or things in your life are so important that you don't think you could bear it if God took them from you?

_____

_____

_____

_____

9 How could that thought or feeling affect your relationship with God?

_____

_____

_____

_____

10 How does God expect us to respond to the tests of life?

_____

_____

_____

11 What basic plan could you design to help you face the uncertainties of life with more confidence?

_____

_____

_____

_____

12 What could you imagine to be the most difficult test of your faith and how might you prepare for this?

_____

_____

_____

_____

13 Choose a specific area of testing in your life right now. Decide on one of two actions: (1) if you don't know what you should do, ask God to clearly show you; (2) if you do know what you should do, then do it. Watch what happens!

_____

_____

RESOLVE
to take action

14 Ask someone who knows you well to tell you what they think are your most important values. God may teach you through them.

_____

_____

A What did God do about Abraham's son Ishmael? How has God created good out of mistakes that you have made?

B How does God identify with those losses we experience which hurt us deeply? Can you remember a time of pain in your life when you realized that God understood what you were going through?

C What was Abraham's reputation with the people in the land? How clearly does your reputation reflect your relationship with God?

D What mission did Abraham give his servant Eliezer? Why was Abraham so concerned about Isaac's future? If you knew someone like Eliezer, how would you feel about trusting them with the same responsibility?

E What were Eliezer's first impressions of Rebekah? How do these compare with the first impressions people get of you?

F Study Eliezer's plan of action in looking for a wife for Issac. Decide on an area or two in your life that deserve the wisdom of this plan.

G What can we learn from Rebekah's response to the decisions that were made about her life?

H How did the servant know that Rebekah was the girl for Isaac? What do Rebekah's actions tell us about her character? What do people know about your character from your everyday action?

I What does this story illustrate about submission and faith?

J Discuss what it means to be part of a chain of faith, where each generation passes on by teaching and example what they have learned of God. Whom are you most directly affecting in the next generation?

K Describe the relationship between Sarah and Hagar. What lessons did God have for each of them? How has he done the same for you?

L How can we most directly apply the lessons about sacrifice that are found in these chapters?

MORE
for studying
other themes
in this section

REFLECT
on your life

1 Which of your parents are you most like? What qualities has each passed on to you?

_____

_____

_____

_____

READ
the passage

Read Genesis 25:19—28:9 and the following notes:

❒ 25:32,33 ❒ 26:17-22 ❒ 26:18 ❒ 27:14

2 What problems did Isaac and Rebekah face in having children? How was God involved? In your difficult times, when do you usually ask for God's help?

_____

_____

_____

_____

3 Why do you think each parent had a favorite son? How would you feel being the child of a family like that? How would you avoid being a parent like that?

_____

_____

_____

_____

_____

_____

4 How did Isaac's traits as a husband and father affect his family?

_____

_____

_____

_____

5 What conclusions can you draw from the well incident (26:12-33) about the way Isaac resolved conflict? What alternatives did he have?

_____

_____

_____

_____

_____

Early in his life, during Abraham's test, Isaac demonstrated a clear quality of submission. By the time he had children of his own, his attitude seems to have changed. His tendency to be passive had an effect on his whole family. There is a fine line which we must walk, between being passive and being submissive. A submissive attitude is a positive decision to cooperate with others, even when our desires might be to do otherwise. The motivation is usually respect for those needing our cooperation. A passive attitude, on the other hand, is a negative decision to go along half-heartedly. There may not seem to be any resistance because it is hidden. The motivation can be fear of failure, fear of conflict, or a sense of inadequacy.

REALIZE
the principle

6 Isaac was often passive when he should have been active. In what situations are you apt to do the same?

_____

_____

_____

7 How could Isaac have taken a more active role in the lives of his wife and sons? In what ways should you become more active in your family life?

_____

_____

_____

_____

_____

8 At the end of Isaac's and Rebekah's lives, what do you think were their sweetest and bitterest memories?

_____

_____

_____

_____

_____

_____

RESPOND
to the message

9 When are you most tempted to be like Isaac and be passive and uninvolved?

_____

_____

_____

_____

10 In what areas of life do you keep moving on and digging new wells? Does one of these conflicts need a new response? What will that be?

_____

_____

_____

_____

11 On the other hand, are there areas of your life that could benefit from a more submissive approach? How might you do that?

_____

_____

_____

_____

12 On what areas of your life should you work to set a better example for your family?

_____

_____

_____

13 When and with whom do you need to be more submissive this week? When and where should you quit being passive and take firm action?

_____

_____

_____

_____

_____

RESOLVE
to take action

A What was the meaning of Jacob's name? How did he live up to that description? Describe his relationship with his brother.

MORE
for studying
other themes
in this section

B What did Esau sell to his brother? Why was this such a critical error for Esau?

C In what ways did Esau give up his future to satisfy a present need? What can you do to strengthen yourself against the temptation to live for the moment?

D Why were Isaac and Rebekah upset about Esau's marriages? What part should parental wishes play in the choice of a mate? What role should God have in our choice of a life-partner?

E What kind of marriage would honor your parents? What kind of marriage would honor God? What can you do to prepare your children to make wise marriage choices?

F What kind of a wife was Rebekah? Given Isaac's character, how can her behavior be explained? What other options would be possible for the wife of a passive husband?

G Put into your own words how Rebekah and Jacob tricked Isaac into giving his special blessing to the younger son. Why was this so important to them?

H In what ways can parents still bless their children? What effect do you think a blessing has on a child? How have the blessings of others affected your life?

I Using Isaac's blessing as a model, develop one you can share with those you love. Decide on a good time for giving.

J What persons in your life could benefit from your blessing? How do you know? How will you give them that gift?

K Why did Esau hate Jacob? When have you been cheated, and how did you respond?

L What parent-child lessons do you see in this story?

REFLECT
on your life

1 Describe a time when you were tricked or cheated. How did that experience impact your life?

_____

_____

_____

_____

_____

READ
the passage

Read Genesis 28:10—30:43, Jacob's Profile in chapter 26, and the following notes:

❒ 28:9 ❒ 28:20-22 ❒ 29:23-25 ❒ 29:28-30 ❒ 30:3 ❒ 30:22-24

2 Why did God give Jacob a dream during his trip away from home?

_____

_____

_____

_____

3 In what ways did Jacob's experiences away from home help him grow as a person?

_____

_____

_____

_____

4 What do the names of Leah's and Rachel's children tell us about their feelings? How could Jacob have been a better husband?

_____

_____

_____

_____

_____

_____

5 Why did Jacob stay an extra six years with Laban after he had earned his wives?

_____

_____

_____

From the beginning, God intended to bless Jacob; and yet over and over we can see Jacob struggling, scheming, and grabbing at what God wanted to give him. Life has a way of wearing off the rough edges, but with Jacob, the job was tough. He was seldom on God's timetable, but God has used his life to teach us all. All of us are prone to think we can take or earn those things that God simply wants to give us . . . like love, forgiveness and his presence in our lives.

REALIZE
the principle

6 Beginning with Jacob's dream in Genesis 28:11, describe how Jacob related to God and his response to the promise. In what ways do you try to bargain with God?

_____

_____

_____

_____

_____

_____

7 How do Jacob and Laban compare in their ability to deceive people? What lessons might they have learned from each other?

_____

_____

_____

_____

_____

8 While he was with Laban, to what degree did Jacob's actions demonstrate that he was trusting God to fulfill His promise? In what ways did he fall short?

_____

_____

_____

_____

_____

RESPOND
to the message

9 In this chapter of Jacob's life, how did he handle those events that were not under his control? How do you handle the unplanned events of your life?

_____

_____

_____

10 During his stay with Laban, Jacob's life seems to have been under construction. What do you think God was trying to change in Jacob? How might God be using events in your life to change you?

_____

_____

_____

_____

_____

11 What schemes in your life are evidence of your lack of trust? How can they be interrupted? What does God want you to do about them?

_____

_____

_____

_____

13 What matters are you taking into your own hands that are better left to God or what timetables are you rushing?

_____

_____

_____

_____

14 If it has been a while since you expressed your desire for God's ultimate control of your life, this might be a good time to tell him that in prayer. Especially consider this if you've never done it before:

_____

_____

_____

RESOLVE
to take action

A Discuss the character of Laban. What was his problem? How would you carry on a relationship with someone like this? How should a person handle their tendencies to be this kind of person?

MORE
for studying
other themes
in this section

B What insights about marriage do you get from Jacob and his four wives? How does knowing about that complicated situation help you clarify what marriage means to you?

C In what ways is this chapter of Jacob's life an example of the statement: "Your sins will find you out"? What illustrations can you find in your own life of this truth?

D Discuss the effects of love in the relationship between Jacob and Rachel. What is the most admirable quality that being in love with Rachel brought out in Jacob? Analyze the quality of your love.

E What can you learn about rivalry between children from Rachel and Leah? How could their example help you understand what might be going on between you and another person in your family?

F Why did Jacob leave Beer-sheba? How was Jacob deceived by Laban?

G How did Jacob change and grow because of his experiences after leaving home? How can leaving home affect our spiritual growth?

H What do the names of Leah's and Rachel's children tell us about their feelings? What made Jacob angry? Why is it easy for us to be insensitive toward our loved ones?

I Add to the chart entitled "Jacob's Children" the meanings of each of the son's names.

REFLECT
on your life

1 What homecoming have you looked forward to the most? Which ones have you dreaded and why?

_____

_____

_____

_____

READ
the passage

Read Genesis 31:1—36:43, Esau's Profile, and the following notes:

❒31:1-3 ❒31:4-13 ❒31:32 ❒31:38-42 ❒32:3 ❒32:9-12 ❒32:26

❒32:27-29 ❒33:1-11 ❒33:3 ❒33:4 ❒33:11 ❒35:10

2 In what ways was Jacob stuck between a rock and a hard place at this point in his life? Describe similar situations in your life.

_____

_____

_____

_____

_____

3 How was Jacob's response to Laban's accusation unwise? How could he have responded better?

_____

_____

_____

_____

4 What do you think has happened to Esau in the twenty years Jacob has been gone? How does the passage of time affect your emotions?

_____

_____

_____

_____

_____

Most of us have relationships that need healing. Usually, both people involved are aware there is a problem, but each is waiting for the other to make the first move. This attitude often comes from a combination of pride and fear—pride in not wanting to be the first to admit a mistake, and fear of having our gesture of peace rejected. Jacob could have learned a lot about graciousness and forgiveness from his brother, and so can we.

REALIZE
the principle

5 In what ways did Jacob show how difficult it was for him to believe that his brother was not holding a grudge against him or planning for revenge? How do you respond to forgiveness?

_____

_____

_____

_____

6 Based on Esau's actions, how would you explain mercy? What could you learn from him about the nature of God's mercy? How have you experienced that mercy?

_____

_____

_____

_____

_____

7 From what you know about Jacob, why was it difficult for him to accept mercy? What makes it difficult for you to accept God's mercy?

_____

_____

RESPOND
to the message

8 Think of the relationships in your life that need healing. Are you playing the Jacob or the Esau role in reconciliation? Which do you want to be in the future?

_____

_____

_____

_____

9 Think again about specific ways in which God has been merciful to you; what should you be thankful about?

_____

_____

_____

_____

10 How have you been resisting or doubting God's mercy? What could you do to change those actions?

_____

_____

_____

_____

RESOLVE
to take action

11 Decide on at least one relationship in your life that needs a homecoming. Below are the basic actions Jacob and Esau took in their reunion. Which one might be helpful for you to try?

    a Sent a message
    b Sent a gift
    c Wrestled with **God** about fear, or unwillingness to forgive
    d Planned an encounter
    e Came with open arms, open heart

A Discuss Rachel's actions in stealing her father's idols and then lying. How do impulsive actions get us into more trouble?

MORE
for studying
other themes
in this section

B In what ways did the oath exchanged between Laban and Jacob settle their relationship? How was it different from what happened between Jacob and Esau? What can you learn from these examples about how to settle disagreements?

C How do the angels in 32:1 fit into the events of Jacob's story? Why did God reveal himself to Jacob in this way?

D Beginning with Jacob's message to Esau in 32:3, discuss the series of events in the reunion of the brothers. Why did each act the way he did? Which of these roles do you think you could have more easily played? Why?

E What were the actions and motives of Jacob's sons in chapter 34? What might we expect to happen when we take justice into our own hands?

F The action Reuben took with Bilhah is only mentioned in 35:21. Later, in 49:3, the consequences of this sin come to light. Discuss how things that we seem to get away with can come back to haunt and overwhelm us later.

G Make note of all the losses Jacob experienced in these chapters. What effect do you think they had on him? How have the losses you have experienced changed your life? How has God used them in you.

H Discuss the honor given Esau in having his descendants listed in chapter 36 even though he was not in the line of the nation of Israel. Why would he deserve that honor? How does this speak of the importance we can have even when we might influence people only indirectly?

I Compare what God told Jacob in 31:3 with God's last words to Jacob in 28:13-15. What do these two statements tell you about the character of God? Think of an illustration of this truth from your own life.

J How do you explain Jacob's actions in chapter 35:1 when God told him to move to Bethel? In what ways do you prepare yourself when you are about to worship God?

K Twice in these chapters God refers to a new name for Jacob—Israel. Why did God change his name? What name do you think would best express the changes you have experienced over the last several years?

L Why were Simeon and Levi outraged? Why did Jacob say their actions "stink among all the people of the land"? When have you been tempted to take vengeance into your own hands?

M Why did Jacob need to destroy the idols to start fresh with God? What should be removed in your life to improve your relationship with God?

REFLECT
on your life

1 What's the best example from your life of what it means to have emotional growing pains? What was the outcome?

_____

_____

_____

_____

READ
the passage

As you read Genesis 37:1—41:57, keep track of the lives of three brothers and their experiences growing up. Read Joseph's Profile (chapter 37), Reuben's Profile (chapter 38), Judah's Profile (chapter 45), and the following notes:

❏ 37:6-11 ❏ 37:28 ❏ 37:36 ❏ 38:1 ❏ 39:2ff ❏ 39:9 ❏ 39:20 ❏ 40:23 ❏ 41:14

❏ 41:38-40 ❏ 41:45 ❏ 41:46

2 What did Joseph do that made his brothers so angry with him? How else might he have handled the situation?

_____

_____

_____

_____

3 How did Joseph respond to suffering? How have you responded to suffering and injustices?

_____

_____

_____

_____

4 Throughout these events, what do you learn about Joseph's relationship with God? In what ways is he a good example for you to follow?

_____

_____

_____

_____

_____

_____

5 How did Reuben and Judah each experience their own growing pains? What has been the hardest lesson for you to learn?

_____

_____

_____

_____

6 What happens to most people when they experience a little success? How was Joseph's character affected by his success in Egypt?

_____

_____

_____

_____

_____

We are shaped more by suffering than by any other human experience. Hardship creates and improves character, and the unexpected hurts in life are what make us the real people we become. The pains that come with mistakes catch our attention and offer us lessons as well. Joseph is a great example of the process. Any one of his ordeals could have broken him. Instead, he responded to the hardships in such a way that they helped him. He discovered the old truth "what can't break me can make me," and he became a compassionate human being who helped others, including those who had intended to kill him.

REALIZE
the principle

7 In what ways did Joseph's difficulties test and improve his character? What made him so different than his brothers? How have you changed through your last hardship?

_____

_____

_____

_____

_____

_____

8 Looking back from his position as ruler in Egypt, do you think Joseph would have changed anything about his life? How does your answer match the feelings you have about your own past?

_____

_____

_____

_____

_____

RESPOND
to the message

9 Think back over your early years. What do you remember doing or saying to parents or siblings that has cast long shadows on your relationships? How could those mistakes be resolved?

_____

_____

_____

_____

_____

10 Does your present position in life allow you to help or hurt people who hurt you in the past? How do you think Joseph would handle your situation?

_____

_____

_____

11 How was God involved in helping Joseph handle what life handed him? How could that same God help you?

_____

_____

_____

_____

12 Think of at least one difficulty in your life that you realize God allowed because he knew it would make you a better person? Take a few moments to thank him for caring enough to let you grow.

13 Joseph had to face most of his growing pains alone. There are probably people you know who feel just as alone with their pain. Find a creative way to encourage them.

RESOLVE
to take action

A How did jealousy affect Joseph's brothers? How can a person resist the tendency to envy others? What do you do when you find yourself jealous of someone else?

MORE
for studying
other themes
in this section

B Have you ever been in a situation like Reuben's, in which you tried to work on both sides? What was his mistake? How would you act in a similar situation?

C In what ways did Joseph's brothers try to handle their guilt over their treatment of Joseph? What can we learn from them about the consequences of guilt?

D What mistakes did Judah make in his relationship with Tamar? What better decision could he have made along the way? What main lesson did you learn from this event?

E How does Judah's attitude toward Tamar's sins compare with his attitude toward his own sins? Why is it so easy to justify our actions?

F How is Joseph's response to Potiphar's wife a good example for how to avoid temptation? At what point do you find its time to run for your life?

G Why might Joseph have felt discouraged? How do you react when you are slandered or wrongly accused?

H While in prison, what did Joseph have in his favor? When we've been devastated by slander or adversity, how does knowing God help us?

I In what ways did Joseph remain faithful to God? How easily do you give up in the face of trouble?

J Use the chart: "Parallels between Joseph and Jesus" to discuss God's constant work of bringing good out of what others mean for evil. How do you relate to the final statement of the chart—"What men did to hurt them God turned to good for all"?

K Why do you think God made it a point to record the number of remarkable women who were a direct part of the human line through which he would come to earth?

L What principles of good management did Joseph demonstrate as he administered in Egypt? Which of these would help you most in your present position?

REFLECT
on your life

1 You've just received a letter from a close friend living far away who has suffered complete family rejection. This person is deeply hurt. What are three or four positive suggestions you would give him or her?

_____

_____

_____

_____

_____

_____

_____

READ
the passage

Read Genesis 42:1—45:28 and the following notes:

❏ 42:7 ❏ 42:8,9 ❏ 42:15 ❏ 43:1 ❏ 43:9 ❏ 44:33 ❏ 45:4-8 ❏ 45:17-20

2 Why did Joseph conceal his identity so long? How did he test his brothers?

_____

_____

_____

_____

_____

_____

3 How did the brothers demonstrate their guilt and guilt feelings over what they had done to Joseph? How does guilt usually affect your life?

_____

_____

_____

_____

_____

_____

4 Describe what you think the brothers felt as Joseph revealed himself and his plans. Can you recall something happening to you that was too good to believe?

_____

_____

_____

_____

_____

_____

5 If Joseph had a motto for his life, what do you think it would be? How would it fit your life?

_____

REALIZE
the principle

_____

_____

_____

_____

Despite setbacks, injustice, and heartache, God's way of living still turns out best. For many years, Joseph's life of honesty and integrity seemed to be a foolish effort compared to his brothers' way of life. But their life of ease was a thin cover over guilt and fear, while Joseph's life of hardship was filled with faith and God's grace. Where is the choice? With God's help, people shape and change circumstances; without his help, circumstances crush people.

The capacity to forgive injustice was Joseph's finest quality. In that action he was closest to the character of God. For many of us, giving and receiving forgiveness is foreign. Joseph's example deserves to be followed!

6 Why was Joseph's plan of forgiveness so complicated? Describe God's plan for forgiving humans.

_____

_____

_____

_____

_____

_____

RESPOND
to the message

7 Why were the brothers so overwhelmed with Joseph's forgiveness? How have you responded to God's offer of forgiveness?

_____

_____

_____

_____

_____

8 In your relationship with God, when and how do you feel like one of Joseph's brothers? What do you think you have to do to deserve his forgiveness? Is that what the brothers had to do?

_____

_____

_____

_____

9 What difference did it make in the brothers' lives when Joseph forgave them? What difference do you think God's forgiveness can make in your life? What prevents you from receiving it fully?

_____

_____

_____

_____

10 Confess to God the ways you have sinned. Hold on to the truth that the same God who taught Joseph to forgive will forgive you!

11 Because you have been greatly forgiven, think of those in your life whom you need to forgive. You can be Joseph to them.

RESOLVE
to take action

A What events in these chapters allowed the brothers to have some of the same feelings of hopelessness that Joseph had experienced years before? How were they affected?

MORE
for studying
other themes
in this section

B How do you understand Joseph's explanations of his trials and triumphs in chapter 45? What would make it possible or impossible for you to look at your life the same way?

C How do you explain Joseph's act of giving his brothers back their money in the sacks?

D How much like Abraham's test involving Isaac's life was Jacob's decision to let Benjamin go to Egypt? What did Jacob have to learn that we also need to learn?

E Review the actions and words of Judah in these chapters. How has he changed since his mistake with Tamar? Describe a mistake that has helped change you. (See the notes on 44:16-34 and 44:32.)

F How is Pharaoh's action in this story an example of God's creativity in helping his people? Have you ever gotten help from an unusual source that God must have been behind?

G Discuss the feelings behind Jacob's reaction to the news that Joseph was alive: "But Jacob's heart was like a stone." Do you find your emotions are frustrators or helpers in your efforts to trust God?

I Where is the justice in this story? Why didn't the brothers get what they deserved? How would this make sense in our lives?

J Look back at Genesis 37:5-7 and compare Joseph's dream with the reality of his brother's visit? How much control do you think God has over the events of our lives?

REFLECT
on your life

1 What is your favorite example of a person who kept their word to you, even when it cost them something? Perhaps a friend came through on a promise, or a store delivered on a guarantee. How do you feel about them now?

_____

_____

_____

_____

_____

_____

READ
the passage

Read Genesis 46:1—50:26 and the following notes:

❏ 46:3,4 ❏ 48:9-20 ❏ 49:3-28 ❏ 49:8-12 ❏ 49:22 ❏ 49:24 ❏ 50:24 ❏ 50:26

2 What is the importance of what God said to Jacob as he set out for Egypt in chapter 46?

_____

_____

_____

_____

_____

3 When Jacob realized his death was close, what did he ask Joseph to promise to do? What would be accomplished by this form of burial?

_____

_____

_____

_____

_____

_____

4 From what you noted in your reading, how important were blessings to Jacob and his family? What was their purpose?

_____

_____

_____

_____

_____

_____

The conversations in these chapters are filled with promises and blessings. To us, they seem little more than words. Talk, we say, is cheap. But it hasn't always been that way. Even today we find ourselves wishing people would stand by their words. When people mean what they say, promises become precious. The danger in our attitude about cheap talk comes when we think that way about what God says. But remember that people who believe what God says become people who treat their own words very seriously. The men and women of Genesis expected God to stand by his words and promises. They also expected to be held to the truth of their words. We also should be people of our words.

REALIZE
the principle

5 In what important ways did Joseph honor his father, while Jacob was alive and after he died? How can we honor our parents?

_____

_____

_____

_____

_____

RESPOND
to the message

6 What examples can you see in this lesson that demonstrate how valuable a person's words were considered in Joseph's day? How much can your words be trusted?

_____

_____

_____

_____

_____

7 How much were men like Jacob and Joseph willing to trust in God's promises? How much are you willing to trust them?

_____

_____

_____

_____

8 Identify several promises of God that you consider essential for your life. Explain what they mean to you.

_____

_____

_____

_____

_____

RESOLVE
to take action

9 List at least five people you care about who could be encouraged by a verbal blessing from you. Decide what you will say, and then choose a time in the next several days to speak to them.

_____

_____

_____

_____

10 If your parents are living, think of how you can make an unexpected gesture of honor to them.

A Describe the feelings and thoughts that must have filled the room as Jacob spoke his blessings to his children. Have you ever had someone make such effective comments on your life? How do you think it would feel to be blessed?

MORE
for studying
other themes
in this section

B Why do you think Joseph postponed his own burial in Canaan until later, when his father had asked for immediate burial in the promised land?

C Using examples from this lesson, explain what a blessing is. Describe a time when you were blessed by someone.

D How have you been affected by your parents' blessings? What about God's blessings?

E Make a list of significant events in people's lives. Include dates like births, marriages, baptisms, birthdays, graduations, and others. Note what kinds of blessings would be appropriate for each of those times—words of encouragement that the person will remember. How do you think God could use you in the giving of blessings?

F Why were the early Hebrews so meticulous about keeping family records? What do your family roots mean to you?

G How do you think Jacob's life was involved in his choice to give the main blessing to Joseph's younger son?

H What does Joseph's response to Jacob's death teach you about the importance of mourning the death of a loved one?

I What do the fears of Joseph's brothers after their father's death tell you about their understanding of forgiveness?

J Why were the brothers still afraid of Joseph? What are some restraints which hold people back from sin? What would the removing of those restraints in your life reveal about your true character?

K How has God been fulfilling his promises to Abraham? How are we the recipients of God's promise to Abraham? What must we do to remain faithful to our part of the covenant?

L In what ways do you feel differently about the real people of Genesis than you felt at the beginning of this study? How has meeting them helped you?

M How has your knowledge of God deepened by seeing these lives he touched? In what ways has he helped you know yourself better?

"For God loved the world so much that he gave his only Son..."

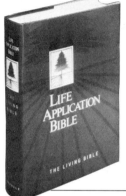

If one verse changed your life . . . think of what 31,172 more could do.

THE LIFE APPLICATION BIBLE
Applying God's Word to real life

The Life Application Bible can give you real answers for real life. We can give you eight reasons why it has all the answers you've been looking for—right at your fingertips.

1. **Unique Life Application Notes** show you how to act on what you read, how to apply it to needs in your own life.
2. **Megathemes** tell you why the significant themes in each book are still important today.
3. **People Profiles** bring alive over 50 colorful and important Bible characters, their strengths and weaknesses.
4. **The Topical Index** gives you over 15,000 entries that tell you where to find real answers for real-life situations.
5. **Bible Timelines** give you dates, names, and places at a glance.
6. **Cross-references** direct you to scores of important passages.
7. **Outline Notes** give you an overview of content plus ideas for application.
8. **Harmony of the Gospels** uses a unique numbering system to harmonize all four Gospels into one chronological account.

Plus: Book Introductions, Vital Statistics, Maps, and Charts!

AT BOOKSTORES EVERYWHERE. Cloth $34.95 Bonded Leather $49.95